TIME, CREATION
AND WORLD-ORDER

TIME, CREATION AND WORLD-ORDER

Edited by
Mogens Wegener

ACTA JUTLANDICA LXXIV:1
HUMANITIES SERIES 72

AARHUS UNIVERSITY PRESS

ISBN 87 7288 804 0
ISSN 0065 1354 (Acta Jutlandica)
ISSN 0106 0556 (Humanities Series)

Acta Jutlandica is published by Aarhus University Press
on behalf of the Learned Society of Aarhus (founded 1945)

AARHUS UNIVERSITY PRESS
Langelandsgade 177
DK-8200 Aarhus N
Fax (+ 45) 8616 4213
www.au.dk/unipress

73 Lime Walk
Headington, Oxford OX3 7AD
Fax (+ 44) 1865 750 079

Box 511
Oakville, Conn. 06779
Fax (+ 1) 860 945 9468

CONTENTS

PREFACE

This series of papers derives mainly from a symposion arranged May 1996 by the Center for Cultural Research, the Department of Philosophy, the Department for History of Ideas, and the Theological Faculty, all at Aarhus University, and the Department for Communication, Aalborg University.

The symposion, devoted to the theme made explicit by the title of the book and dedicated to the memory of Cardinal Nicholas of Cusa, theologian and cosmologist, gathered a number of specialists from all over the world: India, the United States, Russia, Switzerland, Scotland, the Netherlands, and Danmark. All agreed that the meeting had been succesful and the discussion inspiring. Its outcome is the present collection of papers.

It should be mentioned that the contributors came from such diverse fields as logics, physics, philosophy, and theology. Some of us are members of *International Society for the Study of Time*, of which David Park was formerly president. André Mercier†, initiator of *GRG*, co-founder of *CERN*, and former secretary general of *FISP*, was a famous physicist who later turned whole-heartedly to metaphysics. Tom Torrance is a very eminent theologian. Our circle was later extended with the inclusion of papers written by invited persons who could not attend the meeting; one of these is J.R. Lucas, former president of the *British Society for the Philosophy of Science*.

Originally it was intended to provide each of the papers with some 'Editor's Comments', to be followed by the 'Author's Response'. This plan, whose implementation delayed the publication considerably, eventually had to be given up due to unforeseen complications. I offer my sincere apologies to those authors who responded in vain.

M.W.

GRG   = *Gravitation et Relativité Générale*
CERN   = *Centre Energetique du Rechérche Nucleaire*
FISP   = *Fédération Internationale des Societés Philosophiques*

PROBLEM CATALOGUE

which was distributed in advance
to the participants of the symposion

1: WHAT IS TIME?

Is temporal flux real or apparent?
Did time once begin? Will it ever end?
Human time versus the time of science

2: TIME & WORLD-ORDER

The noble art of contriving world-models
Which are the fundamental laws of nature?
How is causal order related to time?

3: TIME & CREATION

What is the sense of assuming God as Creator?
What difference would this assumption make to us?
What does our view of nature imply to ethics?

$$= // =$$

INTRODUCTION

Although this is not the proper occasion for a genuine jubilee, it has been decided to dedicate the symposion to the memory of Nicolas of Cusa (1401-64): theologian, philosopher and cosmologist, Catholic cardinal with ecumenical engagement, a pious believer who yet inspired the revolutionary teachings of Giordano Bruno, the prophet of infinity and freedom, burned at the stake for heresy in 1600 A.D.

We celebrate Nicolas by reprinting his little dialogue entitled:

De Deo Abscondito (cf. Isaiah 45.15)

(On the Hidden God, or, freely: On the God who plays hide and seek)

Herein we witness a fictitious conversation between a Christian and a heathen, expressing the ecumenical attitude of Nicolas. The work, however, is not specifically Christian in its teaching: there is no invocation of the Holy Trinity, nor is any mention made of the Incarnation of God as Son of Man. But the dialectic reasoning of the master, bearing the name of Christian and seeking to explain in words that very Truth which remains unfathomable and inexpressible - God - leads us with the firm yet frolic steps of a ballet-dancer up towards the peak of pure reason from where we can forebode that Divine Greatness which, in another work, is called *Coincidentia Oppositorum* and, in still another, *Non Aliud* - both ideas which are akin, if not identical, to the Absolute Paradox of Søren Kierkegaard.

Nicolas is not very precise regarding time. In his main treatise:

De Docta Ignorantia (On the learned, or enlightened, ignorance)

he follows Plato by depicting time as a moving image of Eternity which is interpreted as simple undivided Oneness. In itself time is nothing but an ordering of the present. This present infolds both past and future, just as past and future unfolds the present. The point seems to be that the present, which is itself of variable duration, includes both the past as a having-been-present and the future as a going-to-become-present.

Oneness, by transcending time, comprises the changeable in an unchanging way. The Divine Providence thus encompasses everything which has happened, is happening, and will ever happen, perceiving what is possible in time as being actualised of eternity. The universe itself, like everything created, had a beginning, though not in time, and may thus be termed eternal in the sense that there was no time before the universe. Eternity, not time, reigned ahead of the creation of heaven and earth; time and world first emanated together - and still emanates - from their only source: Eternity.

The main work of Nicolas has three parts.

Part One treats of God as that Oneness which is the Coincidentia Oppositorum, being both the Absolute Maximum and the Absolute Minimum. This idea is elaborated by means of geometric analogies which in important respects anticipates insights peculiar to the later invented systems of non-Euclidean geometry. We may interpret the idea by characterising God as the Actual, or Absolute, Infinite. The created universe, by contrast, is the merely Potential, or Contracted, Infinite.

Part Two treats of the World as that Wholeness which is the Unity of the infinitely many, both a Contracted Maximum and a Contracted Minimum. To describe the second idea Nicolas uses another geometric analogy, namely that of a sphere which has its center everywhere and its periphery nowhere. This idea stems from the Hermetian writings where it is applied to God; but Nicolas, who probably knows it from the *Itinerarium Mentis in Deum* (5.8) of St. Bonaventure, brings it to bear on the created universe. By this ingenious move he gains a metaphor of astonishing depth and strength which contains in its germ the basic principle of modern cosmology: "center everywhere", originally signifying the Ubiquity of God, now claims the formal equivalence of all socalled fundamental observers, while "periphery nowhere", originally signifying the Infinity of God, now claims the structural invariance of the universe to all fundamental observers. The metaphor can also be interpreted as an expression of the idea of Cosmic Isotropy which, assuming a relation between the structure and its contents, involves also Cosmic Homogeneity, both properties characterising all the standard-models of modern cosmology. But Nicolas did not stop here. Rejecting both a geocentric and a heliocentric world, his intuition of an astrocentric universe of limited or potential infinity leads him to suggest that the stars are heavenly bodies similar to the sun, that no heavenly body can constitute a perfect sphere because perfection is a prerogative of the highest, or divine, nature and that innumerable globes are populated with living conscious beings like ourselves.

Part Three elucidates Man before the Fall as a Created God, the Unity of Creator and Creation, Absolute and Contracted Greatness, whereas Man after the Fall is exposed as a nature corrupt and stained, depending for its salvation on that Mercy of God which is obtainable solely through faith in the Divine Mediator, Christ. Anticipating the crucial doctrine of Martin Luther, Nicolas expressly wrote: '*Humanitas in Christo Iesu omnes omnium hominum defectus adimplevit ... Non est iustificatio nostra ex nobis, sed ex Christo ... quem cum in hac vita per fidem formatam attingamus, non aliter quam ipse fide iustificari poterimus.*' (DDI, iii.6)

Nicolas was evidently inspired by Meister Johann Eckhart whose mystical doctrines are reminiscent of Hinduism and Buddhism, though, of course, there is no question of any direct influence. According to Eckhart: 'The eye whereby God beholds me is the same as that whereby I behold God: it is all one eye, one sight, and one love'. He also said: 'If God could separate from Truth, I would follow Truth and skip God'. These words, which might be chosen as a maxim for the entire development of science in modern times - the very *motto* of modernity - need an addition, however. What Eckhart meant to state was in the end nothing but a simple *assumptio ex impossibile*. In fact, as he added: 'God cannot separate from Truth, for God is Truth!'.

With this homage to Nicolas, and to spirits kindred to his, we want to indicate that science is not the only source of truth, and that religion need not hamper reason. Both lessons are important in an age still intoxicated by the prejudices of positivism. If knowledge could ever eradicate religious belief it would have done so long ago. The warfare of science against religion may turn out to be the most spectacular instance in history of an unsuccessful attempt at falsification; this insight is an urgent warning against all premature judgment, as well as a fascinating inspiration to a renewed search for open dialogue and intellectual synthesis.

M.W.

EDITORIAL NOTE

Italics are used for the accentuation of words and linguistic phrases, and for longer quotations where usual quotation marks are easily overlooked.

Shorter quotations are denoted by single quotation marks, whereas peculiarities are denoted by double quotation marks.

Editorial insertions within quotations are put into brackets.

NICOLAS OF CUSA

DIALOGUS DE DEO ABSCONDITO

A CONVERSATION BETWEEN TWO PEOPLE,
ONE OF WHICH IS A PAGAN AND THE OTHER A CHRISTIAN,
ON THE GOD WHO HIDES HIMSELF

(editor's translation)

Pagan: I see how you kneel, full of awe, and how tears of love flow from the depths of your heart without any sign of falsity! Please tell me: Who are you?
Christian: I am a Christian.
P: Whom do you worship?
C: God!
P: Who is the God you worship?
C: That I don't know.
P: But how can you seriously worship something you don't know?
C: I worship him precisely because I don't know him.
P: How strange to see a man affected by something he does not know.
C: Yet stranger if he could be affected by something he meant to know.
P: But why?
C: Because his knowledge of that which he thinks to know is less worth than his knowledge of that of which he knows he is ignorant!
P: Please, explain that to me!
C: One must be crazy if one thinks to know something that cannot be known!
P: In my opinion you must be even more crazy to say nothing can be known!
C: By knowledge I understand: the full grasp of Truth. If someone professes knowledge he thereby claims for himself a full grasp of Truth.
P: And I believe you are right.
C: But how can Truth be grasped except by itself? For you don't grasp Truth if grasping differs from grasped so that the first is earlier and the latter later.
P: I don't understand why Truth can only be grasped by itself.
C: Do you think it can be grasped in any other way, by something else?
P: Yes!
C: Then you err, for nothing can be true without Truth itself, just as nothing can be circle without circularity and nobody can be man without humanity. So you find nothing true outside Truth, whether it be in or by something else.
P: How, then, can I know what a man is, or a stone, or anything else of all that which I know so well?

C: Truly, you know nothing of all this - you only opine that you know! For if I asked you about the very nature of that which you believe that you know, then you would be obliged to admit that you could never express the truth of any man, or even the truth of a stone. The fact that you know that a man is not a stone is not based on a true knowledge of both man and stone and the difference between the two, but only on their accidental properties and their various appearances and operations which you, separating one from the other, give different designations. However, all these various designations depend only on the separating motion of thought.

P: Now, is Truth one, or is it a plurality?

C: There is no Truth except one, for there is no Unity except one, and Truth coincides with Unity, since it is true that Unity is one. And just as there is in number no unity except one, so among the many there is no truth except one. Therefore one who knows nothing of unity will know nothing about number, just as one who knows nothing of the unitary Truth is unable to know anything at all. And albeit someone believes to know something truly, he may easily find out that all what he believes to know can be known even more truly. The visible, for instance, could always be perceived more truly, by a clearer sight, than it is now seen by you; also you never see the visible as it is in truth; and for audition and all the other senses the same holds true. Hence, as all that which is known is never known as truly as it could be, but otherwise and by something else - for Truth can never be known by anything other than itself - so he must be out of his mind who believes to know something truly and yet ignores Truth. Do we not consider that one to be crazy who is blind and yet pretends to distinguish unperceived colours?

P: What man, then, has knowledge if nothing can be known?

C: Only he has knowledge who knows his own ignorance, and only he honours Truth who knows that without Truth he knows nothing, neither to be, nor to live, nor to understand.

P: Maybe that makes you worship: your desire to be in Truth?

C: Precisely! I worship God - not that one whom you pagans falsely invoke and believe to know, but the only true God who verily is the unfathomable Truth itself.

P: I entreat you, brother: Since you invoke that God who is Truth, and we do not want to invoke a god who is not truly God, what difference is between us?

C: There are many, indeed; but the greatest and most important is that we invoke the absolute, simple, eternal and unfathomable Truth itself, whereas you do not invoke it as it is in itself, but as it is in its effects, that is, not as absolute Unity, but as the unity of number and plurality. In this you err, for that Truth which is God cannot be communicated to anything else.

P: I beseech you, brother: Be my guide, that I may grasp how you know God. Please tell me: What do you know of the God whom you worship?

Nicolas of Cusa

C: I know that all I know is not God, and that everything I grasp is unlike God, since He excels everything.

P: Hence God is nothing!

C: He is not nothing, since such nothing bears the name of nothing.

P: If he is not nothing, he must be something!

C: He is not something, since something is not everything; but God is not rather something than everything.

P: How strange: You claim that the God you invoke is neither nothing nor something. No human reason can comprehend that!

C: God transcends both nothing and something! Does not nothing obey his command so that something is made? In this is God's omnipotence clearly manifested! By his very power God transcends everything, both that which is and that which is not, and in the same way everything obeys his command - that which is, and that which is not. Thus he is nothing of that which is subordinate to him and to which his power is prior, for he makes being arise from not-being, just as he makes being expire into not-being. Therefore he should not be called this rather than that, since he is the source of everything.

P: Can he be called by any name at all?

C: Truly, all names are inadequate. He whose greatness is inscrutable is for that very reason also inexpressible.

P: So he is inexpressible?

C: He is not inexpressible. Rather he is expressible above all, since he is the cause of all that which can be named. How could he lack a name - he who gives a name to everything?

P: Then he is both expressible and inexpressible!

C: No, God is not the root of contradiction, for he is the very root of that simplicity which is prior to everything else! Therefore you cannot call him both expressible and inexpressible.

P: But what will you then say about him?

C: He can neither be named nor be unnamed, nor can he both be named and unnamed; but nothing that can be said, whether by conjunction or disjunction, by unanimity or disagreement, can ever express his exalted infinity which as the ultimate source of everything transcends all that can be thought.

P: So God cannot even be said to be?

C: You are right!

P: So he is nothing, after all!

C: Neither is he nothing, nor is he not, nor is he and is not, for he is the source and well-spring of all the principles of being and not-being!

P: So God is the source of all the principles of being and not-being?

C: No!

P: But you just said so!

C: I spoke truth when I said so, and I am speaking truth when I now deny it, for if there are any principles of being and not-being at all, then God is prior.

Nicolas of Cusa

But the principle of not-being is not not-being, but being. Hence not-being is in need of a principle in order to be what it is, namely not-being, and without such principle it would not even not-be.

P: Is God not Truth?

C: No, for he is prior to all truth!

P: Is he something other than Truth?

C: No, for he has no share in othernes, and he infinitely surpasses all that which we name as truth.

P: You nevertheless call God by the name of God!

C: Yes, indeed!

P: You then speak truly or falsely, I suppose?

C: Nothing of the two! For we do not speak truly when we say that his name is Truth, neither do we speak falsely, for it is not false that his name is Truth. Neither do we speak both truth and falsity at the same time, for the simplicity of God is prior to all that which either can or cannot be called by any name.

P: Why do you call him God, when you do not know his true name?

C: This we do for the analogy which this name bears to his perfection.

P: Please, explain that to me!

C: The very name 'God' (Lat. *deus*) is derived from Greek θεωρῶ, I see. The reason is that God is to us what vision is to colour, for colour can only be perceived by vision. Now the very center of vision lacks all colour in order that the various colours may be equally well perceived; but vision itself, lacking all colour, is not on a par with colour. Hence, with respect to colour, vision seems to be closer to nothing than to something. Beyond its own region colour has no share in being, as it implies all being to be within its own region, and vision does not belong to that; therefore vision, having no colour, is inexpressible in the region of colour, since the name of no colour can be applied to it. Nevertheless it is vision that gives to every colour its peculiar name. Thus all naming in the region of colour depends on vision, and yet we have seen how the name of the source of all names is closer to nothing than to something. So God is to all as vision to the visible.

P: I agree with what you have just said, and now I clearly grasp why neither God, nor his name, is to be found in the region of created things. I also grasp why nothing is comparable to God and why He, not having the appearance of a creature, can never be found in the region of created things, but surpasses everything that we can grasp. Likewise I grasp that all naming is a composing and that in the region of all composition we do not find what is simple, since the composite is not of itself, but stems from what is prior to composition. And though the composite is what it is through simplicity, yet this simplicity, being non-composite, must remain unknown in the region of the composite. Praise be to God, who is hidden to the eyes of worldly wisdom!

Nicolas of Cusa

DAVID PARK

WHAT IS 'TIME'?

One day the ruler of Wei invited *Confucius* to advise him on matters of administration. Confucius's followers asked him what was the first thing he planned to do. He replied, *What is necessary is to rectify names.* When the followers protested, he went on (Confucius 1971, p.263):

If names be not correct, language is not in accordance with the truth of things. If language be not in accordance with the truth of things affairs cannot be carried on to success. When affairs cannot be carried on to success, proprieties and music will not flourish. When proprieties and music do not flourish, punishments will not be properly awarded. When punishments are not properly awarded, the people do not know how to move hand or foot.

- I have heard that *Chairman Mao* often mentioned this sage advice.

I intend for a few pages to follow Confucius, but am not quite sure it is a good idea. Does the search for correct terminology make discussion more fruitful or does it poison it? I think all readers have had the experience of both outcomes. The Dutch physicist *H.A. Kramers* once said (Kramers 1956, p.1):

My own pet notion is that in the world of human thought generally, and in physical science particularly, the most important and fruitful concepts are those to which it is impossible to attach a well-defined meaning.

- Surveying some of what is written about time, one might conclude that time is such a concept, but I don't see why this should be so. The ruminations to follow are intended to help clarify the question.

In situations like this one always begins by quoting *St. Augustine*: *Quid enim est tempus*? If nobody asks, he knows... but does he? His remark tells me that he doesn't really know. In many of Plato's dialogues *Socrates* focuses on some term: love, justice, goodness, which his auditors use; he finds that none of them can tell what it means and again the implication is that they don't really know. One can substitute these and many other words for time in Augustine's question: for example, being, or becoming, or reality (a word that *Niels Bohr* said we must patiently learn to use, but which leaks meaning through so many holes that physicists, at least, rarely say it any more).

What then is 'time'? It is a word. *Karl Popper* once warned us that dictionaries should be read from right to left, rather than from left to right.

There is a phenomenon, a process, an experience that we want to talk about; first we identify it and then we give it a name. So what is the phenomenon, process, or experience to which mankind has given the name 'time'? There is no way to find out what a word means except by studying how it is used, and here we find such extremes of variety that there is no immediate question of "attaching a well-defined meaning", but only of checking the meanings that are offered and trying to see if any are useless or do not make sense.

Here are a few of the ways in which people use the word 'time':

#1. *The rush of experience.* - Each day, event follows event, we are caught up in every process that touches us and there is nothing we can do about it. - As *Marcus Aurelius* wrote, *The universal cause is like a torrent: it carries everything along with it.*

#2. *A general tendency of change* which it is hard not to describe without referring to ideas of motion. *Ronsard* writes, *Le temps s'en va, le temps s'en va, Madame! Las, le temps reste, et nous nous en allons.* I have found by talking with people that about nine out of ten, like Madame (if the second line is her reply), think of themselves as voyaging forward in time from past toward an unknown future; the tenth stands like a rock in a river of time.

#3. *Newton* finds *absolute space and time* necessary in order to explain his system of dynamics, though not to apply it. He writes, *Absolute, true, and mathematical time, of itself and from its own nature, flows equably without reference to anything external,* and never mentions the matter again. What do his words mean? If nobody asks me, I know. But if someone asks a reasonable question about this flow, for instance how fast it moves, I do not know. People who think that Newton has stated a fact sometimes venture out onto very thin ice: Time flows at the rate of one second of time during each second on my watch. The second on my watch, then, is not part of the general flow? Or if it is, what exactly has been said? That way lies nonsense. Newton's remark is a tiny fly-speck on a great monument of marble and bronze.

#4. *A motionless intellectual framework* of seconds and days and years, representable as a graph in which time is measured upward and a sample spatial coordinate is measured to the right. In this graph an object is represented by what is called a world-line, vertical if the object is not moving, slanted or curved if it is. Along this line the present burns its way upward like a spark along a fuse. Some unstated principle enforces a common present. Here is a problem: What determines the line beyond the level representing the (continually advancing) present moment? Do we say that there is a future but we do not know what it is? Or do we say that the line is continually being

David Park

extended? If so, the question obtrudes itself: How fast? So-called "time travel"[1] can be represented on this diagram if the spark representing the present is imagined as moving backward instead of forward, or forward faster than usual. The diagram can be drawn with relativistic refinements; it is then called a Minkowski diagram, but no new considerations result.

#5.   The same graph, but this time it is only *a bundle of lines*. Nothing changes, nothing progresses. The upward coordinate represents time as it might be given by my watch, but there is no 'now' that gets later and later. The graph can be read upward or downward or one can study it point by point. The (usually vertical) time scale does not participate in time as it does in #4. In the same way, the newspaper prints a graph of the performance of the stock market during the week, but the coordinate which represents the price of stocks does not itself have any monetary value. We may call any arbitrary time the present if we wish, but there is no reason to say that my present is the same as your present. Nothing enforces a common present, except that if you and I talk together the rapidity of the signal secures a rough kind of simultaneity. So-called "time travel" is undefined; what exactly would be travelling? This is the time of physics.

This fifth representation, which has been called "the block universe", needs a little clarification, for it has been severely criticized for assuming that if one takes any given moment as the present, events in its future are already determined, whereas no one any longer believes this is possible. Of course, deducing the past from a knowledge of the present involves Bayesian retro-diction and is even more complicated than deducing the future, and so by the critics' own criterion, consistently applied, it is impossible to draw a world-line at all, but they seem not to notice this. More fundamentally, their criti-cism stems from a misunderstanding of what physicists do. Physicists deal with models. Most physicists potently believe, lacking anything resembling proof, that there is a real universe out there, but for the construction of theories they substitute mathematical models that they can analyze rationally. These models omit everything that is not relevant to the matters they are designed to explain. Experiments are another way of establishing a relation with what (if anything) is out there, but they too are described and inter-preted in terms provided by a model. As *Einstein* remarked, *it is theory that tells us what we can observe* (Heisenberg 1983, p. 114). When experiment and theory agree and other criteria of clarity and simplicity are also met one says that the model is a good one, and continues to study its implications.[2]

David Park

The term "block universe" suggests that the diagram is intended to represent the universe, i.e., reality, and that since in the real world exact prediction (or retrodiction, for that matter) from a given moment is impossible, the "block universe" represents a non-existent state of affairs. But this is an irrelevant objection. Physicists have no tools for dealing with "reality", whatever that may be. The diagram represents a model concerned with some portion of space and time in which it is assumed for convenience that we are able to represent events with sufficient accuracy by drawing lines as I have described. The diagram is a good way to represent physical processes, but since it does not accommodate our consciousness of a present instant it is a bad way to represent our experience of these processes. We are still a long way from a physical explanation of consciousness.[3]

Of the five ways of talking about time listed above, some express the human experience of time; others intellectualize time and try to describe it without immediate reference to experience. A planet moving in its orbit is governed by physical laws that relate its position to some universal time scale, and yet it is not considered to be experiencing time. A planet does not need the word 'now'. How can we express the human experience of time? As definitions #1 & #2 show, we tend to use metaphors that involve motion. I do not see how anyone can object to this, provided that metaphor is recognized as metaphor. But again and again, in writings about time, metaphor is taken as fact. Marcus Aurelius's metaphorical river of experience becomes Newton's absolute time which "flows equably". *Hans Reichenbach* once wrote a whole book called *The Direction of Time* in which he assumes at the beginning that time flows, without ever explaining what that might mean or how he knows it is true, and thereafter nothing makes much sense.

It is easy to object to the foregoing remarks: *You just said that time is a word and therefore can be made to mean anything we want. Why shouldn't we define it in terms that express human experience, for example à la Marcus Aurelius?* The difficulties become plain if we consider another metaphor and see what happens when we take it literally. As a schoolboy I could recite a poem by *Alfred Noyes* which asserts: *The Moon was a ghostly galleon, tossed upon cloudy seas.* Consider what happens if one chooses to take this literally: it raises more questions than it answers. How did the ghostly galleon get up there? Is it in orbit? If so, why does it move so slowly? Why doesn't it look more like other galleons? Definitions should match each other as well as our experience of the world in general.

David Park

One is of course free to refuse the common understanding. *Blake*, in *A Vision of the Last Judgment*, explodes: *'What', it will be question'd, 'when the Sun rises, do you not see a round disc of fire somewhat like a guinea?'* - *O no, no, I see an innumerable company of the Heavenly host crying 'Holy, Holy, Holy is the Lord God Almighty'*. But Blake does not expect other people to accept this as a statement of what the Sun is. It is a private vision. I do not object to anyone's using words metaphorically. We do it all the time. If we say that music or a spice or an electric wire or a car is hot,[4] everyone understands that we are talking metaphorically. It is because we agree on the primary meaning of 'hot' that metaphorical meanings proliferate around it. The power of metaphor is that it enriches our imagination by uniting different worlds of discourse, but that is not what is needed in a primary definition.

It would be useful to specify a primary area of meaning for 'time' to which reference can be made when one is trying to be exact: a single tree, perhaps with many branches, surrounded by a garden of analogies. There is nothing simple about this when the word has been used for a very long time. The 1933 edition of *Oxford English Dictionary* enumerates fifty uses of 'time', giving several examples of each to illustrate its history. Only number 24 aims to be a general definition: *Indefinite continuous duration regarded as that in which the sequence of events takes place*. Following this, the first example quoted is from *John de Travisa* (1398), *Tyme is mesure of chaungeable thynges, as Aristotel seith*. The OED's fifty meanings are mostly idiomatic. Very few are metaphorical, and it is striking that none of these refers to our common notion of time as a flow. There must be a reason for this.

Consider the problem of defining the word 'green'. The dictionary on my desk defines green as the color of growing grass, but it does not tell what growing grass looks like. The experience of green is private and uncommunicable, though the color-blind can testify that the rest of the world seems to have this experience. It is the same with time. How can we describe or explain the experience of living in time? Unfortunately the analogy between spatial extension and temporal extension presents itself and then, in a very imprecise way, the procession of events in which we are continually involved becomes something like motion from place to place, except that motion is change of place with respect to time; the analogy, if one permits oneself to think about it, becomes a change of time with respect to time, and it leaves us no wiser than we were[5]. If the dictionary is not expected to describe the experience of seeing the color green I do not see why it should be expected to describe the experience of living in time.

David Park

What, then, can one say about time without actually defining it that is just plain common sense, that agrees with experience without trying to describe it and is not rooted in metaphor and does not go beyond the facts of observation and is a useful basis for discussion? For this I would, as Travisa and the editors of the OED have done, follow *Aristotle (Physics Book iv)*:[6] *Time is the number of change[7] with respect to before and after, and it is continuous because it is an attribute of what is continuous .. It is clear that time is not described as fast or slow, but as many or few, or as long or short .. Further, there is the same time everywhere at once .. Not only do we measure time by change, but also change by time, since they define each other.*

Note that the idea of time is introduced in two stages: first comes change, implying the existence of before and after but nothing more; then comes a scale of measurement which allows one to say that a certain change happened slowly or quickly. This scale is what Aristotle names time.

We use the change in the position of the hand of a watch to judge the performance of an athlete, explaining this procedure by speaking of time. The word *time* is here used as the quantitative measure that distinguishes one athlete's performance from another - it is, as Aristotle says, an attribute of it. This time is, in essence, the time of physics, cf. #5. It is the quantity t in the physicist's equations of motion, involved in every process in the universe.

Every sentence of Aristotle's that I have quoted withstands critical examination and comparison with what we know or what we think we know,[8] but still something is missing, the words that would connect the definitions with our experience of living in time. Aristotle tries to do this in the same book[9], where he talks about *the now* ($\tau\grave{o}$ $\nu\acute{v}\nu$); now, he says, is carried along (by change? by events?, using the passive voice he does not have to say) just as a thing is carried along. In one sense *now* is always the same, in another it is not, just as is true of the thing. Aristotle here introduces the idea of temporal flow: the *now* does flow, *time* doesn't.[10]

I have earlier argued against insisting that time flows, but my argument does not apply to change. Many familiar kinds of change occur continuously - a peach ripens, a cloud shades the sun, someone walks past our window - others are more abrupt; but enough are continuous that it is not absurd to say metaphorically that we experience the world as a continuous flow of changes. Events are the markers of time, and change is what causes us to have any impulse to talk about time at all. In fact, I have long maintained that most metaphysical discussions of time become more clear if one drops the word 'time' entirely and substitutes one of the words 'event' or 'change'.

David Park

What do we really need the word 'time' for? For an answer to this, consider the fifty kinds of use listed in the OED. The word is useful in a great variety of situations, and there is no single definition that covers all of them. On the other hand, there are times when we do not even need the word 'time'. The invitation to the meeting at which this paper was presented invited us to ask ourselves, *Is temporal flux real or apparent*? I suggest that it is neither. For reasons already mentioned I cannot regard it as real, while if 'apparent' means 'observable', what I observe is not time itself, whatever that may be, but events, whether in the outer world or in my private mental stream.

But, on the other hand, when Hamlet says that *time is out of joint* we need not worry about definitions. The greatness of such an utterance is that it gives us a singular insight into the way Hamlet views his personal situation. That's the use of metaphors; they illuminate a specific situation by connecting it with the rest of the world, and they may even help if one is trying to get at the truth, but not if they are taken literally. I see no reason why the moon should not be a galleon, or a car should not be hot, or time should not flow or stand still, as long as no one confuses literal and metaphorical meanings.

If there is to be a central, literal meaning of the word 'time', I suggest that Aristotle's definition says what needs to be said and no more, and most of the usages in the OED are consistent with it. Thus thoughtful people seem to have settled on a well-defined area of meaning. This is the grand tradition of language, it is how those words are established which we all understand in the same way. In English, they tend to be short and to be of Anglo-Saxon origin. They are old words. They are the foundation of clear reasoning and speech, the bedrock of our thought, and 'time' is among them. It is a word which, even if we do not agree on its meaning, we are learning to use.

References

1.   Confucius, 1971: *Confucian Analects, the Great Learning, and the Doctrine of the Mean* (trans. J. Legge), Dover, NY.
2.   Heisenberg, W., 1983: *Encounters With Einstein*, Princeton.
3.   Kramers, H.A., 1956: *Collected Scientific Papers*, North-Holland.
4.   Lucretius, 1910: *On the Nature of Things*, transl. C. Bailey, Oxford.
5.   Park, D., 1988: *The How and the Why*, Princeton.
6.   Reichenbach, H., 1956: *The Direction of Time*, Berkeley.
7.   Schilpp, P.A., ed., 1949: *Albert Einstein, Philosopher-Scientist* (Library of Living Philosophers) Evanston.

David Park

Notes

1 "Time travel" is an unfortunate term. Every day we feel ourselves travelling through time into an unkown future. "Time travel" posits that at a point on one's world line corresponding to a given moment in one's life, one's consciousness corresponds to some other time.

2 Of course, this is not the real way scientists talk. Nobody wants to drone on and on about models. But if they say an experiment shows that a theory is false because it incorrectly describes what really happens, they are using language in a sense that everyone understands and that only occasionally leads to philosophical problems. About the use of models, see Park 1988 p.74.

3 For Einstein's troubled assessment of this situation, see Rudolf Carnap's recollection of a conversation with him (Schilpp 1963 p.37).

4 For those who are not American, a hot wire is one that carries an electric voltage and should not be touched; a hot car is one that is stolen and should not be touched.

5 See Aristotle, *Physics* 218^{b}17

6 See *Physics* 220^{a}25 & 220^{b}16, compare 218^{b}10.
Lucretius, in his *De rerum natura*, I. 463, says the same thing:
No man feels time by itself, apart from the motion or the quiet rest of things.

7 I translate Aristotle's *kinesis* as 'change'. Toward the beginning of his discussion (*Physics* 218^{b}19) he specifies that for the moment he will not distinguish between *movement* (*kínesis*) and *change* (*metabolé*). He is not talking about *rate of change*, for that would make his definition a tautology.

8 Special Relativity questions absolute simultaneity, but relativistic cosmology re-establishes an absolute frame of reference (that of the universe as a whole) relative to which Aristotle's statement about a universal present makes sense.

9 *Physics* 219^{b}13-34

10 Aristotle's time does not flow, but it makes perfect sense to talk (metaphorically) of a flow of events, effects following causes in a regular sequence determined by *the inherent tempo of nature*. This tempo is of course what the physicists' laws of nature and the sociologists' principles of societal change are concerned with.

David Park

ANDRÉ MERCIER †

GOD, WORLD, AND TIME [1]

1.　　The Organizer of this Symposium has raised a number of questions, the first of which asks, ***Whether the Temporal Flux is real or apparent***?

Etymologically, reality is thingness; but 'thing' is indeterminate, so that what it means is first made precise by what either precedes or follows it; and appearance means becoming visible, mostly by attention or imagination, i.e. with*in* time, which makes it difficult to connect thingness or appearance with temporal flux, since both already are time-dependent, so the question can be neither a linguistic, nor a significant alternative.

Since the question concerns a flux which itself means something of the nature of time, the very question amounts to asking, whether what flows does flow! This conclusion is not very kind towards the questioner, especially since he had something profound to put forth! Actually, one has to go one step further, namely to the second question about the *Origin* of Time: Is there a beginning of Time, maybe a cause? Yet we must be careful not to enter into a vicious circle which would define a term by this very term.

In order to avoid that, we must *choose* between Time as the support of what passes, dies and is no more, and Time as the bearer of what is to come and will be. This choice is necessary if we are to conceive of *existence*, i.e., the property of things to indubitably come into one another's presence: from the Latin *ex-sistere*. This presence is rigorously relative to that instant called the *present* which is devoid of duration since it is the cut between what all languages and cultures have understood as past and future.

Hence the prime question to be put as an alternative is rigorously the relationship between the by-gone and the to-come: Is Time the passage from the past to the future, or is it the passage from the future to the past? If it is the latter, *and this shall be our choice*, then Time is created by an Agent itself absconding behind (or should we say before?) the to-come (in Latin *futurum*: the future). This would explain the nature of the so-called *deus absconditus* spoken of by theologians (e.g. *Cusanus*; see his *Dialogus de deo abscondito*, as distributed by the Organizer of the Symposium).

If, by contrast, Time is the continuous passage from past to future, then it cannot support anything, since every happening is immediately past, i.e., already no more with-in, but with-out (outside) time; and if by believing that one could attribute to a Creator that which made its appearance in the past, that very Creator would have to be Himself behind the past, from where He could neither punish, nor pardon,[2] nor even change anything in the funct- ioning of things which He might have created "in the past": a determinism absolute and rigorous if at all! Whereas in absconding behind, or before, the to-come (in German *vor der Zukunft*, in French *derrière l'avenir = l'à-venir*), the Creator keeps all Freedom (e.g. to punish or to pardon).

These statements seem to allow for one choice only according to which time is the flux of the to-come. This flux, through the present as alone perceptible by the senses and intelligible to thought, adds itself to the accumulating past, thus constituting history. Our conclusion is therefore that the flux of time is neither real, nor apparent, because these adjectives need Time if they have to bear the very meaning which is theirs.

Although it differs from a more than millenary interpretation among humans, the only *reasonable* choice is that of *Time-as-the-To-come* and not as the accumulation of a past which does not constitute anything else than mere history. In other words: *Time is not history*. What is furthermore remarkable about our choice is that it constitutes a Proof of God.[3]

Under these conditions, Time is intelligible only through the fact that things change and thus constitute World; thus things, which constitute World, can only change in the course of Time. God does not change and is therefore not a part of World. Together, Time and World constitute Divine Creation.

But mind, please, that not only the intelligibility of Time is implied, but the intelligibility of *three* terms in their relationship: the intelligibility of God, of World, and of Time. Thus merely two verbs not to speak of one only, do not suffice to ground that intelligibility: we need both the French "il y a le monde etc." (with the verb 'to have'), the English "there is the world etc." (verb 'to be'), and the German "es gibt die Welt etc." (verb 'to give').

The dyad 'to be' and 'to have' (as considered e.g. by *Gabriel Marcel* in his *L'Etre et l'Avoir*) do not suffice; but the triad *to be, to have*, and *to give*, together complete our understanding of Divine Creation.

Whence we can move to the next question asking what meaning there is in assuming precisely a Divine Creator - even though He may, as we have suggested, abscond. This question is:

André Mercier

2.   Whether Time "had a beginning" and "will have an end"?

In our hypothesis of Flux, with To-come like a tide the front of which would glide up the sand-strand and vanish into the past, the beginning of Time coincides with that front, yet entering the past in an irreversible way. This is the right interpretation of *Virgil*'s formula *'fugit irreparabile tempus'*. Perhaps that front and what follows leave a "trace" in history - but so feable, however, that it is impossible to verify its origin in the "big bang"?

We may further ask: What is the "thing" that "banged" that "big"? The scientist who first suggested it: Father *Lemaître,* the astrophysicist at Louvain, spoke about the explosion of what he called "the primeval atom". But even if that explosion did happen, this could have been the true beginning of *neither* Time *nor* World, since the atom had to "be there" for it to explode. Consequently, its existence had to be given as a fact "before" that explosion. But, we may ask: How "long" before?

So, even if God did initiate the explosion, this would not amount to the beginning of World nor of Time, since before exploding the said primitive atom had to be "already there", which is absurd. I remember *Wolfgang Pauli* ostentatiously declaring such a hypothesis of a primitive atom "inacceptable". But in case the "big bang" did happen without a primitive atom "being there", it could only happen as a consequence of God's free decision to create Time and World - maybe by "tearing them off" from His own Being?[4]

Now, God has always been and by all the thinkers who involved Him in their thought as the *Perfect* Being, i.e., as implying the highest, most beautiful, most true, and best possible idea. Could then such a tearing off leave the said Divine perfection untouched, intact? Yes, since even though World thus created should be found greater than all what Man has so far been able to measure and though Time should be older than any lapse Man may conceive, both World and Time have remained *commensurable* to Man. This seems to support the idea of a beginning.

As far as an end is envisaged, would that be a sudden stop owing to simply screwing down the tap from which Time flows at the source of the To-come from whence it issues? Then World would not be anything more than a past without a present where things (including human beings) could no longer communicate, nor have any consciousness of one another, not even with the help of light or some other physical agent! Such question doesn't even make sense. Or would it rather be a sudden cataclysm at the source of the to-come, worse than anything suggested by some Holy Scripture?

André Mercier

All such questions justify a further question, viz. whether one ought to distinguish the time of science from a human conception of Time. Whence the third Question as put by the Organizer of the Symposium under the form of an alternative:

3.   Human time *versus* Time of Science: Does it suggest that there are indeed two thinkable Times between which we have to choose the right one? Or does it mean, that there are indeed two necessarily different times?

If Time were a *concept*, it could indeed be *conceived* such or such, just as one can conceive of a space with one, or two, or three, or even more dimensions, be it Euclidean, or curved, e.g. Riemannian, or Finslerian, or what have you: Physics, as the first of the sciences (called positive), uses for various purposes such differently conceived spaces, in order to propose *models of Reality* which it then tries to understand; another, second science like biology, or a third one, say sociology, may need further concepts of space to be defined each by a set of axioms. In doing so, geometry does not itself work as a science, i.e., as a *knowledge* (*eine Wissenschaft*), but as a *power* (*eine Könnenschaft*), part of a more universal power called mathematics.

Mathematics use concepts which are created by our mind as if by pregnancy. Basic terms as used by the sciences are not concepts, but notions which our mind guesses by discovering them. Popularly said: Science (or the sciences) discover, mathematics invent; and it makes sense to put mathematics in the plural just as there are several, plural sciences. But then one must understand that there is no space as reality, whereas there is Time as such, just as there is World as such, both created by God. Only artificially is Man given a rôle of a will-be exceptionality, other things being nothing but plain things devoid of thought, elements of Nature which Man pretends to dominate as if he were outside, or above, it - i.e., outside World and superior to things. Yet Man is - not just a reed, even though a 'thinking one' (*Pascal* dix.) - but constitutes a species within the animal kingdom.

In Nature as encompassing all such data, there is but just *one notion* which appears alone and unique of its kind, yet common to all things; it is *Time*: Time of World in its whole and its parts, hence of Man too. Hence the alternative is not between physical (or scientific) and human time. If there is an alternative, then it is between the commensurable and the incommensurable, calling not only for physics and the other ordinary, socalled positive, sciences, but also for metaphysics, which is dedicated to the study of the incommensurable, the very science of the incommensurable, if you please.

André Mercier

The alternative is, by the way, not only present within the so-called *objectivity* of *Science*, including metaphysics, but similarly within the *subjectivity* of *Art*, including the highest possible poietics, and within the *conjectivity* of *Morals*, including the relationship between man and His Creator, God.

If there were no Time, there would be no World. Yet there is Time, and the problem arises to make for ourselves adequate models of the latter.

4.   The Art of inventing World Models.

A model ought to ressemble the original to such a degree that if one would build in reality an object accordingly, that object should be so near the original as to make it quasi impossible to say which one, of the original and that object, is the true original. Yet World is the original of the totality of things, so much so that even to be nearest the original, one had to be God Himself in order to remake it *de facto* in its totality. Since we are not God, the model can at most be a mental construct, and even though it would differ in one or other respect it should, in order to be perfect, be mathematical, for mathematics alone are indisputable, i.e., free of faults, since they constitute the system of unattackable proofs. Now, according to *Aristotle*, κόσμος ἐστὶ σύστημα ἐξ οὐρανοῦ καὶ γῆς: World constitutes a totality as composed of heavens and earth: such was the representation of Antique Greece of yon World conceived as beautiful and perfect (κόσμος). And *Plato* maintained that ἀεί ὁ θεός γεωμετρεῖ: God always thinks in geometry!

But a truly mathematical (notably geometrical) construct of a World model by human intelligence was achieved much later, for two main reasons: one being the fact that the mathematics at the disposal of thinkers remained rather poor until after the Renaissance, despite the development of Euclidean geometry; the other being that the true cosmos does not simply coincide with "Heaven and Earth", because to begin with the latter is but an insignificant ball among the celestial bodies, and owing secondly to the fact that scholars had not yet understood that there are *at least* (namely on a scale equal or superior to the human one) two distinct phenomena as manifested in World: Universal attraction, and light.

That World be "luminous" does not seem to have caught anybody's attention (except authors of *Genesis* who quoted - *Gen. 3*: "there be light") insofar as it is part of that *cosmic*, i.e. *mathematical* order, and *Descartes* did for the first time produce a *theory* of reflection and refraction of light rays as these are conceived as the trajectories of its propagation. Moreover and by analogy, the same *Descartes* has elaborated a "model of the vacuum" - say

André Mercier

rather the model of an empty world where only light rays could be propagated, of which he did not conceive that they might bear an energy capable alone of exerting an influence upon the nature of World.

For sure, *Descartes* did put forward the principle of a physical determinism, which is more than suggesting a (geometric) model of World. Yet it was *Newton* who first understood the need to postulate a *trinitarian relationship* between notions concerning the nature of World, viz. time, momentum, and force, and to *enunciate* so-called natural laws describing the forces as capable to act upon momentum. In creating both rational mechanics in particular, and theoretical physics in general (called natural philosophy), *Newton* achieved two things: he modified the approach toward an explanation of World by substituting for the idea of a mere mathematical, or geometrical, model that of a mechanism as moved by a "force", and he founded - without noticing that he did so - a brand new chapter of philosophy, viz. the branch called theory of knowledge (in Greek: epistemology) wherein *notions*, beside *concepts*, are being suggested by relationships of mathematical form which are assumed to determine what is going on within World *and* Time.

That was the new efficacious means to ground a model explanation of how World works without any reference to Biblical or other genesis. In precisely this way *philosophic* thought (then called natural philosophy) became *complementary* (in a sense more general than the later complementarity as expounded by *Niels Bohr*) to religious thought without making the latter either false or superfluous. Such a *postulate* is not a "law of Nature"; it is rather what *David Hilbert* later called an *implicit definition* (a mutual implication of more than two terms), as opposed to the explicit definitions that dictionaries are expected to yield.

From its foundation, Newtonian Mechanics yielded as a model of World nothing but an explanation of the so-called *universal gravitation* (except some few local frictions which are not important on the cosmic scale). It was later elaborated further, from the middle of the 18th Century on, mainly by mathematical physicists in France and elsewhere around the *Encyclopedia*, e.g., *d'Alembert, Lagrange, Hamilton* and their followers, by finally reducing the "model of World" to a "principle of variation". Yet from the beginning of the 19th Century on, a new law of force was added to universal gravitation: first as separated into two supposedly distinct forces: the electric and the magnetic ones (*Coulomb, Ampère*), led back to fields (*Faraday*); this, from Maxwell on, was electromagnetism, by which light, as forgotten in the Newtonian conception, was reintegrated into a larger picture of World.

André Mercier

With *Einstein*, in his first proposal from 1905, electromagnetism alone is included in a four-dimensional model, while in 1916 gravitation is re-introduced owing to a Riemannian, instead of a Euclidean, geometrical description, thus opening the door to further generalisations of his relativity theory allowing for the description of further forces, preferably called inter-actions, assuming if necessary higher dimensionality than just a four-dimen-sional description in spaces which have totally lost any nature of the old reality of things. In all these later models, the so-called velocity of light is supposed to assume a so-called invariance.

In the Program as submitted by the Organizer of this Symposium, the next and fifth question concerns precisely that very point:

5.   What are the fundamental invariants of Nature?

Here, the word Nature has been substituted for World. We remember by the way that, according to *Spinoza*, Nature stands for God, as he put it in the Latin phrase: *Deus sive natura*. So far, in the present paper, such an idea of God is unthinkable. *Spinoza* was forbidden to enter the Synagogue after he said so. Later, *Einstein* put forward a similar idea by identifying God as Pantheos with World as described by generally relativistic models. Should he have been submitted to the same condemnation?

Within religious thought, pantheism is the extreme generalisation of animism by which a soul (of divine nature) is attributed to any particular object or thing in World: a tree, a mountain or what have you. In pantheism, World as single universal thing is identified with God as its soul - as such, it cannot be but perfect. Call it Nature if you please, and you join *Spinoza*. One great danger in doing so is, that the epistemological distinction between postulate and law collapses; there is then no room left for discovering natural laws of a universal validity as ruling, or reigning in, World.

If one asks questions about invariants, one assumes that there may be invariants as well; but what is then the kind of changes in reference to which there may be variance and/or invariance? The answer to that question is: possible changes of parameters within the description of world models. And since no other means of description than geometrical ones have been invented so far, such changes cannot be but changes in the parameters used in geometry, i.e.: coordinates, as they had for the first time been introduced by *Descartes* inventing Analytic geometry. Some magnitudes have been found to be invariant in that sense; the most conspicuous among them is the velocity of light. Invariants of such nature become then what one might call the universal

André Mercier

measures of World. They could, and should, then replace conventional units like the c.g.s. of international conventions. They are then the warrants of the commensurability of World. Apparently, knowing their values would close the problem of knowing how "big" the "bang" was at the creation of World.

Yet in fact and in truth, that is not the case: It was discovered in the middle of the 19th Century that a model of World is not achieved within the mere Newtonian or within a Newtonian-like epistemology. This was made obvious by *Sadi Carnot*'s establishment of thermodynamics with two so-called principles (which are neither of the nature of Newtonian postulates, nor of the nature of laws of Nature in the Newtonian sense). One of these principles expresses a general *conservation*, which is of manifestly temporal nature, the other one expresses what may specifically be called *death*, which is also of manifestly temporal nature. The physics chapter dealing with these principles is called thermodynamics - a chapter very much neglected in teaching at many physics departments of our Universities, and which is wrongly, though widely, thought to be reducible to mere probability calculus.

Further comments on these topics would take too much time. They would lead to conclusions in radical disagreement with certain contemporary ideological opinions held about Freedom. In any case, the Initiator of our Symposium very rightly calls our attention to his next question:

6.   How is causal order related to Time?

It is most important today to understand, that *Minkowski*'s old interpretation of what he called 'space-time' cannot be kept anymore: Indeed, physicists and scientists at large have unfortunately come to believe, that owing to the introduction of a four-dimensional manifold in the description of electromagnetism, World "is" that manifold in which Time t, as multiplied by ic, plays nothing more than the rôle of a fourth dimension. This belief seemed reinforced by the successful attempts to integrate the description of gravitational happening into that description: World seemingly became a four-dimensional, complex, geometrical manifold!

Time was no more considered a fundamental notion of its own, whereas Space, as a complex manifold, assumed the rank and honour of being World itself! If electromagnetism *and* gravitation had remained the only physical interactions as observable by any physical means, that conceptual view of World might have won the competition over the older one: Space would seem to possess Reality, Time having lost the statute of a notion, being reduced to the mere rank of a concept. But World was soon found to include

André Mercier

more interactions: strong and weak, and possibly further ones, and compelled physicists to enlarge the frame of description; especially, a four-dimensional manifold was found insufficient: So-called 'grand unification' speaks of, e.g., a ten-dimensional manifold.

In brief, the correct interpretation is not one, by which time is declared a supplementary, imaginary coordinate to be glued upon a spatial sub-manifold in order to constitute a homogeneous geometric model of World. Quite the contrary: *Time is and remains the bearer of Reality*, the geometric description of which is feasible by adjoining to it as many 'dimensions' of a mathematical imaginary nature, i.e.: not Time, but the parameters to be used in World description are to be used as complex numbers: Why not? The most elegant known description of electromagnetism rests already on the use of hypercomplex numbers, called *Clifford* numbers; spinors as used in quantum field theory have been found to belong to a sub-manifold of the corresponding Clifford algebra. In short: all progress made in the mathematical construction of models of World show that Space is, and remains, conceptual and *is not* a *notion* that has been "discovered", but is a *concept* that has been "invented", whereas the rôle as attributable to Time is, and remains, that of a *notion* which reflects the Reality of a Created World.

This is the reason why the problematics of Creation, or the Origin of World, must be approached. Yet to say that an original Big Bang is the only possible answer is inacceptable, since an already created thing had to explode, i.e., unless God *as a metaphysical Person* did tear World off His own Being. And that yields a proof of God, which is also the proper answer to give to the Next Question as put on our Agenda (**7.**).

8.   As to the further Question, asking what sense there is in assuming **God as a Creator**, it is very doubtful whether God is to be considered a mere "assumption", for either God imposes Himself to the human mind with full certainty, or He remains ignored by those who do not feel His evidence.

9.   Finally the Question **What does our view of Nature imply to ethics?** This has received an answer in my paper published 1992 and dedicated to *Karl Popper* on the occasion of his 90th birthday, in which World is not considered a mere mirror of God: World does not belong to Heaven for, in that context, Heaven does not mean the sky as studied by the astronomers; rather, it designates the *abode* of the absconding God of which we now know that it is located behind the to-come as its origin and source.

André Mercier

Appendix

Papers read at the Symposium were followed by three panels, and as many general discussions. These were listed as dealing successively with the following items: *What is Time? Time & World Order. Time & Creation.*

The three Items of the discussions just mentioned were meant to put some order in the questions which the Organizer of the Symposium had originally sent to the participants; these questions were exactly as follows:

1. Is temporal flux real or apparent? 2. Did time once begin? Will it ever end? 3. Human time versus the time of science. 4. The noble art of contriving world-models. 5. Which are the fundamental invariants of nature? 6. How may causality be related to time-space? 7. What is the sense of assuming a Divine Creator? 8. What difference would this assumption make to us? 9. What does our view of nature imply to ethics?

In opening one of the panel sessions, Professor *David Park* put forward the opinion that the unity of all these items might be summarised in the one Question: *What is time?* and he even took the trouble to write that one question in big letters on the panel board.[5] In a certain sense I could agree with that, in another one I could not! For if, on the one hand, Time has been a main notion around which all prepared lectures have been held and the panel discussions would have to keep in mind, on the other hand one main concern of the Host of our Meeting was evident from the specific invitation we had received as well as from the nine questions reproduced a few lines above: The feasibility of connecting the topic of Time with that of God.

Since Professor *Park* summed up the first of these topics in the plain question: *What is Time?*, I suggested to sum up the second of these topics, and wrote it on the board, by asking, not 'what', but 'who', viz.: *Who is God?*

In a private discussion which followed, Prof. *Park* agreed, that it would not have been proper to use the interrogation pronoun *what* in referring to God, whereas the use of the pronoun *who* is correct, for God, *if He is at all*, is neither a thing, nor a vague assumption: *God is a Person* - i.e., as I added as a kind of definition: One who is in a position 'to speak in the first person'; (cf. *Concise Oxford Dictionary*, 6th ed. 1976, p.824, items 5 and 6).

On the whole, the scholars attending the Symposium did not seem inclined to discuss a possible connection between the topics of Time and God. A number of them were physicists, and maybe physicists in general prefer to avoid touching upon such subject-matter of speech. Yet why be so reserved?

André Mercier

Moreover, there were also philosophers, especially metaphysicians, and even theologians (at least one most respected of such), and it is a fact that among contemporary scholars, the question of an understanding between science and theology, even religion, has become a matter of concern on a world-wide scale (cf. *Who's Who in Theology and Science*, which fills 400 pages).

It was therefore a disappointment to me that the general discussion remained restricted to questions foreign not only to religion proper, but even to *metaphysics*. The more so as I have in my lecture taken care to remind that, according to *Niels Bohr*, scientific thought (especially that of physics, but also that of philosophy) is related by way of complementarity to religious thought. This kind of *generalised complementarity* deserves to be studied and clarified not only by scientists, but also by theologians.[6]

This is the reason why I took care to explain the difference which allows us to distinguish *metaphysics as the science of the incommensurable* from physics proper and the other ordinary sciences of the commensurable. Metaphysics thus reaches the domain of Divine Nature, whereas ordinary science keeps to worldly matters. Time, however, appertains likewise to the physical *and* to the metaphysical enterprise of the human mind.

This was also the reason why I felt compelled to raise a fairly strong objection when someone maintained that time is the object of measurement. This mistake is repeatedly made by many physicists when talking about time. But I claim that time is never the object of any measurement - indeed, time is not reducible to the status of being an object at all!

That I am right can be made clear by the following line of reasoning. If, to begin with, one intends to measure the length of a rod - and this does indeed make sense - he will put his rod along another bigger rod upon which regular marks have been engraved according to the choice of a unit of length. Such rods may be made of wood, of iron, of platin-iridium, or what have you - but they are never made of time, as "time-rods" would not be repeatable.

Time flows as the to-come goes by, but the present, called the 'now', which separates the to-come from the by-gone, has no duration since it is a "cut" between the two. There are no lasting durations, no temporal intervals, that can be repeatedly measured by putting them in parallel with other fixed, invariable intervals chosen as units. At this point of my argument a naive physicist may wish to interrupt me and say: Oh yes, there are such intervals: what about the course around the sun of a planet coming back to a same point of its trajectory, or the tick-tock of a pendulum attached to a clock?

André Mercier

Planetary motions indeed seem to be extremely regular, yet they are not radically free from tides which may bring them to a stop after a quasi infinite length of time. Swiss watches are considered to be very reliable, but they must be wound up if fashioned in the old mechanical way, or refilled with new batteries if based on electric power. Thus, it seems as if intervals of time can be compared such as, e.g., those covered by the competitors in a skiing championship when running down from the same hill.

Yet it is wrong to consider these examples as measurements of time or as measurements of temporal intervals to be compared with one another. So let me repeat: the length of one and the same rod can be measured again and again, to make sure that no mistake has been made; but neither duration as such nor temporal intervals can ever be measured at a given time for the simple reason that the same durations or instants never occur twice.[7]

There are natural clocks, or calendars, e.g. the motion of the Earth, rotating around its axis with regard to the Sun (yielding the day and its hours, minutes, seconds), or moving around the Sun (yielding the year) along a trajectory that is quasi-unchangeable for millenia. There could be other and less conspicuous clocks or calendars as derived from astronomical or physical phenomena such as motions and even radioactivity. All this is well known. Yet it has misled a number of scholars into believing that time is measurable. But clocks and watches are not measuring devices; they are quasi-calendars.

Physicists claim to be exact. Then let them be indeed. What is correct to say about time is that it can be *numbered*. Therefore, if we want to answer the question of Prof. *Park* by saying what Time is not, we should agree that Time is not a measurable property of anything, least of all a property of World. Rather Time, by being numbered, is a necessary condition for the possibility of measuring properties disclosed by our observation of phenomena.

Turning then to my own question - *Who is God?* - I shall answer: *God is the Donor of Time*, thus making it possible for Man to develop physics and to devote himself to a lot of other useful and meaningful activities.

Editor's remark

Professor André Mercier, after some time of weakness, departed on his birthday, April 15th, 1999, 86 years old. We shall all remember him as a great scientist, an impressive personality, and a loveable human being.

When presenting this paper to the participants of the symposium, he described it as his "spiritual testament".

André Mercier

Notes

---

[1] Under the same title the author has published a book (P. Lang, Bern 1996).

[2] The alternative between 'pardon' and 'punishment' was a favourite example used by *Niels Bohr* when HE discussed the meaning to be attributed to the concept of *complementarity* with regard to circumstances outside the restricted field of physics proper.

[3] Yet not of the so-called existence of God, which is a meaningless concept, since only things do exist, their existence being dependent upon God, whereas God Himself does not depend upon existence, since He is not a thing.

[4] As far as I am aware, this last conjecture has been uttered for the first time by the Swiss philosopher *Jeanne Hersch*.

[5] *Prof. Park notes* that the reason he wrote 'Time' (instead of simply: Time), on the blackboard and in his paper, is that he does not know what Time is.

[6] It is interesting to point out that the 1976 edition already quoted above of the *Concise Oxford Dictionary* contains the word 'complementarity' whereas early editions of the same, especially the first one from 1911 and further ones, do not: The concept of complementarity as explainability of micro-physical phenomena as either waves or particles jointly was namely put forward by *Bohr* in the late twenties after *Louis de Broglie* had founded his wave mechanics in 1924. Attempts by *Bohr* (and some of his pupils, incl. the author of the present Report) to enlarge the dialectical significance of the concept of complementarity, go back to the middle and late thirties.

[7] All such commentaries allow us to declare as a fake the saying that "time is money": time is not money; but the speed at which business comes to a successful achievement is rewarded by money. If time were money, money ought to be time, which is evidently not the case, while money can be said to be a form of energy, e.g. in paying the bill for electric power used during a month, i.e., a period of time; which is something else.

André Mercier

LAWRENCE FAGG

IDEAS OF TIME & COSMIC ORIGIN

1. The Early Universe According to Modern Physical Cosmology

Certainly one of the most fundamental questions arising from the contemporary study of cosmology is whether time had a beginning. Currently most physicists and cosmologists as well as Western theologians (following the lead of St. Augustine) tend to associate the beginning of time in some way with the beginning of the universe. For the physicists, with some exceptions, this beginning is described by successively amended versions of the Big Bang Theory (BBT), now mostly termed the "Standard Model" by cosmologists. This model rests on three principal pillars of experimental support:

1) The universe is observed to be expanding. This expansion was first observed and reported by M.L. Humason and E. Hubble in 1929 and early theoretical interpretations of it in terms of the Big Bang concept were given by G. Lemaitre and G. Gamow among others. 2) The observed abundances of the light elements agree with predictions of the BBT, although this has been subject to some recent controversy to be discussed later. 3) Observations of the temperature and frequency spectrum of the cosmic microwave background (CMB) of remarkable accuracy also agree with predictions of the BBT.

With this as background I would like to describe my understanding of the presently accepted Big Bang scenario which will include the phenomena that provide the three pillars of experimental support mentioned above. In this scenario the universe is thought to have expanded from an extremely compactified source whose length and time scales were of the order of 10^{-33} cm and 10^{-43} sec respectively, characterised by enormous temperature and energy densities. This has often been called the Planck domain or Planck era. In this condition the universe was so compactified that the classical laws of general relativity can no longer describe it and time and space no longer have their usual meaning. The universe was a quantum object, only describable by a quantum theory. On the other hand the universe as we know it is described by a classical theory: general relativity. This brings us to the central issue of cosmology today: can a theory be found that unites the quantum and general relativity theories into a satisfactory theory of quantum gravity?

So far this has not been achieved. I will come back to the issue later, but for now I would like to describe the rest of the Big Bang scenario that occurs after the Planck era. It must be emphasised that the earliest parts of this scenario are generally considered rather speculative and unamenable to experimental confirmation. We first need to note that, in the Planck era of quantum gravity, the four forces of nature (nuclear, electromagnetic, weak, gravitational) are taken to be united and describable by one set of equations. As the universe expands, the forces begin to separate stepwise into four distinct forces while the particles begin to unite into more complex particles. Let us consider the forces first. As the universe emerged out of the Planck quantum realm, the gravitational force separated off from the other three at around 10^{-43} sec leaving these three still united and hopefully describable by one of a number of so-called Grand Unified Theories, or GUTs. It has often been noted that such a pretentious title is unjustified, since the GUTs only unify three forces. At around 10^{-35} sec the nuclear force separates leaving the remaining two still united. Finally, at roughly 10^{-10} sec, the weak and electromagnetic forces separate leaving the four separate forces we see today.

However, there is now a thus far successful theory uniting the electromagnetic and weak forces, the electroweak theory, which received its first major support from experiments at the CERN accelerator in Switzerland some 15 years ago. The particle energies that the CERN accelerator produced yielded energy densities characteristic of the universe at about 10^{-10} sec when the universe was still thought to be subject to the electroweak unification. The electroweak theory is the first major unification of forces since Maxwell unified electricity and magnetism over 120 years ago, and provides the motivation for finding a theory that includes one or both of the other two forces. However, to experimentally confirm even one of the GUTs, incorporating the nuclear force with the electroweak formulation, would require an accelerator at least the sise of the solar system (Hawking 88, p.74).

Let us now discuss the particles. Between 10^{-43} sec and about 10^{-35} sec the universe was an intensely hot "soup", wherein quarks and electrons were indistinguishable. Then at around 10^{-35} sec there was a "freeze out" or condensation to a lower temperature "soup" of which quarks and electrons can be considered for our purposes here the most significant constituents - and it was in this era that the universe, according to most theoretical cosmologists, experienced what has been called an inflation, i.e., it underwent an incredible exponential expansion, much faster than any expansion before or after, which was completed at about 10^{-30} sec, after which the universe continued to expand

Lawrence Fagg

in a non-inflationary mode (Guth & Steinhardt 84; Linde 87). The concept of inflation was added to the Big Bang scenarios some 15 years ago to help explain a number of features of the universe that the original BBT could not. Since that time there have been a number of variant inflation theories, with little chance at this time of confirming which is correct (Linde et al. 94).

In any case, the quark-electron soup began to "freeze out" to a still lower temperature soup at about 10^{-6} sec wherein the quarks combined three at a time to form protons and neutrons, of course, still accompanied by electrons. At roughly 1 sec the protons and neutrons began to unite to form light nuclei, such as deuterium, helium, and lithium in a soup of a still lower temperature. The BBT's prediction of the relative abundances of nuclei in agreement with observations provide the second basis of experimental support for the theory. Although astronomic observations essentially affirm the relative abundances, very recently some clearly conflicting data on the deuterium abundance have been reported (Physics Today 8/96, p.17).

Eventually, at about 300,000 years the universe had expanded and cooled sufficiently to allow electrons with negative electric charge to attach themselves to nuclei with positive electric charge to form electrically neutral atoms; this event made it possible for electromagnetic radiation, or light, to move freely without being trapped in a constant interaction with the plasma of charged particles which characterised the previous higher temperature era. It is the degraded remnant of this radiation that constitutes the cosmic micro-wave background (CMB) today, first observed in 1965, providing the third major source of experimental support for the BBT's predictions.

In the '90's this confirmation became far more impressive, due to extremely accurate measurements of the CMB. These measurements showed:

1) that the temperature and frequency spectrum of the observed CMB down to an accuracy of about one part in one hundred thousand was in remarkable agreement with the BBT, predicting a universe that was on average homogeneous and isotropic; but 2) at the most sensitive levels of temperature measurement down to a level of about three parts in a million, however, there were slight variations in the temperature (Smoot et al. 92).

The discovery of these minute temperature variations in 1992 was vital to the survival of the BBT. The variations are considered to reflect quantum fluctuations in the universe's mass at a very early stage of its evolution soon after inflation. These slight accumulations of mass are thought to serve as the seeds for the gradual gravitational accretion of matter that ultimately formed the galaxies we see today.

Lawrence Fagg

Thus this observation helped resolve a vexing contradiction that prevailed until 1992: how could the CMB indicating a universe that was isotropic and homogeneous be reconciled with the observed fact that the universe was lumpy with stars and galaxies. The current conviction in the cosmology community that the temperature variations observed in the CMB are signatures of minute mass fluctuations in the very early universe brings us back to the question of this primordial era. In fact I would like to return my attention to the Planck regime and briefly treat the issue of a quantum gravity theory, which, as I noted earlier, is necessary when the universe, ordinarily describable by general relativity, was incredibly small, finding itself in this regime where some form of quantum physics must come into play.

A whole spectrum of attempts at a theory of quantum gravity were proposed in the early and mid '80's. Among them were what is known as string theories wherein the ultimate elements are tiny strings instead of point-like matter. Also included in some theories was the concept of what is known as supersymmetry, which proposes essentially that the elementary particles which are the material building blocks of our world, such as electrons and quarks on the one hand, and particles which are carriers of the forces between the above particles, such as photons in the case of the electromagnetic force on the other hand, exchange rôles. Thus according to supersymmetry there are two sets of particles, one set consisting of the particles we know and another set a kind of mirror image of the first.

In the late '80's and early '90's things were relatively quiet on the quantum gravity, string theory, and supersymmetry front. But the last couple of years have seen a resurgence of string theories, especially in their supersymmetric form, as leading candidates for ultimately finding a theory of quantum gravity. Indeed, according to Ed Witten at Princeton, the study has narrowed down to only a few string theories, and they may possibly be all equivalent, so that there may ultimately be only one left (Witten 96).

Even if an apparently satisfactory theory of quantum gravity is formulated so that in principle the Planck era could be better understood, the problem of experimentally confirming such a theory remains formidable, if not impossible. Whether or not such a new theory is formulated, theoretical cosmologists are nevertheless still interested in formulating a theory for how the universe originated, in particular, how the Planck era itself originated; attendant with this, of course, is the haunting question of whether time began. Many theorists hold that time did not begin at a precise instant, but somehow evolved to its present form with the emergence from the quantum realm.

Lawrence Fagg

The theories that try to deal with these problems do not actually come to grips with developing a theory of quantum gravity. Some of the most well-known are based on the somewhat controversial assumption of applying quantum mechanics to the entire universe. They set up a quantum wave function for the whole universe and attempt to determine initial conditions that in one way or another describe a universe evolving essentially from nothing.

Two efforts, which have drawn attention the two last decades, are the so-called "no boundary" and "tunneling" theories. In the "no boundary" theory proposed by J. Hartle and S. Hawking (cf. Hartle & Hawking 83; Hawking 88, p.136f), the universe in its earliest stage when subject to quantum effects is seen as having no specific spatio-temporal initial state or "$t=0$ boundary". For this to be true theory implies time to be imaginary in the quantum regime. This is not imaginary in the conventional sense; it is a mathematical term. In mathematics any number multiplied by the square root of minus one is called 'imaginary'. The effect of the procedure is to endow time with another kind of dimensionality wherein time actually assumes a space-like character. A feature of this theory is that there is no clearcut beginning of the universe and time, that is, there is no time boundary. Time has no real meaning in this early era which is analogous to north having no meaning at the north pole. In the tunneling process proposed by Andrei Vilenkin the universe "tunnels" from essentially nothing to proceed henceforth in its expansion (Vilenkin 84). This tunneling process is roughly comparable to that which occurs in the radioactive emission of an α-particle (essentially a helium nucleus with two protons and two neutrons) from a heavy nucleus such as uranium. In this case quantum theory shows that it is possible for the α-particle to "tunnel" through the barrier imposed by the collective effect of the strong nuclear force provided by the neighboring protons and neutrons.

However, what is probably of most interest here is: *'What is nothing'*? It is certainly not anything remotely material. It is most often compared with the vacuum. That is, vacuum as we know it or what you would get when you pump all of the gas out of a vacuum-tight container. Even this vacuum is not really nothing. Quantum electrodynamics tells us that it is alive, with fleeting particles that appear for an instant and then vanish, generally in pairs, the most well-known example of which is an electron-positron pair spontaneously emerging and disappearing. Such particles are not directly observable, hence they are called 'virtual particles'. They do not violate the law of conservation of energy because the product of their masses and life-times are such that Heisenberg's Uncertainty Principle says they are undetectable; nevertheless,

Lawrence Fagg

we know they must be there, for if they were not included in the calculations, quantum electrodynamics could not yield the incredibly accurate agreement with experimental measurements it does, to better than one part in ten billion. So at least something like this vacuum may be hypothesised as the "nothing" from which the material structure of the universe may have arisen.

The foregoing is my understanding of what today's theoretical cosmology can say about time in the early universe and about the idea of the universe evolving from nothing. However, it is very important to emphasise even though the basic elements of the BBT that I have described so far appear to be valid, the theories that describe the very beginning of the universe are highly speculative and could easily be replaced by something considered to be better within a few years.

2. Religious Creation Myths and the Parallels with Physical Cosmology

Now I would like to change focus and briefly discuss some religious sources for the concept of *creatio ex nihilo*. For me the concept rests on the interpretation of the creation myths that initiate the cosmologies of a number of religions throughout the world. Undoubtedly the most familiar in the Western world is the Genesis account which starts with the famous words: *"In the beginning God created the heavens and the earth"*. Most biblical scholars consider it to be derived from Canaanite and Mesopotamian myths.

It was St. Augustine's interpretation of the Genesis scenario that left a lasting impression on Christian theology. According to Augustine, God has created the world and time along with it. Thus the world was not created in time: there was no time before the creation because there was no "before". As is well known, this is all clearly laid out in Book XI of his *Confessions*. Augustine also states that God created the world from nothing. Quoting again from Book 11: *Nor did you have in your hand anything from which you could make heaven and earth, for where could you have obtained matter which you had not yet created, in order to use this material for making something else? Does anything exist by any other cause than that you created it?* The same conviction was stated by St. Thomas Aquinas in his *Compendium of Theology*: *God was not in need of any pre-existing matter from which to fashion things*.

But Judeo-Christian-Islamic cosmology is not the only one wherein this interpretation can be made. Myths may be found in a number of religious traditions throughout the world which speak of a creation out of nothing in even more specific terms than the Genesis account. There are a whole host of creation myths that posit a variety of ways by which the world originated.

Lawrence Fagg

There are what Charles Long termed "emergence" myths which speak of a birth from Mother Earth; these are found in the Navaho and Pueblo Indians of North America as well as in some South Pacific cultures. Closely related are the "world-parent" myths of Babylonia, Polynesia, and Egypt, wherein, e.g., the earth is mother and the heavens father. Greek, Finnish, Upanishadic, and Tahitian traditions depict creation from chaos and/or from a "cosmic egg". There are also the engaging "earth diver" myths describing a divine being, usually an animal, who dives into the water to bring up the first particles of earth, the germs from which the whole universe grows (Long 63).

However, for this discussion, the most significant and relevant are the *creatio-ex-nihilo* myths. In addition to the Hebrew creation myth, among others are the Zuni, Mayan, Tuamotuan, and Maori myths; all are *ex nihilo*. According to Long, the religions in which these myths are imbedded tend to be characterised by some form of monotheism. They also tend to have a relatively long developmental history, often initially involving some form of polytheism, but later the multiple gods are gradually subsumed by one totally independent omnipotent god (Long 63, p.146ff). It may be that my thought is colored by my Western Judeo-Christian heritage, but I believe that compared to the other kinds of creation myths, the *ex nihilo* myths are indicative of a greater theological, if not spiritual, maturity. This is because the creator god is truly one, omnipotent, and unconditioned. There is no primordial substance which the god uses to create the world, no world parents, no cosmic eggs, no particles at the bottom of the sea - nothing but one omnipotent god.

To summarise, four characteristics of *ex nihilo* myths are pointed out by Long: 1) the creator is all-mighty and does not share power with any other deity or force; 2) the creator is alone in the void; there is no material reality prior to the creation of the cosmos out of the void; 3) the mode of creation is conscious, ordered, and deliberate, revealing a clear plan; 4) the god is free, not bound by the inertia of any prior reality (Long 63, p.114-9f).

I want to give some few examples from Maori and Polynesian myths. Consider first the Maori myth of Io: *Io dwelt within the breathing space of immensity, and the universe was in darkness. And he began by saying these words: 'Let there be light unto Tawhito, a dominion of light, a bright light', and suddenly a great light prevailed* (Long 63, p.173) A similar example is the Polynesian myth of Taaroa: *He existed, and Taaroa was his name. In the immensity there was no earth, there was no sky, there was no sea, there was no man. Above, Taaroa calls. Existing alone, he became the universe. Taaroa is the sand. It is thus that he is named. Taaroa is the light.* (ibid, p.172)

Lawrence Fagg

Do these ex nihilo creation myths have anything in common with the Big Bang scenario that I have described earlier? I suggest that there are three fundamental properties common to the physical and religious scenarios that I have discussed: 1) there was indeed some kind of beginning from "nothing", 2) light was an early feature of the process, 3) the process took place in stages. As regards the stages, no attempt is intented to correlate, e.g., the days of the Genesis story with the ages of evolution, whether cosmologic or human. My only point is that the complete creation did not take place all at once.

What, if anything, is to be made of this broad similarity in physical and religious processes of creation and evolution? In response to the question one must be careful. It is not primarily a matter of religion being right about cosmology all along, or of science proving the validity of a religious claim. It is a matter of according some credibility to the profound spiritual insight that vitalises these religious traditions. It is a matter of sensing that when scientific and religious descriptions have such general similarity, a special immanence of meaning, a special inner resonance is accorded that description that it otherwise would not have. It is a matter of realising that a world view that is solely scientific is incomplete and unsatisfying.

3. Theological Interpretations of Some Views of the Origin of Cosmos

It is undoubtedly realisations such as the foregoing that have at least in part motivated some scholars to seek meaningful theological interpretations of the current status of physical cosmology concerning the universe's origins. For example, Ted Peters has pointed out the significance of the *creatio ex nihilo* doctrine in Christian theology being consonant with the picture of the universe's beginning as indicated in the Big Bang cosmology (Peters 88).

This is a view with which I am in sympathy and one which has been examined extensively by philosophers and theologians in recent years. But Peters goes on to express a concurrent need to more deeply understand and evaluate the concept of *creatio continua*, wherein God is seen as a creator-sustainer of the cosmos in its evolution. His primary reason for supporting these concepts jointly is that "the primordial experience of God doing something new leads us in this direction" just as the Old Testament prophets saw God promising something new in Israel, and as Jesus and Paul in the New Testament promised something new for Christian believers.

However, the primality of the *creatio-continua* principle has long been supported by Ian Barbour, who sees the universe continually undergoing creation: *Today the world as known to science is dynamic and incomplete.*

Lawrence Fagg

Ours is an unfinished universe which is still in the process of appearing. Surely the coming to-be of life from matter can represent divine creativity as suitably as any postulated primeval production of matter "out of nothing". Creation occurs throughout time (Barbour 66, p.385). In more recent work (Barbour 95, p.396) he reinterprets the idea of *creatio ex nihilo* to apply to "the whole of the cosmos at every moment, regardless of questions about its beginning or its detailed structure and history". He maintains that the purpose of creation myths is to place present human experience in a meaningful cosmic context, and not primarily to explain distant past events. In a word he holds that *creatio ex nihilo* is an ontological, not an historical, assertion.

The dialectic concerning the relative significance of *creatio ex nihilo* and *creatio continua* in terms of ontological versus historical origination has also been studied by Robert Russell (93, p.307ff.) in an article that is in part devoted to seeking theological interpretations of the Hartle-Hawking no-boundary proposal discussed earlier. Russell proposes that expressions of the historical origination be imbedded within "the broader context of ontological origination". He sees the scientific support for the universe having a finite age according to the Big Bang scenario, as "empirical evidence for the support of ontological origination". In a word, he suggests that central to theological research is the hypothesis: "*creatio ex nihilo* means ontological origination".

However, my viewpoint is most congenial with that of Ted Peters, wherein equal credence and value is accorded historical and ontological origination. I further maintain that the mythical bases for the Genesis creation story and for numerous creation myths worldwide is evidence that there was in the psychic makeup of perceptive early men and women an apprehension of an historical beginning, a creation insight. Though this insight is expressed in a multitude of different creation scenarios, it nevertheless expresses one commonality among them: that there was a beginning, a beginning that was sensed as having both an ontological as well as historical basis.

These endeavors to interpret theologically the empirical evidence furnished us by modern cosmology I see as a sincere groping for our own story of cosmic evolution (Rue 96), a story that is rationally understandable and that emotionally and spiritually rings true in the hearts of today's men and women. It is the essence of our humanness to now seek a modern myth of creation and evolution of the cosmos for the 21st century, a myth that somehow harmonises the facts of physical cosmology with the realisation that we did not make ourselves and that we are a part of the universe, a universe whose existence is at least consistent with a belief in a Creator.

Lawrence Fagg

4. The Irreversible Nature of Time. Cosmic Expansion
Thermodynamics, and Electromagnetism

I would like to comment briefly on the irreversible nature of time. A number of contemporary scholars and writers have cited some three to six natural phenomena by which the passage of time is gauged and which they choose to term "arrows of time." However, I will only discuss the two most fundamental phenomena in the physical world by which time is sensed.

From a cosmic viewpoint, the primary process offering a means of gauging time is the expansion of the universe. When the universe completed its inflationary phase at about 10^{-30} seconds after the Big Bang, its expansion proceeded at a much slower rate. It is a rate that is thought to be gradually decreasing and so is probably not exactly constant. But on time scales of say millions of years can be considered close to constant. As such the expansion of the universe has therefore been cited as the "cosmological arrow of time".

However, the temporal gauge that has received the most attention in the scholarly as well as popular literature has been the "thermodynamic arrow of time." Based on the Second Law of Thermodynamics, it associates the passage of time with the general tendency in nature on average to proceed irreversibly to greater states of disorder, the measure of which is entropy. This irreversibility is to be considered to correlate with the time asymmetry observed in the macroscopic world of everyday experience.

On the other hand, this asymmetry is in direct contrast to the time symmetry or reversibility that characterises almost all of the interactions in the microscopic world of quantum physics, except for the decay of the neutral K meson and maybe the neutral B meson. That is, the equations that describe the interactions in the quantum world apply equally well for the interaction to proceed in one way as well as the reverse way. This brings us to the central question still under some controversy to this day: how is it that phenomena in the macroscopic everyday world are characterised by irreversibility, while almost all of the individual microscopic events comprising this macroscopic world are amenable to a time symmetric or reversible description?

The question was first addressed by Boltzmann with his statistical thermodynamics over a century ago, but has recently received the attention of Prigogine (Prigogine 80; Prigogine & Stengers 84; Prigogine & Driebe 95). Among Prigogine's conclusions, the most controversial (see Verstraeten 91) seems to be that microscopic phenomena are time irreversible too, a view also held by Fadner (Fadner 92). Both Prigogine and Fadner make use of quantum mechanics in order to show the microscopic irreversibility of time.

Lawrence Fagg

However, considering the macroscopic level, I would like to present a more specific reason for irreversibility based on a well-known electromagnetic phenomenon known as *bremsstrahlung*, occurring in all electron, atomic, and molecule collision processes. Whenever an electrically charged particle is deflected in a collision it undergoes an acceleration and it emits photons whose energy varies depending on the kinetic energy of the particle and the angle of deflection (for electron scattering see Schwinger 49).

Such emissions also occur in collisions between neutral atoms and molecules, for instance by virtue of van der Waals forces, which come into play in particular if the atoms or molecules have a non-spherical distribution of orbital electrons. But a lack of symmetry can also be induced in a collision between two neutral atoms which are otherwise spherical (Amusia 88), resulting in so-called polarisational *bremsstrahlung* In these cases very low energy *bremsstrahlung* photons can be emitted. Such photons, as well as high energy photons from more energetic collisions, are lost in the medium; that is, the collision by the amount of this loss, however small or large, is irreversible. This behaviour of bremsstrahlung photons is in addition to that of the photons ultimately lost to the medium, which were emitted and absorbed by atoms and molecules via transitions among their energy states. To my knowledge this explanation for macroscopic irreversibility in terms of electromagnetic interactions has not previously been suggested.

I would like to conclude by making some general remarks concerning religious views relative to the irreversible nature of time, whether or not it has a microscopic or macroscopic basis. Most of the major world religions in one way or another place a singular importance on the living moment, the here and now. Furthermore they also generally provide some form of a moral goal in terms of salvation through unity with an eternal God or enlightenment by union with a transcendent Reality.

Accordingly, these religions furnish a new dimension to the time in the physical world characterised by transience, continuity, and irreversibility. For them the ongoing lived moments are *value-endowed time*; and it is *goal-directed time* by being set in the context of the search for a Divine eternity or for a timeless transcendent Reality.

Lawrence Fagg

References

1. Amusia, M.Y., 1988: *Physics Reports* 162.5, p.249.
2. Barbour, I.G., 1966: *Issues in Science and Religion*, Prentice-Hall.
3. Barbour, I.G., 1995, in: *Cosmic Beginnings and Human Ends*, eds. Matthews & Varghese, Open Court, Chicago.
4. Fadner, W., 1992: *Bull.Amer.Phys.Soc.* 37, p.965.
5. Guth & Steinhardt, 1984: *Scientific American*, May.
6. Hartle & Hawking, 1983: *Phys.Rev.* D 47, p.2950.
7. Hawking, S.W., 1988: *A Brief History of Time*, Bantam, NY.
8. Linde, A., 1987: *Physics Today*, September.
9. Linde, Linde & Mezhlumian, 1994: *Phys.Rev.* D49, p.1783.
10. Long, C.H., 1963: *Alpha, The Myths of Creation*, G. Braziller, NY.
11. Peters, T., 1988, in: *Physics, Philosophy, and Theology*, eds. Russell, Stoeger & Coyne, Vatican City State, p.273.
12. 1996, *Physics Today*, August, p.17.
13. Prigogine, I., 1980: *From Being to Becoming*, Freeman, S.Francisco.
14. Prigogine & Stengers, 1984: *Order out of Chaos*, Heinemann London.
15. Prigogine & Driebe, 1995: 'Time, Chaos, and the Laws of Nature', submitted to *Scientific American*.
16. Rue, L., 1996, lecture on the Epic of Evolution, at Conference of the Institute of Religion in an Age of Science, Star Island, NH.
17. Russell, R.J., 1993, in: *Quantum Cosmology and the Laws of Nature*, Russell, Murphy & Isham, Vatican City State.
18. Schwinger, J., 1949: *Phys.Rev.* 75, p.898.
19. Smoot, G., et al., 1992: *Astrophys.Jour.Lett.* 396, p.?
20. Verstraeten, G., 1991: *Phil.Science* 58, p.639.
21. Vilenkin, A., 1984: *Phys.Rev.* D 30, p.509.
22. Witten, E., 1996: *Physics Today* 49, p.24.

Lawrence Fagg

LUDWIK KOSTRO

RELATIVISTIC SPACE-TIME INTERPRETED AS A NEW ETHER
THE VIEW OF ALBERT EINSTEIN

Introduction

Einstein's relativistic ether concept remains today almost unknown among physicists, philosophers, and sometimes, also, historians of physics. Albert Einstein has acquired, among them, the reputation of having destroyed the concept of the ether. Today, this view is still put forward in textbooks, encyclopaedias, and scientific reviews. It is true that, from 1905 until the end of his life, Einstein denied the existence of an ether as it was conceived in 19th-century physics, in particular of Lorentz's ether, which was in the first place a privileged reference frame. He denied its existence because it violated his principle of relativity, according to which there is no privileged reference frame for the formulation of the laws of nature. Nevertheless, in 1916, after having offered a definitive formulation of the general theory of relativity, Einstein proposed a completely new conception of the ether. According to this conception, the new ether does not violate the principle of relativity because the space-time of the theory of relativity is conceived of as a material medium *sui generis* that can in no way constitute a frame of reference.

In Einstein's letter to Lorentz of June 17, 1916, in which he introduced for the first time his new notion of ether, we read:

I agree with you that the general theory of relativity is closer to the ether hypothesis than the special theory. This new ether theory, however, would not violate the principle of relativity, because the state of this $g_{\mu\nu} =$ ether would not be that of a rigid body in an independent state of motion, but every state of motion would be a function of position determined through the material processes.[1]

As we see, physical space (intimately connected with time) the local state of which is described by the components $g_{\mu\nu}$ of the metrical tensor g was regarded by Einstein as the new ether. In this new conception, the ether is no longer considered as a rigid quasi-object to which we can apply the notion of motion and which is independent of the material processes but it is conceived as a medium the structure of which depends on the presence and motion of material bodies and which determines their inertio-gravitational motion.

Ludwik Kostro

According to Einstein, the concepts of motion and of velocity can be applied only to the ponderable bodies composed of particles but not to the new ether. Einstein denied the existence of an ether for only 11 years, from 1905 to 1916. Then he began to consider his denial as an opinion which was too radical. In the so-called 'Morgan Manuscript', in 1919, he wrote:

In 1905, I was of the opinion that it was no longer allowed to speak about the ether in physics. This opinion, however, was too radical.[2]

In a letter to Lorentz, written also in 1919, he likewise regretted his former denial of the existence of an ether:

It would have been more right if I had limited myself in my earlier publications to emphasising only the non-existence of an ether velocity instead of arguing the total non-existence of the ether, for I can see that with the word ether we say nothing else than that space has to be viewed as a carrier of physical qualities.[3]

As we can see, Einstein identifies the new ether with physical space. According to him, the ether simply is physical space endowed with real physical properties. These properties are describable in the general theory of relativity by the components $g_{\mu\nu}$ of the tensor g.

On the basis of Einstein's papers and letters we can say that, in 1916, Einstein's physics of space-time became the physics of a new ether. Thus, the notion of an ether in the theory of relativity found a new and interesting application. Einstein wrote in 1938:

We may still use the word ether, but only to express the physical properties of space. This word ether has changed its meaning many times   in the development of science. At the moment it no longer stands for a medium built up of particles. Its story, by no means finished, is continued by the relativity theory.[4]

The history of Einstein's ether concept is very interesting. I have presented it in several papers,[5,6,7] and in a book entitled:

Albert Einstein's Relativistic Ether Concept,
its History, Physical Meaning and Philosophical Background.[8]

In the present paper I would like to give its physical interpretation. A physical interpretation of a concept used in physics can be conceived and performed in different ways. One of them consists in an enucleation of its physical meaning. Such an enucleation must be done, of course, not only verbally (i.e., using only words) but also mathematically (i.e., using symbols). I shall attempt to offer a similar physical interpretation, at the same time following closely Einstein's original argumentation.

Ludwik Kostro

At the end of this introduction let us note that, today, we are dealing with a renewal of several ether concepts - especially that of H.A. Lorentz. We can even say that we are dealing with a 'Neo-Lorentzian' interpretation of Einstein's relativity theory. In this context, the works of S.J. Prokhovnik and F. Selleri are particularly interesting.[9,10] I would like to say that Einstein was provoked to invent and to introduce his new ether concept by H.A. Lorentz.[11,1] J. Illy is convinced that Einstein's ether constitutes a version of Lorentz's ether.[12] Einstein himself maintained that his relativistic ether can be derived from Lorentz's ether through relativisation.

In his Leiden lecture, in 1920, Einstein said:

The ether of the general theory of relativity can be transformed intellectually into Lorentz's through the substitution of constants for the spatial functions which describe its state, thus neglecting the causes conditioning the latter. One may therefore say that the ether of the general theory of relativity is derived through relativisation from the ether of Lorentz.[13]

The influence of Lorentz on Einstein and Einstein on Lorentz was mutual. Lorentz similarly tried to relativize his ether. According to J. Illy,[12] Lorentz presented, in 1918, a model of ether with a constant state of rest. In this model the ether was at rest with respect to every reference frame and not only with respect to the privileged one.

1. Einstein Identified The Ether with Physical Space

Einstein never considered the ether as something in space, he always identified it with physical space. He did this when he denied its existence and also when he introduced his new ether. We see here P. Drude's great influence on Einstein who with great interest studied Drude's textbooks and papers. For Einstein, as for Drude, the ether was identical to physical space endowed with real physical properties.

Einstein was also under a great influence of E. Mach. According to Mach, space (particularly absolute space) constitutes a metaphysical intercalation or foreign matter which must be removed from physics as an experimental science. Absolute space must be removed from physics because it has not experimentally accessible properties. Until 1916, Einstein was convinced that Mach was right. In 1905, when formulating his special relativity which rejected the existence of absolute space (identified with the old ether), he was convinced that he was realising Mach's programme.

In his 1905 paper we read:

Ludwik Kostro

Examples of this kind, together with the unsuccessful investigations the purpose of which was to ascertain the motion of the earth relative to the 'luminiferous medium', lead to the conclusion that neither the phenomena of mechanics nor those of electrodynamics can be assumed to possess properties corresponding to the notion of absolute rest.[14]

As we can see, according to Einstein, in line with Mach, "properties typical of physical phenomena do not correspond to the notion of absolute rest", and therefore they must be removed from physics. Since Einstein identified the concept of space at absolute rest with that of the old ether, the latter proves, according to him, to be superfluous:

The introduction of a 'luminiferous ether' will prove to be superfluous inasmuch as the view here developed will not require an 'absolutely stationary space' provided with special properties.

This quotation taken also from Einstein's 1905 paper testifies that he identified the old luminiferous ether with absolute space.

In Einstein's mind, the notion of a frame of reference was closely connected with the notion of space, accordingly he identified the notion of a privileged reference frame with the notion of absolute space. Therefore, when he removed from special relativity the privileged reference frame, he was convinced that he removed absolute space from physics.

Subsequently, when he arrived at the conclusion that in his general relativity he had succeeded to remove the privileged set of inertial reference frames, and when he became aware that, in his new theory of gravitation, the co-ordinate systems had lost all physical meaning, he became convinced that his general theory of relativity had achieved Mach's goal and had removed space and time as metaphysical intercalations from physics.

According to him the only thing which remained were the space-time coincidences of events. In 1916, in his general relativity paper, he wrote:

That this requirement of general covariance, which takes away from space and time the last remnant of physical objectivity, is a natural one, will be seen from the following reflection. All our space-time verifications invariably amount to a determination of space-time coincidences.[15]

In a letter to Moritz Schlick, on December 14, 1915, he stated:

Thereby [through the general covariance of the field equations] time and space lose the last remnant of physical reality.[16]

In a letter to Ehrenfest, on December 26, 1915, he emphasized:

Ludwik Kostro

The physical is real in what happens in the world (as opposed to what depends on the choice of the reference system) consists of spatio-temporal coincidences (added in a footnote: *and nothing else!*).[17]

During the period from 1913 to 1916, Einstein did not believe in the existence of a physical space endowed with real physical properties. In a letter to Ernst Mach, in late 1913 or early 1914 he wrote:

For me it is absurd to attribute physical properties to 'space'.[18]

In a paper of 1914 he stated:

As much as I am not disposed to believe in ghosts, I do not believe in the enormous thing about which you are talking and which you call space.[19]

Since, for Einstein, ether meant physical space with real properties, therefore, at that time, he solidified his disbelief in the existence of the ether.

In June 1916, however, Einstein changed his ideas. In his mind the notion of space broke off from the notion of reference frame. The physical space ceased to be, in his opinion, a reference frame. And so he could recognise the reality of space. It no longer violated his principle of relativity. Under the influence of a letter written by Lorentz[11] he arrived at the conclusion that physical space does really exist and is endowed with real physical properties that, in the general theory of relativity, are described by the components $g_{\mu\nu}$ of the metrical tensor g but it can no longer be considered as an enormous quasi-body composed of points which could serve as a frame of reference.[1] In such a way the notion of ether was resurrected in the relativity theory. Einstein emphazised this fact, in 1919, in the so-called 'Morgan Manuscript':

Thus, once again 'empty' space appears as endowed with physical properties, i.e., no longer as physically empty, as seemed to be the case according to special relativity. One can thus say that the ether is resurrected in the general theory of relativity, though in a more sublimated form.[2]

According to Einstein, the notion of ether was resurrected not only in the general theory of relativity but also in the special one. Therefore, in 1920, in his Leiden lecture Einstein said:

More careful reflection teaches us, however, that the restricted principle of relativity does not compel us to deny the ether. We may assume the existence of an ether; only we must give up ascribing a definite state of motion to it .. The special principle of relativity forbids us to assume the ether to consist of particles observable through time, but the hypothesis of an ether in itself is not in conflict with the special theory of relativity.[13]

Ludwik Kostro

Let's note that Einstein, when reincorporating the notion of the ether into the special and general relativity theory, always identified the ether with physical space. He did not consider the new ether as something in space but as space itself endowed with physical properties. In the above mentioned lecture he said:

There is a weighty argument to be adduced in favour of the ether hypothesis. To deny the ether is ultimately to assume that empty space has no physical qualities whatsoever ... space is endowed with physical qualities, therefore, there exists an ether.[13]

We find the same identification of the ether with space in Einstein's attempts to construct a relativistic unified field theory in which he considered the gravitational field and the electromagnetic field as states of the same physical space. In 1934 he wrote:

Physical space and the ether are only different terms for the same thing; fields are physical states of space. If no particular state of motion can be ascribed to the ether, there does not seem to be any ground for introducing it as an entity of special sort alongside of space.[20]

When Einstein is speaking about 'physical space' he means space closely connected with time i.e. space-time. Therefore, as he emphazised it, in 1924 in his paper 'Über den Äther', his new 'ether became, to some extent, four-dimensional'.[21]

2. Three Models of the Relativistic Ether

After 1916, Einstein published several papers in which he interpreted his models of space-time as so many models of the ether. In these papers one can make a distinction between three models of the relativistic ether:

α.   The first one is the ether of the special relativity theory. In this model the ether is identified with the flat space-time which, according to the terminology used by Einstein, possesses a pseudo-Euclidean metric. Since, in the flat space-time of special relativity, there are co-ordinate systems in which the 10 components of the tensor $g_{\mu\nu}$ are constant and presented by the symbol $\eta_{\mu\nu}$:

$$g_{\mu\nu} = \eta_{\mu\nu} = \begin{bmatrix} 1 & 0 & 0 & 0 \\ 0 & 1 & 0 & 0 \\ 0 & 0 & 1 & 0 \\ 0 & 0 & 0 & -1 \end{bmatrix}$$

Ludwik Kostro

Einstein considered the components $\eta_{\mu\nu}$ as the mathematical tool to describe the metrical behavior of the special relativity ether. In connexion with the fact that in reference frames in which $g_{\mu\nu} = \eta_{\mu\nu}$, freely moving test particles behave according to the inertia principle, i.e. they are at rest or move with constant velocity on straight lines, Einstein called the ether of special relativity 'inertial' ether, like the ether of Newtonian mechanics.[22]

Because of its flatness, the inertial ether is extended towards infinity. According to Einstein it is also rigid and absolute (i.e. the presence of matter and the matter movement do not exert an influence on its structure) like the Newton's absolute space and the three-dimensional ether of Lorentz.

Physical space and the ether are only different terms for the same thing .. The four-dimensional space of special theory of relativity is just as rigid and absolute as Newton's space.[20]

The rigid four-dimensional space of the special theory of relativity is to some extent a four-dimensional analogue of H.A. Lorentz's ether.[23]

In brief, using present-day terminology and symbols, we can say: The pair (M,η), where M is the four-dimensional differential manifold and η the Minkowskian metric on M, represents the ether of special relativity.

β.   The second model of the ether is that of general relativity. Einstein identifies this ether with a space-time which possesses a pseudo-Riemannian metric and the metrical behaviour of which is described by the 10 components $g_{\mu\nu}$ of the symmetrical tensor g. The components $g_{\mu\nu}$ represent mathematically the physical properties of the new ether, i.e. the gravitational potentials. Einstein, therefore, called this ether 'the gravitational ether'.[13] According to Einstein the general relativity theory ether is no longer rigid and absolute in the above mentioned sense because it 'not only conditions the behaviour of inert masses, but it is also conditioned in its state by them'.[13]

The ether of general relativity is mathematically represented by the four-dimension differential manifold M together with its imposed differentiable field of the symmetrical tensor g, (i.e. together with pseudo-Riemanian (Lorentz metric). In brief, the pair (M, g) designates the new ether in the general theory of relativity. Note, however, that although both of them (i.e. M and g) represent the new ether, only the components $g_{\mu\nu}$ of the tensor g represent its physical distinctiveness, i.e. the gravitational potentials.

γ.   The third model of the new ether is the one that appears in Einstein's attempts to construct a relativistic unified theory. This model has as many versions as the number of Einstein's attempts to unify the electromagnetic field with the gravitational one.

Ludwik Kostro

Their common characteristic is Einstein's supposition that the 10 components $g_{\mu\nu}$ of the symmetrical tensor g (where $g_{\mu\nu} = g_{\nu\mu}$) no longer describe completely the structure of the real space-time. The structure must be richer than the Riemannian one because, in reality, we are dealing in space-time not only with a gravitational field but also with an electromagnetic one. Therefore, Einstein looked for "a theory of the continuum in which a new structural element appears side by side with the metric such that it forms a single whole together with the metric".[20]

In the two relativity theories of Einstein, the electromagnetic field appears as something that 'fills space', i.e., something not belonging to the structure of space-time as described by the components $g_{\mu\nu}$ of the tensor g. Therefore Einstein looked for a mathematical entity which could represent the "total or entire field" (*Gesamtfeld*). In his different editions of a unified theory Einstein used very different mathematical entities to express the *Gesamtfeld*. In the version of the unsymmetrical unified field theory, the unsymmetrical tensor $g_{\mu\nu} \neq g_{\nu\mu}$ with 16 components was such an entity, 10 components representing the gravitational field and 6 the electromagnetic one. In the version of bivector fields, the socalled symmetrical bivector represented both. In still another version, the Hermitian metrical tensor $g_{\mu\nu} = \overline{g}_{\mu\nu}$ did it.

In short, the manifold M, together with the different geometrical structures imposed on it, constituted the different versions of the third model of the relativistic ether. The imposed structures were conceived as mathematical representatives of physical properties of space-time, i.e. of the new ether. None of them, however, is today considered satisfactory.

3. From a Rigid-Body Conception of Space to a Field Conception of it

Following Einstein, the transition from the old ether to the new one consisted in the transition from a rigid body conception of space to a field conception of it. According to him, we are inclined to conceive physical space as *a unique, infinite, enormous, all permeating rigid body* to which we relate the position of all physical bodies. This all-permeating body is inaccessible to our senses, but was invented by mankind for the convenience of our thinking:

When considering the mutual relations of the location of bodies, the human mind finds it much simpler to relate the locations of all bodies to that of a single one rather than to grasp mentally the confusing complexity of the relations of every body to all others. This one body, which is everywhere and must be capable of being penetrated by all others .. is not given to us by the senses, but we devise it as a fiction for convenience in thought.[24]

Ludwik Kostro

According to Einstein, also in Newtonian mechanics the rigid body became the prototype of the concept of absolute space. The absolute space of Newtonian mechanics constitutes an idealisation of an enormous rigid body composed of particles. Points of the absolute space are idealisations of these particles. Space, therefore, is conceived of as an infinite flat quasi-object composed of points. These points do not change their position with respect to each other and therefore the absolute space is rigid.

Also the inertial reference spaces which are at rest or move with respect to the absolute space were conceived in the same way. They are infinite flat rigid quasi-objects that move with respect to the absolute space and with respect to each other.

Thus, the rigid body remained the archetype for the concept of space in Newtonian physics. The rigid body remained also as prototype in several conceptions of the ether, e.g. that of Lorentz.

According to Einstein, a new prototype of the concept of space begin to play its part when Faraday and Maxwell introduced into physics the concept of field. First the field was conceived of as a state of a mechanical medium, therefore the luminiferous ether was invented. But, step by step, such a mechanical carrier of the field became superfluous. All mechanical interpretations of electromagnetic waves failed. According to Einstein:

The emancipation of the field concept from the assumption of its association with a mechanical carrier finds a place among the psychologically most interesting events in the development of physical thought.[23]

In the theory of relativity in which we, according to Einstein, are dealing with the relativisation of the concept of absolute space, or of that of the privileged reference frame, a new prototype of space - namely the field - plays its fundamental part.

The final victory of the concept of field over the concept of absolute space became possible only because the concept of the material object was gradually replaced as the fundamental concept of physics by that of the field. Under influence of the ideas of Faraday and Maxwell the thought developed that the whole of physical reality could perhaps be presented as a new kind of field whose components depend on four space-time parameters. If the laws of this field are in general covariant, that is, are not dependent on a particular choice of the system of co-ordinates, then the introduction of an independent, or absolute, space is no longer necessary. That which constitutes the spatial character of reality is then just the four-dimensional character of the field. There is then no empty space - i.e., there is no space without a field.[25]

Ludwik Kostro

When Einstein identified his new ether with physical space-time he did it in the framework of this new field conception of space:

α.　　The physical properties of the 'inertial' ether which determine the inertial behaviour of test particles in the special theory of relativity are represented mathematically by the field of the tensor η.

β.　　The physical properties of the 'gravitational' ether which determine the inertio-gravitational behaviour of the test particles in the general theory of relativity are represented mathematically by the field of the tensor g.

γ.　　And the physical properties of the 'Gesamtfeld ether' determining the inertio-gravitational and electromagnetic behaviour of test particles in Einstein's attempts to construct an unified field theory are represented by the respective fields of respective mathematical entities like the field of the unsymmetrical tensor with 16 components, $g_{\mu\nu} \neq g_{\nu\mu}$.

4. The Relativistic Ether is an Ultra-Referential Fundamental Reality

In identifying the new ether with physical space, Einstein made a very clear distinction between physical space as such ('Der Raum als solche'), conceived as indicated above, and the reference spaces ('Bezugsraume'). According to Einstein there is only one single physical space as such which manifests itself through field properties that are represented mathematically by the components $\eta_{\mu\nu}$ of the tensor η in special relativity, by the components $g_{\mu\nu}$ of the tensor g in general relativity, and by the components of respective mathematical entities in the various versions of Einstein's unified field theory. Physical space as such is composed neither of particles, nor of points, and is indivisible in parts. The new ether is identified with this space.

There is also an infinite number of reference spaces which are artificial extensions of reference bodies. We introduce a reference space through an infinite number of points which we connect with a reference body. Therefore, every reference space is composed of points, just as every material medium is composed of particles.

Every reference space, just like every material medium, can serve as a reference frame. If we move with respect to a material medium we feel a wind or a change of temperature. When we move with respect to reference space we 'feel a wind of points'. The particles of a material medium, or the points of a reference space, can be followed in time. Therefore, the concept of motion is, in the full sense of the word, relative to material media and reference spaces. The reference spaces move with respect to each other.

Ludwik Kostro

The concept of motion and velocity, however, cannot be applied at all to the new ether, or to physical space as such, because *the ether* constitutes *an ultra-referential fundamental reality* which is neither composed of points or particles, nor of parts, the motion of which can be followed in time.

But, this ether may not be thought of as endowed with the properties characteristic of ponderable media, as consisting of parts that may be traced through time. The idea of motion may not be applied to it.[13]

According to Einstein, the new ether cannot be identified with any of the reference spaces because that would mean that one of them is privileged as compared to others, and this would contradict the principle of relativity. The ether, in such a case, would be connected only with one reference space and would be reducible to a simple material medium in the usual sense.

The new ether constitutes a material medium - but in another sense: It is material in the same sense in which we attribute materiality to a field. With the gravitational and electromagnetic field is connected a certain density of energy and in this sense they are material.

Physical space as such, when identified with the relativistic ether, constitutes an ultra-referential reality. This means that physical space subsists "over", or "behind", all reference spaces. With respect to these, it constitutes a more fundamental background, which makes possible the existence and the motion of reference spaces, although it is neither in motion nor at rest itself. The ultra-referential physical space manifests its existence through real field properties. Its structure determines the behaviour of free moving bodies.

5. The Relation between the New Ether and Ponderable Matter

In the first paper on the new ether, physical space, as identified with the ether, was still conceived of as being secondary to ponderable matter and actually generated by it. Step by step, however, Einstein changed his opinion. The first signs of this can be found in his paper 'Spielen Gravitationsfelder im Aufbau der materiellen Elementarteilchen eine wesentliche Rolle?'.[26]

The opinion, according to which physical space playing the role of the new ether constitutes a reality prior to ponderable matter, was expressed by Einstein e.g. in a lecture delivered in 1929 in Berlin.

We may summarise in symbolic language. Space, brought into light by the corporeal object and made a physical reality by Newton, has in the last few decades swallowed ether and time and also seems about to swallow the field and the corpuscles, so that it remains the sole carrier of reality.[27]

Ludwik Kostro

In a particularly emphatic way, ***the primacy of physical space*** was expressed by Einstein in a speech at the University of Nottingham:

The strange conclusion to which we have come is this - it now appears that space will have to be regarded as a primary thing and that matter is derived from it, so to speak, as a secondary result. Space is now turning around and eating up matter. We have always regarded matter as a primary thing and space as a secondary result. Space is now having its revenge, so to speak, and is eating up matter. But that is still a pious wish.[27]

Einstein said 'that is still a pious wish' because, at that time, he had not found solutions of the field equations that might be interpreted as representing corpuscles. In 1935, he was convinced that he found such solutions. Together with Rosen, he published a paper in which they presented solutions of the centrally symmetric gravitational field equations that were interpreted by them as representing both neutral and electrically charged particles. Having found these, they stated with emphasis that:

The neutral as well as the electrical particle is a portion of space.[28]

This result, however, is today considered as being unsatisfactory. Nevertheless, the search for a unified field theory, not only of gravitation and electromagnetic fields, are continued with a certain success. Summarising, we can say that in Einstein's intentions, expressed for the first time already in 1924, all structures imposed on the differential manifold M, which represent mathematically the physical distinctiveness of physical space, must be included in the notion of the new ether. In his paper 'Über den Äther' we read:

One can defend the view that this notion [the ether] includes all objects of physics, since according to a consistent field theory, ponderable matter and the elementary particles from which it is built also have to be regarded as 'fields' of a particular kind or as particular 'states' of space.[21]

Let's quote here Peter Bergmann, the collaborator of Einstein and co-author of some of his papers:

In the last decades of his life Einstein was concerned with unitary field theories of which he created a large number of models. So I think he was very conscious of the distinction between the differential manifold ... and the structure you have to impose on the differential manifold (metric, affine or otherwise), and that he conceived this structure or set of structures as potential carriers of physical distinctiveness and including the dynamics of physics. Now, whether it is fortunate or unfortunate to use for the latter the term like ether? I think that, from the point of view of Einstein ... we could, if we wanted, use the term ether for the latter.[29]

Ludwik Kostro

References

The abbreviation 'EA', and the numbers in brackets, refer to the control index of the Einstein Archive at the Hebrew University of Jerusalem.

1.   A. Einstein, 1916: Letter to H.A. Lorentz, June 17 (EA 16-453).

2.   A. Einstein: 'Grundgedanken und Methoden der Relativitatstheorie in ihrer Entwicklung dargestellt' (EA 2-070, 'Morgan Manuscript', unpubl.).

3.   A. Einstein, 1919: Letter to H.A. Lorentz, Nov.15th (EA 16-494).

4.   A. Einstein and L. Infeld, 1938: *The Evolution of Physics. The growth of ideas from early concepts to relativity & quanta*, Simon & Schuster, NY.

5.   L. Kostro, 1987: 'Einstein's conception of the ether and its up-to-dated applications in the relativistic wave mechanics', in: *Quantum Uncertainties*, eds. W. Honig & E. Panarella, Plenum Press, NY, pp. 435-49.

6.   L. Kostro, 1988: 'Einstein's new conception of the ether',
in: *Physical Interpretations of Relativity Theory*, ed. M.C. Duffy,
British Society for the Philosophy of Science, London, pp. 55-64.

7.   L. Kostro, 1992: 'An outline of the history of Einstein's relativistic ether concept', in: *Einstein Studies Vol. 3, Studies in the History of Gen.Rel.*, eds. J. Eisenstaedt & A.J.Kox, Birkhauser, Boston/Basel/Berlin, pp. 260-80.

8.   L. Kostro, 1992: 'Alberta Einsteina koncepcja eteru relatywistycz-nego. Jej historia, sens fizyczny i uwarunkowania filozoficzne',
Wydawnictwo Uniwersytetu Gdańskiego, Gdansk.

9.   S.J. Prokhovnik 1992: 'A cosmological basis for Bell's views on quantum & relativistic physics', in: *Bell's Theorem & Found. of Mod. Physics*, eds. Merwe, Selleri, Tarozzi, World Scientific, London, pp. 388-96.

10.   F. Selleri, 1990: 'Special Relativity as a Limit of Ether Theories', in:
Physical Interpretations of Relativity Theory, ed. M.C. Duffy,
British Society for the Philosophy of Science, London, pp. 508-14.

11.   H.A. Lorentz, 1916: Letter to A. Einstein, June 16th, (AE 16-451).

12.   J. Illy, 1989: *Archives for History of Exact Sciences* 39, pp. 247-89.

13.   A. Einstein, 1920: *Äther und Relativitatstheorie*, Springer, Berlin.

14.   A. Einstein, 1905: *Annalen der Physik* 17, pp. 891-921.

15.   A. Einstein, 1916: *Annalen der Physik* 49, pp. 769-822.

16.   A. Einstein, 1915: Letter to M. Schlick, Dec.14th (EA 21-610).

17.   A. Einstein, 1915: Letter to P. Ehrenfest, Dec.26th (EA 9-363).

18.   A. Einstein, 1913: Letter to E. Mach, Dec. (EA 16-454).

19.   A. Einstein, 1914: *Scientia* 15, pp. 337-48.

Ludwik Kostro

20.   A. Einstein, 1934: 'Das Raum-, Feld- und Äther-Problem der Physik',
in: A. Einstein: *Mein Weltbild*, Querido Verlag, Amsterdam.

21.   A. Einstein, 1924: *Schweiz.Naturforsch.Gesellsch.*,Verhandl.105, p. 85.

22.   A. Einstein, 1967: 'Fundamental ideas and problems of the th. of rel.',
in: *Nobel Lectures*, Elsevier Publ. Comp., Amsterd.-London-NY.

23.   A. Einstein, 1960: 'Relativity and the Problem of Space',
in: A. Einstein: *Ideas & Opinions*, Crown Publishers, NY, pp. 360-77.

24.   A. Einstein, 1930: *Forum Philosophicum* 1, pp. 173-184.

25.   A. Einstein, 1954: Foreword, in: M. Jammer: *Concepts of space*,
Harward Univ.Pr., Cambridge-Mass., pp.13-14.

26.   A. Einstein, 1919: *Sitzungsberichte Preuss.Akad.Wiss.*1.Tl., p. 349.

27.   A. Einstein, 1930: *Science*, 71, pp. 600-10.

28.   A. Einstein & N. Rosen, 1935: *Physical Review* 48, pp. 73-77.

29.   P. Bergmann, 1988: Comment, recorded on tape recorder, to a lecture given at
the 2. Internat.Conf. on the History of Gen.Rel., Luminy, France.

Acknowledgment

The author would like to express his sincere thanks to the Volks-wagen-Stiftung for a scholarship that made also this research possible, and to the Hebrew University of Jerusalem for kind permission to quote from Einstein's papers and letters.

Ludwik Kostro

ALEXEI V. NESTERUK

TEMPORAL IRREVERSIBILITY
THREE MODERN VIEWS

INTRODUCTION

Among philosophers there is, in general, a clear understanding of the difference between *irreversibility of time* and *irreversibility of processes*. By contrast, physicists when attacking the problem of irreversibility mostly presuppose that irreversibility as disclosed through processes which happen *in time* will somehow show the way how to treat the irreversibility *of time*. We can refer to different historical sources on this account, starting with a quotation from the Jewish philosopher, Philo of Alexandria (1981):

Time began either simultaneously with the (Divine) Word or after it. For since time is measured space as determined by the world's movement, and since movement could not be prior to the object moving, but must of necessity arise either after it or simultaneously with it, it follows of necessity that time also is either co-eval with, or later born, than the world.

From this it follows that Time, originating from the Divine Word of Creation, must disclose a special kind of "reality" which must be immanent to the world, but which probably does not exist *before* or *without* the world. One can even strengthen the last proposition saying that time does not exist *beyond* the world and has nothing to do with a transcendent reality.

By saying this, we restrict our subject matter to those aspects of time which are accessible to the senses and to the understanding. For people who possess an advanced mystical or religious experience the last statement will hardly be valid since, for them, the mystery of transpersonal existence points out towards another temporal reality that could be described by such rational words as "timelessness", "eternity", "immortality", etc.

Such terms indicate a feature of temporal reality, in fact the only one to reach beyond this world, namely, the *trans-temporal*, which reveals itself as a kind of religious truth (Lossky 1995). It is clear that reflection upon such revelations cannot be the task of positive science, and that is why scientific experience is destined to accept dispassionately the time of the material world which manifests itself through the change of sensible things.

In spite of this, however, it is amazing to witness how scientific knowledge, being part of the human cognitive faculties, incessantly leads to the production of multiple theories of time. Nevertheless time, this fascinating feature of all existence in the world around us, threatens to escape from our scientific understanding into a spiritual world of ideas, becoming again the subject of mystical experience; but this time it is the experience of meditating scientists, not that of devoted believers or practising magicians.

This shows that there is something with time which will always escape from any attempt of human science to look at it "under microscope". The present paper intends precisely to deal with the meditations of scientists. Meditating about the irreversibility of physical time, the scientist silently lifts his thoughts beyond the physical world, transferring the problem from the sphere of physics into the sphere of ideas. The proper way to treat the problem here, however, is by applying to it the *methods of philosophy*.

By saying that physics understands time through material processes we implicitly execute an act of reductionism that might diminish the meaning of the proposed research. We are not afraid of that, however, because this reduction is only used as a starting point for our discussion. We are convinced in advance that any truth about time we may discover will inevitably urge us to modify our reductionism and that, in consequence, the subject of time will hence be reinstated to its proper place in the sphere of human ideas.

Nevertheless, being respectful to science and its attempts to obtain a glance of the unfathomable depths of a reality which underlies the everyday world of our senses, we shall start with some of its accounts of irreversibility. So we shall outline *three modern scientific views* of the irreversibility of time, all of them implying that it should be treated in terms of the irreversibility of processes. These views are associated with names of three eminent scientists: viz. I. Prigogine, R. Penrose and J. Wheeler. We shall see that, irrespective of their differences, they are *all searching for some ultimate truth about time*. This truth, further, turns out to be *metaphysical*, hence *philosophical*.

1.   ILYA PRIGOGINE: Irreversibility from a New Dynamics.

Let us first consider some interesting statements of Prigogine (1991): "The arrow of time expresses a relation among objects, be it among particles or fields; (however) time is not in the objects, but results from the dynamics". "Irreversibility is not related to particles but to relations among particles".

Alexei V. Nesteruk

The rationale of these two statements is straightforward: time is not some ontological being that transcends the relations linking the components. In other words: there is no time in itself, and the arrow of time is not some mysterious metaphysical entity, but rather an "epiphenomenon" of dynamics. So, according to Prigogine, if we want to explain the irreversibility of time, we should explain why certain processes turn out to be irreversible.

To state this in another way, Prigogine seems to assume that the irreversibility of time can be explained by reference to some hidden features of an underlying reality which may be responsible for irreversibility in general. Regrettably, this in no way brings us closer to solving the riddle of time. Prigogine's heroic attempt to solve the mystery of time unawarely exposes the problem of irreversibility to the search-light of philosophy.

Prigogine and the paradox of "time's arrow"

Let us trace some of the stages in Prigogine's way of tackling the problem of time. We start from the well known fact that classical dynamics, whether in Newtonian or in Einsteinian form, do not give us the right tools to trace irreversible changes of physical systems which could represent a history. *In short, all processes are time-reversible within classical physics.*

The reason is that the dynamics of such processes is determined by standard differential equations requiring a set of initial conditions to specify their solution. This set can be chosen at liberty at any time, there being no difference between initial or final conditions, which further implies that all instants in this dynamics are equivalent, or indistinguishable. The symmetry of past, present and future here means that there is no past, present, or future. *Thus we may claim that, in an ideal reversible process, there is no time at all.* It is a world of timelessness where no temporal distinctions can survive.

This "time paradox" appears as an obvious contradiction between classical physics and our everyday observations of the world wherein we live with its evolving complexity, its variety of temporal orders, and its creation of novelty in chemical, biological, geological and other phenomena.

Let us formulate the essence of the time paradox in technical terms. From a formal point of view, the whole dynamics of a single free particle is given by a trajectory in phase space which is a one-dimensional manifold with two boundary points marking the initial and the final phase of its evolution. But, as underlined above, these points are equivalent in the same way as they are equivalent to all other points on the trajectory.

Alexei V. Nesteruk

The "time" which in this description functions as a parameter of the curve, or particle trajectory, is easily reversed to the opposite direction so that the dynamics remains the same, although the logical order becomes reversed. Such reversible dynamics has nothing to do with evolution in a proper sense of this word: there is no real change in the system and no novelty emerges.

We may now state our main conclusion: If for some given physical system a trajectory representation of its dynamics is possible, then the system is time-reversible and yields no indication of the arrow of time.

One might hope that, considering ensembles of free (non-interacting) particles, we would be able to put an element of irreversibility into dynamics. But this is not the case, which we can easily demonstrate if, instead of a single trajectory, we consider a whole "tube" of trajectories in phase space described by a density function ρ. The dynamics of this tube is described by a Liouville equation which generalises the Hamilton equations for a single particle:

$$i\frac{\partial \rho}{\partial t} = L\rho$$

This differential equation can be solved in closed form (integrated). A formal solution of this equation can be written in the following form:

$$(1) \qquad \rho(t) = U(t)\,\rho(0)$$

where $U(t) = e^{-iLt}$ is the *evolution operator*. The eigenvalues of L being real, solution (1) describes an infinite stationary process with a constant amplitude. The function ρ just oscillates, indicating no irreversibility, no arrow of time.

The same situation occurs in the quantum world, where the dynamics of objects is given by the famous Schrödinger equation for a wave function:

$$i\frac{\partial \Psi}{\partial t} = \hat{H}\Psi$$

Again, an evolution-operator $\hat{U}(t)$ gives rise to a formal solution:

$$\Psi(t) = \hat{U}(t)\,\Psi(0) \ . \ \hat{U}(t) = e^{-i\hat{H}t} \ . \ \hat{H} \sim E_n \ . \ \hat{U}(t) \sim e^{-iE_n t}$$

It also yields exactly the same result: the function Ψ oscillates with constant amplitude $|exp\text{-}i\hat{H}t| = 1$. As E_n are all real numbers, there is no distinction between past and future, no irreversibility, and no arrow of time.

A transition to the ensemble description in quantum mechanics gives nothing new because the density matrix, which is the analogue of Ψ,

$$\rho \sim \ <x|\hat{\rho}|x'> \ \sim \ <p|\hat{\rho}|p'>$$

obeys the Liouville-von Newmann equation which is integrable in analogy to the Liouville equation for a classical ensemble yielding a stationary oscillating solution with constant amplitude showing no irreversibility, no arrow of time.

All this gives rise to the suspicion that the idea of "time's arrow" constitutes a serious paradox to modern physics.

Alexei V. Nesteruk

TWO VIEWS OF NATURE

(Diagram 1)

MÁKRO-KOSMOS
General Relativity
Field-Equations

MÉSO-KOSMOS	→ (?) →	*OÍKO-KOSMOS*
Classical Mechanics		*Phenomenology*
Differential Equations		*Observations*

MÍKRO-KOSMOS
Quantum Mechanics
Wave-Functions

UR	OS
Underlying Reality	*Observable Surface*
Processes Reversible	*Processes Irreversible*
Perfect Knowledge	*Imperfect Knowledge*
Deterministic	*Indeterministic*

The Greek words were suggested by the editor
(oíko-kosmos = the world as the dwelling of man)

Alexei V. Nesteruk

Reversibility and Irreversibility - two opposite views of nature

Past attempts to resolve this paradox were based on a common belief that it originates from the specificity of the scientific description of the world. Historically we can distinguish two different views of nature (see Diagram 1).

One of them believed that the world as described by classical physics is transparent, and that our knowledge of it is in principle perfect, or closed. Another view was derived from everyday experience and from those parts of physics which demonstrate the existence of irreversible processes in nature. Scientists tried to explain this irreversibility as due to our lack of knowledge concerning microscopic particle-motions involved in macroscopic processes. If we could know all parameters with unlimited precision we might achieve a knowledge so perfect that it would exclude irreversibility.

What is most striking is that nobody expressed any doubt concerning the perfection and exactitude of the Underlying Reality (UR) - i.e. ontology - assumed to produce or determine the Observable Surface (OS) of phenomena. Nobody could believe that UR itself may be too complex to be reversible.

This led to a strange dualism in the views of nature - in a sense, a contradictory dualism: a dualism where both views were trying to trespass a forbidden area, not realising that they were dealing with different realities. There was a need for changing the scientific paradigm. Precisely such change was intended by Prigogine when he attempted to resolve the time paradox. His ambition was to find a theory which can explain the transition from *UR*, the fundamental level, to *OS*, our everyday world.

Classical physics taught us that there was no ultimate explanation of the arrow of time observed to hold in the *oíko-kosmic* world (cf. Diagram 1). In other words, classical physics had to recognise that its conceptual basis was not sufficient to tackle the problem of the arrow of time. In spite of this it was tempting to claim that there must be a physical origin of the arrow of time. The belief in the ultimate character of the arrow of time, combined with the obvious inability to explain it rationally, created an epistemological situation which can be described in Kantian terms as a cosmological antinomy.

Antinomy of classical physics, relating to the arrow of time

• *Thesis*: The world is governed by some unknown fundamental physical law which expresses a necessary and sufficient condition for the arrow of time.

• *Antithesis*: No unknown physical law, expressing a necessary and sufficient condition for the arrow of time, can be compatible with classical physics.

Together the two conflicting theses indicate that the arrow of time manifests itself as a brute fact, one which cannot be explained by positive science.

Alexei V. Nesteruk

Prigogine's treatment of the arrow paradox

According to Prigogine, the key to a (dis-)solution of the paradox of time's arrow is this: the laws of dynamics should be generalised in such a way that they can explain the emergence of irreversibility on a fundamental level. So the task is to construct a dynamics which is inherently irreversible, and the key concepts for solving this task are: *interaction* and *non-integrability*.

The idea that interactions may produce irreversibility in systems of many particles goes back to Boltzmann: he pointed out that the evolution of particle ensembles tends towards disorder due to collisions (interactions), and he viewed the increase of disorder, or entropy, as a possible measure of time. We must assume such macroscopic parameters of description as time, entropy and interaction to be intimately related for irreversible processes.

Since classical physics always aspired to exclude from theory any ingredients which could affect its time-reversible status and bring uncertainty into the description, the question was posed whether it is somehow possible to exclude interactions from the dynamical description of large physical systems; the tacit assumption was that dynamical systems are always integrable.

Poincaré introduced a fundamental distinction between integrable and non integrable dynamical systems (1892). In integrable systems one can eliminate potential energy of interaction between parts or particles through a suitable transformation of the canonical variables: $J \rightarrow J'$, whence:

$$H = H_o(J) + \lambda V(J, \alpha) \rightarrow H_o^* = H_o^*(J')$$

The system is then isomorhpic to a system of non-interacting particles.

In 1892 he also showed that in "Large Poincaré Systems" (*LPS*) it is impossible to get rid of interactions due to resonances between the degrees of freedom: if there are "enough" resonances the systems cannot be integrated. Later it was shown by Kolmogorov, Arnold and Moser (cf. Arnold & Avez 1968) - that particle interactions involving resonances lead to unpredictable trajectories: determinism is lost, we get irreversibility and an arrow of time.

As a result of that, classical determinism (which was assumed to be an inevitable consequence of classical reversible dynamics) is attributed only to very special cases in our days. Time reversible dynamical systems represent a very narrow class of atypical physical situations with no interaction, no increase of entropy, no evolution, and no time (Prigogine 1988).

We realise now that irreversible processes are the inevitable outcome of the existence of large complicated dynamical *LPS*-systems in the universe. To the purpose of generating irreversible processes at least one *LPS* is needed. *In fact, the evidence for evolution indicates that the universe itself is an LPS.*

Alexei V. Nesteruk

Coming back to Prigogine's intention to construct a new dynamics, we can state his motives more clearly: his hope to introduce irreversibility on the fundamental level of description was associated with an attempt to change the dynamics in such a way that the trajectory description is no longer valid.

What are the philosophical implications of this program? First of all, when we say that the time-reversible behavior of some physical system makes it possible to think of this system as following a trajectory in a phase space, we imply that phase space itself is a more fundamental aspect of physical reality than the variety of observable phenomena, and that the macroscopic properties of the system are somehow predetermined by its development in the underlying phase space. But phase space is *not* an element of physical reality. It is an abstract mathematical object which is believed to have some physical meaning, but its ontological status is unclear.

We are here confronted with an interesting epistemological paradox. We sometimes observe time-reversible phenomena on the macroscopic level, describing them in terms of factual appearances. Our understanding then summarises the multitude of disconnected facts under its own categories in order to produce some unifying conceptual totality that explains this variety. A striking feature of this description is that it makes use of mathematical constructs which have no direct correlation with anything in physical reality. Hence, in order to explain the phenomena observed, one appeals to elements belonging not to the world of physical reality, but to a foreign world of ideas. In this approach, the responsibility for the time-reversible character of some processes is not ascribed to the world of physical phenomena, but to some kind of conceptual "underlying reality", viz. matemathical phase space (S).

From this point of view Prigogine's program to eliminate trajectories, and thereby to explain the irreversibility of macroscopic physical processes, means the following: in order to introduce irreversibility into the description of macroscopic processes it should be attempted to recover the dynamics not from the physical world of phenomena, but from an abstract construction, viz. a matemathical phase space clearly transcending our capacities of experience. Hence, if it were possible find a mechanism that explains the elimination of trajectories in phase space, we would be able to claim that this mechanism, underlying the new dynamics, is responsible for macroscopic irreversibility.

An amazing feature of this program is that in order to invent a mechanism that can eliminate trajectories from phase space, one has to make a further appeal to another "reality", UR', that underlies and explains $UR=S$. This "reality" we shall provisionally identify as so-called Hilbert space, H.

Alexei V. Nesteruk

The basic idea can then be formulated as follows: for a standard trajectory in S we substitute the superposition of all possible trajectories, or histories, in H. What we interpret as the history of a certain system was formerly represented by its trajectory in S. Now its history is instead represented by the continuous sum, i.e. the integral, of all its logically possible histories of the system in H.

The achievement of Prigogine's group is to have demonstrated that, for *LPS*, the presence of the resonances makes the amplitude of the transition between two histories in the Hilbert space H be a Fokker-Planck operator:

$$< k|e^{-iLt}|k' >$$

This destroys all trajectories in S, implying a diffusion in momentum space H. As a consequence, a macroscopic irreversibility emerges which is expressible in terms of a flow of correlations among particles. This flow makes it possible to introduce a mechanism of ageing into many particle systems of the *LPS* type and thereby to provide time with an arrow (cf. Prigogine 1995).

Since the interactions among particles may be understood as a flow of correlations from two particles to three particles, from three particles to four particles and so on, the increase of entropy as a measure of this kind of irreversibility will be an unending process due to the tremendous amount of particles in the Universe. Since irreversible processes in this way turn out to be inevitable ingredients of physical reality, it is assumed accordingly that they are responsible for all constructive processes in the Universe such as the creation of the large-scale structure of the universe, of galaxies, stars, planets, and human bodies, etc. These structures manifest the effects of long-range coherence due to interactions and instabilities (Prigogine 1980 & 84).

Philosophical meditations on the program of Prigogine

Let us reflect a little upon the results outlined above. One can express the epistemological presuppositions of the quest for a source of irreversibility, undertaken by Prigogine and his group, by means of the following diagram:

Diagram 2
Epistemological assumptions latent in the program of Prigogine

Phenomena	←	Phase Space S	←	Hilbert Space H
Irreversibility*		Trajectories of Systems		Superposition of Histories
OS		UR_1		UR_2

* This *á priori* assumption was later abandoned in favour of complementarity.

Alexei V. Nesteruk

Diagram 2 demonstrates that, in order to explain the evolution in the macroscopic world (*OS*), physicists persistently construct their models of its underlying mechanisms (UR_{1-2}) by means of mathematical structures that are freely created by the human intellect. Such structures, of course, do not belong to the world of physical phenomena. Classical physics introduced the idea of a phase space *S*, identified as UR_1. Quantum physics then introduced the idea of Hilbert space *H*, identified as UR_2, where the factual history of a system is being replaced by a construct: the result of a superposition of all logically possible histories of the system. But *S* and *H* are only two peaks of the continued evolution of our physical theories where we steadily have been forced backwards from the abstract to the yet more abstract, always explaining the coarse and solid by means of the fine and ethereal.

It was once hoped that classical physics could retain the structure:

$$OS \leftarrow UR_1 \leftarrow UR_2$$

for the description of irreversible processes, where UR_1 & UR_2 were treated as perfect worlds governed by deterministic and time-reversible laws of physics. The origin of irreversibility was ascribed to the hidden nature of the relation:

$$(UR_1 \oplus UR_2 \equiv UR_{rev}) \rightarrow (OS_{irr} \in OS)$$

The Prigogine groups in Brussels and Austin showed this hope to be in vain. It turned out that the structure of our Diagram 2 is applicable to reversible processes only and that it had to be replaced by a completely new structure. Hence, in order to describe irreversibility on the macroscopic level we must change the underlying physics from UR_{rev} to UR_{irr} so as to obtain instead:

$$(UR_1^* \oplus UR_2^* \equiv UR_{irr}) \rightarrow (OS_{irr} \equiv OS)$$

We have now shown how the necessity of explaining UR_1 by means of UR_2 demonstrates the impossibility of a trajectory description of the dynamics. Thus a new UR_1 makes no sense if interpreted as a phase space of trajectories. A generalised dynamics of some UR_2^{**} that could justify an UR_1^{**} would take us far beyond Hilbert space (Prigogine & Petrorsky, 1995)

This is a consequence of Prigogine's paradigm which enables us to reformulate the dualism about the nature of reality represented in Diagram 2. It must be clearly understood how deep the chasm is between reversible and irreversible physical processes: they differ not only on the surface of physical phenomena (*OS*), but their fundamental underlying physics (*UR*) is different. Hence, in order to understand the physics of the irreversible processes, we must change our fundamental description of classical physics!

Alexei V. Nesteruk

We will not ascribe irreversibility to a deficiency of our description. On the contrary, we have reason to insist that irreversibility necessitates a consistent and coherent description, albeit another than the classical one. When translated into philosophical terms this means that we shall have to invent an epistemology that can cope with the new physics of irreversibility. We say epistemology, not ontology, because most models of an underlying reality yield only a fragment of a theory of those processes which are clearly and undeniably irreversible, moreover a fragment which by far transcends the sphere of our immediate cognitive access as they exploit abstract ideas of explanation which are foreign to the world of observable phenomena.

Before, we had a dualism between the surface world of observable phenomena (*OS*) and the underlying reality of perfect physical laws (*UR*). Now, following Prigogine, we have arrived at a more sophisticated dualism stating that there are *two complementary kinds of processes* in the universe: (α) *reversible processes*, described as OS_{rev} and explained by UR_{rev} within the framework of classical physics, and (ω) *irreversible processes*, described as OS_{irr} and explained by UR_{irr}, within the framework of his new dynamics. However, *no kind of dualism can ever satisfy our searching intellect*.

We feel intuitively that it is a fundamental feature of reality to be in motion, to evolve, to pass in time, to produce novelty. We also intuitively feel that the future is open, and not fixed or determined in advance, *ab aeterno*. This understanding stimulates our search for a cause of the passage of time. However, evolution, irreversibility, passage of time, always mocks and eludes our rational attempts to grasp everything by subordinating it to our realism; moreover, it leads us astray from the starting point of its search: experience. The only explanation we have been able to construe for irreversibility and the arrow of time thus refers to an abstract world, UR_{irr}, where the physics is concocted by a "superposition" of logical and mathematical ideas!

Since *UR* in none of these views on nature can be observed directly, one might guess that natural causality is unable to bridge the chasm between *UR* & *OS* - only a "causality of reason" can do that. The belief that *UR* as the fundamental reality is responsible for the variety of phenomena of *OS* is very close to the philosophical idea of "things-in-themselves" affecting our senses. But this simply amounts to "naïve realism" - and a very naïve realism, indeed. What is interesting here is that the dualism outlined poses a complementarity between two kinds of "things-in-themselves" and "things-for-us", cf. Kant:

$$UR_{rev} \rightarrow OS_{rev} \quad \& \quad UR_{irr} \rightarrow OS_{irr}$$

Alexei V. Nesteruk

This can be further illustrated by means of the following diagram:

$$(OS_{rev} \in OS) \leftarrow (UR_1 \oplus UR_2 \equiv UR_{rev})$$

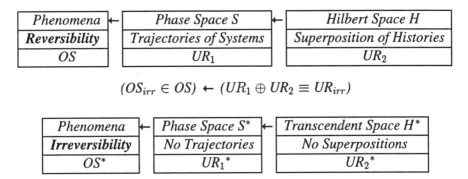

$$(OS_{irr} \in OS) \leftarrow (UR_1 \oplus UR_2 \equiv UR_{irr})$$

Phenomena	Phase Space S*	Transcendent Space H*
Irreversibility	*No Trajectories*	*No Superpositions*
*OS**	*UR_1^**	*UR_2^**

Diagram 3:
epistemological representation of the dualism of nature

We are now in a position to answer the question, whether something has changed in the epistemological status of the idea of time's arrow after this dualism in views of nature was brought into physics by Prigogine's ideas. Unfortunately we have to state that nothing has changed: In spite of the fact that his dynamics indicates a source of macroscopic irreversibility to inhere in physical reality, the problem of the ontological status of UR_{irr} is unsolved. Since, from a philosophical point of view, we cannot point to any evidence of the objective existence of any UR_{irr} - i.e., such kind of existence which could be formulated in terms of physical space and time - we cannot claim that the source of time's arrow belongs to the physical world. What we can do, and have done, is to invent incompatible hypotheses regarding the nature of *UR*. This is what leads the present author to treat time's arrow as an antinomy.*

Antinomy of time's arrow latent in the physics of Prigogine:
• *Thesis*: The world is ruled from some unknown fundamental physical level, UR_{irr}, containing the necessary and sufficient condition for the arrow of time. This is the view of a dogmatic idealist physicist accepting UR_{irr}
• *Antithesis*: There is simply no unknown fundamental physical level UR_{irr} which constitutes the necessary and sufficient condition for the arrow of time. This is the view of a dogmatic empiricist physicist denying UR_{irr}

So the ultimate character of time's arrow is inaccessible to science.

---

* In a couple of papers, Verstraeten (1986,1991) has criticised Prigogine's idea of the microscopic irreversibility of time from a different angle.

Alexei V. Nesteruk

2.   ROGER PENROSE: Irreversibility from Boundary Conditions

We will now discuss an alternative attempt to locate the origin of irre-versibility in the initial low entropy boundary conditions of the universe itself. This approach, which is due to Penrose (1979), is based on a firm belief that: *If all important laws of nature are time-symmetric, then the place to look for an origin of statistical asymmetry is in the boundary conditions.*

Classical dynamics teaches us that boundary conditions can be posed either in the past or in the future. But as our macroscopic experience shows, the way of imposing the boundary conditions in the future presupposes an infinitely precise arranging of the velocity distribution of particles composing the system, so that it would need an infinite amount of information to obtain the present state of the system. Such boundary conditions are separated by an "entropy barrier" (Prigogine 1980) from what is physically possible.

If we lack information about the states of a system we ascribe to it a high measure of entropy. By contrast, the imposing of boundary conditions, whether past or future, corresponds to a low, or minimal, measure of entropy. The imposition of future low-entropy boundary conditions implies that the system will evolve in the direction of entropy decrease which goes against the second law of thermodynamics. In order to evade this conflict one can instead think of the future low entropy conditions as "time reversed past conditions". In other words, low entropy states are possible in the future because of even lower entropy states in the past which then predetermines the future.

The relatively small entropy of the present state of our universe, which is evidenced by the existence of stable structures, must stem from the low entropy conditions at its initial state, assumed to have been a "Big Bang". The irreversible evolution of the universe towards states with high entropy must hence have its origin in low-entropy conditions at the initial singularity. These are the cause of time's arrow as indicated by the irreversible processes. Notice that "time's arrow" is just a shorthand term for the predominant tenden-cy of the majority of observed processes. According to Penrose (1979, p.588): *The entropy concept .. refers to classes of states .. not individual states.*

This shows that the definition of entropy depends on what kind of changes we observe and what way of description we choose. The very idea of irreversibility, which is associated with the growth of entropy, is relevant not to distinct objects following well-known dynamical laws, but rather to aspects of collective behavior of these objects which is normally observed.

Alexei V. Nesteruk

In Prigogine's model of time, the growth of entropy in the universe is driven by the flow of correlations among particles, and the arrow of time which is related to this mechanism of ageing of a system is associated with a flow of correlation towards complex states involving more and more particles. One must, however, answer a fundamental question: what is the ultimate reason for this flow of correlations to start at all? According to Penrose, the answer is that the origin of this flow, and of the arrow of time, is hidden in the low-entropy initial conditions for the evolution of the universe.

In itself, the expansion of the universe does not explain time's arrow. Already in 1979, Penrose pointed out that there was no direct link between the expansion of the universe, the growth of entropy, and the arrow of time. It is easy to understand that, in the approach connecting increase of entropy with a flow of correlations, there is no object in equilibrium in the universe, and the increase of entropy continues forever independently of the universal evolution, whether it be due to expansion or to contraction.

This eliminates the idea of a thermal death of the universe which is inevitable if evolution be considered only in terms of binary correlations.

Low initial entropy conditions of the universe

Classical physics considered entropy to be some attribute of matter attached to such ingredients as radiation and particles. It is usually assumed that the state of matter near the Big Bang is approximately in thermodynamic equilibrium with a maximum of entropy. However, at present, the state of the universe displays an entropy whose value is not high enough to prevent the emergence of states showing precise macroscopic after-collision correlations. These correlations, observed in a variety of structures, are evidence that a state preceding the present one must show an entropy which is much less. This contradicts the hypothesis of maximum-entropy at the Big Bang.

To overcome this paradox, Penrose (1979) has pointed out that one should take into account the gravitational degrees of freedom of the universe. He proposed to ascribe to the gravitational field some new property indicating an entropy later called the gravitational entropy (GE). Evaluating the possible amount of entropy which can be produced in the universe during the whole period of its evolution from Big Bang to Big Crunch, he discovered that there is a tremendous lack of entropy in the baryon universe we observe now, viz. 10^{88} as compared to the possible value 10^{123}. The reason for this was thought to be found in the low GE condition at the Big Bang.

Alexei V. Nesteruk

To express this condition in geometrical terms, it was noticed that the growth of *GE* corresponds to a clustering of matter that is accompanied by an increase in the degree of anisotropy of the gravitational field which is itself described by $C_{\alpha\beta\mu\nu}$, the so-called Weyl Curvature (*WC*). This led Penrose to propose a scenario for the development of the universe in which the evolution begins from a low *GE* state corresponding to weak gravitational anisotropy and evolves to a high *GE* state marked by strong gravitational anisotropy, granted the assumption that *WC* is a possible measure of *GE*. A more precise statement of this idea is his well-known Weyl curvature hypothesis (*WCH*): *The Weyl curvature tends to zero at all past singularities, as the singularity is approached from future directions* (Penrose 1979,1981,1986,1989).

The physical implications of the *WCH* for the present state of the universe can be expressed as follows: we regard the character of the actual state of the universe, assuming that it began with a Big Bang and $C_{\alpha\beta\mu\nu} = 0$, as being more and more of the "precise-correlation" type and less and less of the "low-entropy" type as time progresses. It is consistent with Prigogine's ideas that the complexity of the universe is due to a steady flow of correlations among particles that can explain a very *special* state of the present universe. The *WCH* is local in time and cannot be derived from macroscopic dynamics. According to Penrose (1979), "there are in fact .. laws which only become important near spacetime singularities, these being asymmetric in time and such as to force the Weyl curvature to vanish at any initial singular point".

It is believed that there must be some laws, local in time, which are responsible for macroscopic irreversibility but, in contradistinction to the ideas of Prigogine, these laws are important only at the singularity, i.e., in the remote past. They have a fundamental importance since they predetermine the entire thermodynamical evolution of the universe. From a methodological point of view such an approach presupposes the search for hidden (unknown) laws pre-existing at the singularity which we can guess only observing its macroscopic appearance in the form of irreversibility.

As Penrose (1979) claims, "the problem of time's arrow can be taken out of the realm of statistical physics and returned to that of determining what are the precise physical laws". The mystery about these physical laws is that they are hidden from the "observable surface" in some "underlying reality". The assumption that *UR* causes the appearances of *OS* by means of some yet unknown mechanism is unusual though open to reason in principle.

Alexei V. Nesteruk

Philosophical reflections on the program of Penrose

In order to make plausible that *WCH* implies such atypical conditions in the early universe, Penrose has appealed to the idea of phase-space which is now thought not as a space of all possible dynamical histories of the universe, but instead as a space of different initial conditions for all possible universes. Taking the figure 10^{123} as a maximum potential entropy for a universe of our type, he estimates the phase-space volume corresponding to its possible initial conditions to be $V = 10^{10^{123}}$. But our actual physical universe corresponds to a phase-space volume of size $W = 10^{10^{88}}$. This shows that the necessary initial conditions constitute an infinitesimal part of V, viz.: $W/V = 10^{-10^{123}}$.

In other words, the probability *a priori* for our physical universe with its arrow of time and its second law of thermodynamics approximates to zero. This is due to the fact that V, as measured by W, remains "almost infinite". Consequently, the amount of information necessary to select our physical universe as a particular region in a space V will likewise be "almost infinite". According to Prigogine this means that any attempt to explain physically the creation of our universe will meet the impasse of an infinite entropy barrier. Penrose's theory seems inadequate to cope with this problem.

The event of creation, when understood as brute fact, is certainly open to description and interpretation in terms of mathematical cosmology. *WCH* is, perhaps, one of the brighter examples of this kind of "explanation"; it is possible as a *phenomenological* explanation from within our own world, but it is certainly not acceptable as an explanation in the *ontological* sense, as the latter kind of explanation would transgress our natural limits of possible experience only to evaporate into the very thin air of abstract speculations. Viewed as ontology, such models are nothing but lofty ideas.

In one of his books (1989, p.343) Penrose elucidates our conclusion. He introduces the idea of a God powerful enough to create all kinds of worlds: only an omniscient Creator may possess the knowledge of that infinite amount of information necessary to pin-point that tiny part of phase-space which describes the initial conditions of our own universe as we perceive it today. The function of this Creator is only to *create* the universe but not to *govern* it. According to Penrose, it is governed by the time symmetrical laws of physics. An arrow of time and irreversibility appear only because of the very special type of the act of creation which can be formulated in the language of physics. From a philosophical point of view this kind of thought is very close to *deism*: God created the world once in the past, but He does not govern it.

Alexei V. Nesteruk

The problem facing us is that we can only give a phenomenological description of that time-asymmetric "law" which is acting at the singularity. In fact, *WCH* describes not the source of the arrow of time and irreversibility, but rather the consequences of the second law when reversed into the past. Probably some kind of cosmological scenario can be devised that incorporates *WCH* and makes this hypothesis plausible within the range of experimentally confirmed theories; but it is still impossible to explain *WCH* by mere physics as this "explanation" would consist in an appeal to the idea of possible worlds and to the mysterious randomness of the mechanism producing our universe. This plurality, treated by Penrose under the symbol *V*, is nothing but another version of the idea of an underlying reality *UR*, known from Prigogine.

All this tells us that understanding, by its attempt to shed light upon the ultimate source of irreversibility, once more falls prey to the tendency to find an explanation not in our own world *OS* but in an imaginary world *UR*.. But this kind of "explanation" proves nothing, except that it evidences our extreme speculative fertility to produce transcendental illusions, or *Schein*. As a consequence we have to face the fact that propositions concerning an underlying reality can only be expressed in terms of the antinomies of reason. Since we cannot logically prove or disprove the ontological existence of *UR*, the only way to make a reasonable judgement of it is in terms of antinomies. There is no way to explain the transition *UR→OS* by physics alone.

Antinomy of time's arrow latent in the physics of Penrose:

• *Thesis*: God, by His act of Creation in $V = UR$, has produced the universe *W* with low initial entropy as a causal condition of the arrow of time in *W*.

• *Antithesis*: No "god" has, by any act, produced the universe *W* with low initial entropy as a causal condition for the arrow of time in *W*.

This antinomy shows that reason both postulates an ultimate source of time's arrow and postulates that there is no such source. Theoretical physics and cosmology seeks to obtain knowledge of temporal appearances (*OS*) through propositions about some ultimate reality (*UR*): the source of time. However, reason cannot find this within the realm of possible experience, but has to extend its search to an imaginary realm of ultimate underlying reality. It thereby trespasses the limits of its own legitimate use as it objectifies its goal in the image of some indefinite *ens perfectissimum*.

This entitles us to characterise the speculative quest for the ultimate underlying source of time as the turn to a theological type of reasoning.

Alexei V. Nesteruk

3. JOHN WHEELER: Irreversibility and the Anthropic Principle

We now start to consider an approach to irreversibility based on an extreme version of the Copenhagen Interpretation of Quantum Mechanics. According to J.A. Wheeler, there is no pre-existing universe in any possible sense of this term, and there is no pre-existing time, or space, or space-time. The observer produces events by making them happen, or by observing them; in this way he brings the tempo-spatial appearance of a world into being.

Consequently, following Wheeler (1988), the very *concept of time* is a *human invention*, and the problems that come with it are of human origin. Time cannot be a fundamental concept, because time does not exist prior to events, and events do not exist prior to our own actions or observations; therefore timelessness is a necessary concomitant of the world of existences: "The word 'timelessness', in summary, stands for the thesis that at bottom there is not, and cannot be, any such thing as time; that we have to expect a deeper concept to take its place. Events yes. A continuum of events no." (ibid.) The concept of an 'event' becomes the fundamental ingredient that constitutes the reality of time as a directed and irreversible process.

The notion of an 'event' as an ingredient of physical description was introduced into *Special Relativity* in the context of *Minkowski 4-Space (M)*. When we say that M is a "4-space" of events, we intend this to mean that M is different from any kind of abstract mathematical space. The difference is rooted in the way such spaces exist. Mathematical space and its elements do exist conceptually, or logically; this kind of existence lacks all temporality. M by contrast incorporates temporality within its own framework of timeless or "frozen" existence; hence the term "block-universe".

When we think of M as an infinite 4-dimensional continuum we are not quite right, as it is the set of events that constitutes the structure of M. However, events as elements of M are not just simple rational constructs: events happen in M, and some element of reality can be attributed to them; obviously, it makes a difference whether some event belongs to reality or not. The phrase "an event has happened" must be understood as implying that some novelty, changing the universe, was brought into being by this event. Such creation of novelty is an irreversible act because once brought into being it can never disappear again; events are, in a certain sense, indestructible. That is why we think of M as a "block universe" of events.

But what is an 'event'? Clearly, events must be elements of reality. What 'reality'? Reality in the sense of Einstein, or in the sense of Bohr?

Alexei V. Nesteruk

The Einsteinian view is founded upon the belief that there is an external world existing independently of any observer, and that it is made up of events which are real in themselves. Time in this approach was treated as a separate spatial dimension in the space-time formulation of Special Relativity. The temporal structure of events was supposed to be predetermined and instead of an evolving universe we had a realm of timeless order fixed *a priori*. But temporal predetermination of events implies their existence in all eternity, all events being given at once (from the point of view of a divine observer).

This view of relativity was severely criticised by H. Bergson (1922) who noticed that the space of our experience is a space of three dimensions and that its amalgamation to a fourth dimension is an operation of our mind. So it is not evident that 4-space as a whole corresponds to anything in reality. If one assumes that 4-dimensional space-time exists as a whole, it means that this space of events exists *a priori*, i.e. in advance of any possible experience. The observer, being described as a world-line, only appears to travel along his own set of pre-existing events; but how is this appearance to be explained? The problem for adherents of the "block universe", such as e.g. H. Weyl, is to explain how the supposed illusion of a flow of time or events can arise at all! In this picture, there is no place for becoming, or the emergence of novelty.

Bohr's alternative point of view can be stated in the form of his well-known principle that "no elementary phenomenon is a phenomenon until it is a registered (an observed and indelibly recorded) phenomenon" (Bohr 1959). Wheeler radicalised this to the sweeping statement that "there is simply no universe out there" (Wheeler 1988). The universe is called into being by us. The way of how we are doing this "depends on what question we put, what experiment we arrange, what registering device we choose" (Wheeler 1985). Events are here treated essentially as quantum observations. It follows that quantum observations, irreversible by definition, constitute our experience. Time as a concomitant of events turns out to be irreversible too.

The question of how to perceive the relationship between events in the sense of relativity theory and events in the sense of quantum theory can be further elucidated as follows. It is natural to attempt an interpretation of the relativistic events making up the structure of M as if they were "projections" of quantum events "onto" M. This view implies a kind of "correspondence" to hold between the set of quantum events $\mathcal{E}_k \in \mathcal{H}$ and the set of their relativistic "projections" $E_{t_k} \in M$, where $\mathcal{E}_k = (\mathcal{E}_p \oplus \mathcal{E}_m)[k]$, indices p & m being short for 'preparation' and 'measurement', and where a world-line in M is constituted by a subset of M completely ordered by the parameter t.

Alexei V. Nesteruk

Now a precise correspondence is ensured if $k \leftrightarrow t_k$; however, this assumption runs into difficulties. The problem is that E_{t_k} & $\mathcal{E}_k$, when they are translated into propositions by means of a temporal operator of "realisation", $R_t[..]$, are subject to completely different truth conditions. In fact, we get:

$$\delta_{t,t_k} = 1 \text{ for } t = t_k$$

(2) $\quad R_t[E_{t_k}] = \delta_{t,t_k}$ where $\begin{cases} \\ \\ \\ \delta_{t,t_k} = 0 \text{ for } t \neq t_k \end{cases}$

$$\Theta(t-t_k) = 0 \text{ for } t < t_k$$

(3) $\quad R_t[\mathcal{E}_k] = \Theta(t-t_k)$ where $\begin{cases} \\ \\ \\ \Theta(t-t_k) = 1 \text{ for } t \geq t_k \end{cases}$

The truth conditions stated above tell us that relativistic events are instantaneous, flashing up and dying away at once, leaving nothing behind, whereas quantum events, once brought into existence, never disappear again; in this way quantum events acquire a future-directed eternity they didn't have! Let us now consider a series of events constituting the world-line of a person, the entire history of her/his life being ordered in physical time t; then we find:

$$(t_1 \leq t_2 \leq t_3 \leq .. \leq t_\nu)$$

$$Hist(\mathcal{P}) = R_t[E_{t_1} \oplus E_{t_2} \oplus ... \oplus E_{t_\nu}] = \delta_{t,t_1} + \delta_{t,t_2} + ..+ \delta_{t,t_\nu} \underset{t > t_\nu}{=} 0$$

$$\mathcal{H}ist(\mathcal{P}) = R_t[\mathcal{E}_1 \oplus \mathcal{E}_2 \oplus ... \oplus \mathcal{E}_\nu] = \Theta(t-t_1) + \Theta(t-t_2) + ..+ \Theta(t-t_\nu) \underset{t > t_\nu}{=} 1$$

Obviously $\mathcal{H}ist(\mathcal{P})$ does not exist physically, for an observer living at $t > t_\nu$. Nevertheless, such observer has permanent access not to events $E_t \in Hist(\mathcal{P}) \subseteq M$, but only to events $\mathcal{E}_k \in \mathcal{H}ist(\mathcal{P}) \subseteq \mathcal{H}$ which do not belong to M and, hence, do not belong to time but to eternity!

However, we must not forget our former presupposition, viz. $k \leftrightarrow t_k$; due to this correspondence, the events $\mathcal{E}_k$ do retain their correlation with time. We conclude that the past events of space-time, or time-space, are never again accessible, whereas their quantised counterparts are preserved for all eternity. This raises some interesting perspectives as regards human morality.

The idea of a future directed eternity of past events, when projected onto the subjective consciousness of some human agent, or observer, means that traces of the past are always preserved - in the brain, or in the universe. Alone the heat which escapes from this globe bears witness to all our acts.

Alexei V. Nesteruk

The idea of an indelible universal memory perserved for eternity can now be visualised by the picture of M as a container of events E_{t_k} which are the ephemeral counterparts of the archetypal paradigm comprising all events $\mathcal{E}_k$. Even physically it seems impossible for man to escape his sinful deeds!

Thus the scientific picture of the world wherein we live and take part offers evidence that the real universe accumulates our experience as a memory depicting what we are now as the integrated sum total of what we have been, thereby persuading us to accept responsibility for every single act of ours simply because any act corresponds to an event subsisting not in physical time but in a timeless logical "space" whose contents are a mirror of eternal truth. This truth, however, is not the proper topic for finite understanding focussing on mere *fainomena*, but for reason transcending to *noumena* (cf. Kant).

The world of experience reflects a world of indelible quantum traces, and the steady increase of irreversible facts implies the accumulation of truth. Events being observed now are in causal connection with quantum events which have taken place in a unique chain of accumulating events constituting the total world-course as witnessed by some imaginary super-human observer. The history of the universe mirrors the irreversible accumulation of events in the quantum sub-world whence it derives its peculiar character of eternal fact, its eternity being limited towards the past but unlimited towards the future. In this sense we can ascribe to history *a finite future-directed eternity*.

It might be conjectured that a finite eternity was "pre-existent" as the "cause" of both worlds: the world of our transitory perceptions, and the world of our steadily accumulating, finitely eternal, experience. The problem with this idea is that it takes the concepts of cause and pre-existence outside their natural sphere of applicability. However, nothing can prevent us from viewing the creation of novelty in nature as associated with the continued processing of information from an Underlying Reality $\mathcal{H}$ to an Observable Surface M. This creation is simply just another expression of time's arrow, time of course being needed for the correlation $k \leftrightarrow t_k$ which connects $\mathcal{H}$ with M.

This once more points towards time as the necessary condition for projecting the sub-world of finite eternity into the realm of human experience. Our ability to arrange observations separated as to their temporal order is connected to the awareness of time by human beings as an irreversible flow. Time is the necessary condition for human beings to carry out observations. This lends some credibility to Wheeler's ideas about the rôle of the observer: Observers by their acting cause events to be and in order to explain the events by reference to an underlying reality they then invent the idea of time.

Alexei V. Nesteruk

This approach to the origin of irreversibility and time's arrow tells us that observers are functioning as necessary beings in a transcendental sense. To explore the contents of this thesis, we shall undertake a transcendental analysis of the "participatory anthropic principle", cf. Barrow & Tipler (1988): *observers are necessary to bring the universe into being* - here restated with regard to the origin of time: *observers are needed to bring time into being.*

The problem is however, "where" do observers exist if not "in time"? From one point of view, observers exist as a phenomenon among phenomena. From another point of view observers call time - and the universe - into being. But from "where" do they call time into being? From "a timeless something"? This makes sense if, and only if, observers are *noumena* as well as *fainomena*. Our "time-version" of the "participatory anthropic principle" (*PAP*) then is:

Philosophical time-version of PAP

Observers, being noumena *as well as* fainomena, *are necessary to produce a world of temporal phenomena from a pre-existing pattern of eternal noumena.* The idea of a *human observer*, accordingly, is the idea of a *necessary being*! This absurdity indicates that the idea of "participation" involves an antinomy:

Antinomy of time's origin latent in the position of Wheeler:

• *Thesis*: The existence of the universe as a totality of temporal appearances presupposes the timeless existence of a transcendental observer.
• *Antithesis*: The existence of the world as a totality of temporal appearances does not presuppose the timeless existence of any transcendental observer.

In the "participatory" universe of Wheeler the cause of time appears to be identified with a kind of *collective consciousness*, here interpreted as a transcendental observer, i.e. an observer transcending ordinary time and space. *PAP*, by introducing the observer as the real cause of our temporal universe, just reproduces the idea of an "ultimate underlying reality" of time.

Hence *PAP* is a statement about *UR*, and the transcendental observer can be interpreted in the way similar to the models of Prigogine and Penrose. The conclusion to be drawn from this is very simple: the ultimate character of time always escapes from our scientific explanations into the world of ideas where a philosophical rather than a physical analysis is appropriate.

Alexei V. Nesteruk

CONCLUSION

Analyzing three attempts to tackle the riddles of irreversibility and of time's arrow we have found similar results. In all the cases considered above, physical reason has brought us to the edge of possible scientific explanation by suggesting models of some ultimate underlying reality which is regarded as being responsible for the observed macroscopic irreversibility of time.

These models represent ideas which, while not being abstracted from experience, are at the same time not applicable to the data of sense intuition. These ideas transcend our ordinary experience in the sense that no objects are given, or can possibly be given, within experience which correspond to them. According to Kant, transcendental ideas are produced because of the natural tendency of the human mind to search for unconditioned principles of unity. The transcendental ideas exercise an important regulative function suggesting scientific explanatory hypotheses. However, all attempts to use the ideas as a foundation of science involves us in logical fallacies and antinomies.

The current ideas about an underlying reality to explain the origin of time all stem from a general tendency of the human mind to add "something else" to the immediate data of consciousness. Using the method of Kant we have in earlier papers illustrated how this tendency works in the context of Quantum Mechanics and in that of Anthropic Cosmology (Nesteruk 1993-4). Looking at these ideas from the point of view of the most general relations in which our representations of them can stand, one can conclude that they more or less tacitly imply a "Meta-Physics" associated with a belief in the existence of some Underlying Reality, interpreted as a kind of Perfect Being.

Any aspiration of the scientific spirit to uncover an Ultimate Reality behind the Observable Surface of appearances amounts in the end to nothing but a misguided attempt to obtain a final unification with this Perfect Being. Nevertheless, the current efforts in this direction discussed above have at least had the purifying effect to reveal that *the mystery of time* cannot be grasped in scientific categories but must ultimately be left over to *mystical experience*. Any attempt to grasp this experience in objective scientific terms, i.e. in terms of mathematical physics, should henceforth be treated as an epistemological mistake of the type termed "transcendental realism" by Kant.

Says Kant: *The realist in the transcendental sense of the term treats these modifications of our sensibility (appearances) as self-subsistent things, i.e. he treats representations as things-in-themselves.* (1933, p.439)

Alexei V. Nesteruk

Further: *The transcendental realist interprets the outer appearances (their reality being granted) as things-in-themselves which exist independently of us and of our sensibility and which are therefore outside us, the phrase 'outside us' being here interpreted in conformity with the pure concepts of the understanding.* (der Verstand) (ibid.p.346).

Therefore: *If we regard the outer appearances as representations produced in us by their objects, and if these objects be things existing in themselves outside us, it is indeed impossible to see how we can come to know the existence of the objects otherwise than by inference from effect to cause. This being so, it must always remain doubtful whether the cause in question be in us or outside us.* (ibid. p.347)

The confusion of mathematical models with physical reality made by all three approaches to uncover the origin of time's arrow clearly shows that the scientific mind by producing its fancy theories of *UR* is still bounded by the categories of *understanding* (Verstand); hence it is indeed a far cry from making use of such a cognitive faculty as *reason*, or *intelligence* (Vernunft). The widespread ignorance among scientists of the deep critical distinction between Verstand and Vernunft (cf. Plato: *noesis* $\neq$ *noûs*) leads into fallacy. It is simply a capital mistake of category that leads us into antinomies to treat ideas like time, being, or creation, under the heading of physics.

Instead of treating the problem of time carefully, using the accepted methods of philosophical inquiry, the authors of the three views discussed all misuse the categories of understanding by pretending that the ultimate cause of time is to be found among the elements of the so-called material universe. But there is an alternative: according to Kant, "we must admit that something (here: *UR*) which may be in the transcendental sense outside us, is the cause of our outer intuitions; but this is not the object of which we are thinking when we speak of presentations of matter and of corporeal things, for these are mere appearances, i.e., kinds of presentation which are never met with except within us, and the reality of which depends on immediate consciousness, just as does the consciousness of my own thoughts" (op.cit.p.347-8)

This precisely shows how the sophisticated "physical" ideas of time, as proposed by the authors of the theories we have analyzed, may evidence the eminent capacities of human reason and the amazing power of its imaginative faculty rather than bear witness to some subtle kind of *UR*.

Alexei V. Nesteruk

REFERENCES

1. Arnold & Avez, 1968: *Ergodic Problems of Classical Mechanics*, NY.

2   Barrow & Tipler, 1986: *The Anthropic Cosmological Principle*, Oxf.

3   Bergson, H., 1922: *Durée et Simultaneité*, Paris.

4   Bohr N., 1959: *Atomic Physics and Human Knowledge*, NY.

5   Kant, I., 1933: *Critique of Pure Reason* (ed. N.K. Smith), London.

6   London & Bauer, 1939: *Theorie de l'observation en meq.quant*, Paris.

7   Lossky, N.O., 1995: *Sensual, Intellectual & Mystical Intuition*, Moscow

8   Nesteruk, A.V., 1993: *The Approach of Transcendental Realism .. etc.*,
    in: *The Origins of the World in Science and Theology*, St.Petersburg.

9   Nesteruk, A.V., 1994: *The correlation between (Minkowski & Hilbert)*,
    in: *Proc. Physical Interpretations of Relativity IV*, Ld, pp.240-54.

10 Penrose, R., 1979: *Singularities & Time Asymmetry*,
    in: Hawking & Israel: *General Relativity, An Einstein Centenary*, Cambridge.

11 Penrose, R., 1981, in Isham: *Quantum Gravity 2*, pp.244-72, Oxf.

12 Penrose, R., 1986, in: Flood & Lockwood: *The Nature of Time*, Blackwell.

13 Penrose, R., 1989: *The Emperor's New Mind*, Oxford.

14 Philo, 1981: *On the Account of the World's Creation*, London.

15 Poincaré, H, 1892: *Methodes nouvelles d.l. mecanique céleste*, Paris.

16 Prigogine, I., 1980: *From Being to Becoming*, Freeman, NY.

17 Prigogine, I., 1988: *La redécouverte du temps*, L'Homme 28,4,pp.5-26.

18 Prigogine & Stengers, 1984: *Order out of Chaos*, Heinemann, London.

19 Prigogine, I., 1991: 'What is time?' in: *I. Leclerc Festschrift*,
    Zogaard & Treash eds., Mount Allison Univ..

20 Prigogine, I., 1995: 'Why Irreversibility?' *Int.J.Q.Chem.* 53,105-18.

21 Prigogine & Petrorsky, 1995: *Extension of classical dynamics*,
    in: *Hommage a Ivanenko*.

22 Verstraeten, G., 1991: 'Some Critical Remarks conc. Prigogine's Conception
    of Temporal Irreversibility', *Phil.Science* 58, pp.639-54.

23 Verstraeten, G., 1986: *Thermodyn. Reduction of the Anisotropy of Time ..*
    Lecture Notes in Physics 278, Springer Berlin, pp.438-40.

24 Wheeler, J.A., 1985: 'Bohr's "phenomenon" and "law without law"', in.
    Chaotic Behavior in Quantum Systems, pp.363-78, Nato Proc..

25 Wheeler, J.A., 1988: 'World, a system self-synthesised by quant. networking',
    IBM J.Res.Develop. 32, pp.4-15.

26 Wheeler, J.A., 1994: *At Home in the Universe*, AIP Press, N.Y.

Alexei V. Nesteruk

THOMAS E. PHIPPS JR.

TIME IRREVERSIBILITY
AN AGENDA FOR PHYSICS

1. Introduction

During 300 years or so of modern science, two principal modes of description have emerged and have polarised physics. These are the point particle mode, deriving from Newton's mechanics, and the continuum mode, deriving from Maxwell's field theory of electromagnetism.

Experience has shown that the continuum mode cannot stand alone; that is, in order to attain detailed descriptive capability, the mathematical constructs known as "fields" must be "quantised". This amounts to arbitrarily imposing the particle mode on the continuum mode, thereby contributing to a patchwork of fix-its deserving of the name "band-aid physics".

Such physics is aesthetically displeasing, because the postulates that force the mixing of oil-and-water concepts are gratuitous and lack any visible foundation apart from expediency. Their apparent necessity is an affront to logical economy. One would like to find ways of thinking that would avoid the "necessity" of foundational ugliness.

Is the continuum mode indispensable? This is the same question as *do we need Maxwell's equations?* Oddly enough, the answer is: *perhaps not.* What we observe or detect is always the final, decisive, irreversible, purely localised aspect of nature, the "process completion". Are other hypotheses, reaching beyond what is observable, essential to the descriptive process?

The earliest form of electromagnetism, [1] which was due to Weber and Neumann, following the pioneering investigations of Ampère, made no use of the field concept, but was an action-at-a-distance theory of Newtonian "forces" between localised objects (susceptible to idealisation as points). It seems to have worked beautifully for all the problems of observable ponderomotive force actions, and perhaps for electromotive actions as well. [2] It failed only where force drops out of the discussion and radiation enters. Even there, since the crucial parameter 'c' also appears in Weber's formalism, it is not impossible that a point-based theory could (at a deeper level) cope. For Kirchhoff has shown that Weber's theory predicts speed-c propagation of signals on transmission lines; and proof has been given that it is possible to model the vacuum formally as a transmission line.[3]

Why was not this promising line of action-at-a-distance inquiry kept alive during our century? Surely the early killing-off of alternatives is not the strategy of technological inquiry that gave mankind the atomic bomb. We know better, strategically speaking, when we set out to find the means to kill people, but forget when it comes to killing ideas or theories. In the latter department physicists elect a "feel-good" strategy of consensus: the herd instinct among experts is encouraged to take over (example: the reaction of nuclear physics professionals to the possibility of cold fusion).

It is well-known (since Herman Kahn) that committees can behave more stupidly than any of their members would, if left to their own devices. Yet consensus of experts is aimed for as today's preferred method of getting at scientific truth. Obviously to any child, seeking consensus within a technical area is how one gets at teachability, not how one gets at truth. We can thank our academies and their pedagogues for perennially confusing these two.

The famous Jury system of jurisprudence might be appealed-to as lending honor or redemption to committee decision-making; but this system operates on the principle of appeal to the adversarially-informed opinion of unbiased non-experts - essentially the opposite of the principle of seeking the consensus of experts. The Jury system employs experts only as witnesses. For those experimentally inclined, it might be interesting to try a little of the Jury principle in science (in place of, or supplementary to, the consensus of experts) and see what happens. For one must never forget the definition of an *expert* as someone who *does not make small mistakes*!

We shall not pursue the matter of alternatives to field theory here, but merely observe in passing that a great amount of empirical evidence [1,2] is accumulating toward the end of this century that the original Ampère law of force actions (at a distance) between "current elements", long dropped from textbooks because of its conflict with the preconceptions of experts, is superior to that of Lorentz, on which standard relativity theory relies implicitly. Indeed an apparently "crucial" experiment has very recently been done, [4] in which nature has plainly spoken in favor of Ampère; but this (following rejections by APS and the Royal Society) is currently mired in the politics of publication of unwanted news.

So, can particle mechanics stand alone? The unhesitating answer of today's physical theorists is: Never! Since Einstein, physicists no longer look for theories of nature but exclusively for *field* theories of nature. They are happy to prejudge - and it is this prejudgment that produces the polarisation of physics alluded to above ... a polarisation whereby this author stands at one

Thomas E. Phipps

pole and virtually all authorities at the other. In its favor, the prejudgment does produce a kind of economy, albeit not logical economy - namely, economy of logical thought. This cheapens the search for truth, of course ("Thrift, Horatio!"), and so pleases the research-funding bureaucrat.

This writer's (speculative) answer is that **mechanics can stand alone** if and only if mechanics is changed in such a way as to be more true to itself. To accomplish this, a covering theory of Hamilton-Jacobi mechanics has been proposed [5-10] that makes rigorous the formal Correspondence governing the transition to quantum-level description. The effect of this rigorisation is to preserve the canonical character (or parametric symmetry) of the mechanical formalism by restoring to it analogs of the lost "new canonical variables". In classical mechanics the latter are identifiable with "constants of motion". The disappearance of these parameters from Schrödinger's mechanics, which otherwise formally resembles that of Hamilton-Jacobi, has been an enduring mystery, never mentioned by physics teachers in the presence of the young.

The rigorisation of formal Correspondence automatically provides an operator mechanics that is **a covering theory** of both classical mechanics and ordinary quantum mechanics, more richly parametrised than the latter. This operator mechanics contains two unknowns, an operand or wave function Ψ, and a new quantity S, the operator analog of Hamilton's principal function. Three classes of exact solutions have been found: 1. the Hamilton-Jacobi classical states of motion, 2. the Schrödinger-Dirac quantum mechanical states, but with the wave function modified by attachment of a phase factor in which the "constant of the motion" analogs enter as "hidden parameters", and 3. a new class identified specifically with nuclear dynamics in which Ψ and S are solved-for simultaneously. It will be argued here that the new phase factor on the wave function (of the second class of solutions) opens the way for treating time irreversibility since it allows event *retro-description* but, owing to the unobservability of phase factors, not event *prediction*.

In this connection it has long been commonly accepted wisdom that mechanics cannot explain process irreversibility, such as is encountered in thermodynamics and incorporated in the second law. We shall argue here, to the contrary, that only mechanics is qualified to explain irreversibility at the quantum level, where it may be considered to originate. Thus the process completion of quantum mechanics, sometimes verbalised as a "reduction" of the wave function or a "severance" of the von Neumann phase chain, is in fact the most elementary form or prototype of a physically irreversible occurrence. More kinds of irreversibility than one should not be needed in any conceptual

Thomas E. Phipps

scheme that honors logical economy. The problem is that that one kind is obtained in present measurement theory only with the help of extra postulates, i.e., through discarding logical economy. We shall suggest that the right way to deal with the problem is by extra parametrisation, not extra postulation.

We proceed to review the formal apparatus necessary to treat such matters. The writer has been over this ground in print many times [5-10] and apologises to any reader who has met it before.

2. Strict Formal Correspondence

In recognition that the major part of our perception-mediated daily experience is describable by Newton's mechanics, and that the most elegant, generalised, and generalisation-inviting form of that mechanics is the energy formulation due to Hamilton-Jacobi (H-J), we begin our search for a more comprehensive point-particulate mechanical foundation of physics with an explicit writing-out of the H-J equations [11]:

$$\text{(1a)} \qquad H = -\frac{\partial}{\partial t}S \qquad H = H(t, q_k, p_k)$$

$$\text{(1b)} \qquad p_k = \frac{\partial}{\partial q_k}S \qquad S = S(t, q_k, Q_k)$$

$$\text{(1c)} \qquad P_k = -\frac{\partial}{\partial Q_k}S \quad k = 1, 2, .., 3m$$

Observe the symmetry between the set of $6m$ old canonical variables (q_k, p_k) and the set of $6m$ new canonical variables $(Q_k, -P_k)$. Classical canonical transformation theory [11] exploits this symmetry (or gives rise to it), the H-J theme residing in the interpretation of the new canonical variables as the constants of motion. That theme will be strictly preserved in all that follows.

The idea behind any formal Correspondence is: *preservation of form.* One seises upon a favored mathematical form and doggedly preserves it. Oddly enough, no form is rigorously preserved in the presently accepted "formal Correspondence" as it is employed in textbooks to "derive" ordinary quantum mechanics. That is a manifest flaw which we shall make a point of correcting here. In particular, the canonical symmetry mentioned above is not preserved, and we shall make it our primary business to correct that.

The stage is now set for a rigorous formal Correspondence. The form we choose to favor is Eq. (1). No effort will be devoted to justifying this choice, apart from pointing out that it is a likely thing to try, in light of the canonical symmetry aspect. (Since the formal mathematical Correspondence is supposed to mirror a continuous physical correspondence, however, we might reasonably ask at what physical discontinuity, in the transition from large to small, any claimed loss of canonical symmetry occurs). The only real justification comes later in the working out of the detailed consequences.

Thomas E. Phipps

Taking Eq. (1) as it stands, we reinterpret all symbols as operators and supply a common operand or wave function $\Psi_f = \Psi_f(t, q_k, Q_k, P_k)$. Thus we postulate the basic equations of a generalised mechanics to be

(2a) $\qquad H\Psi_f = -\frac{\partial}{\partial t} S\Psi_f$

(2b) $\qquad p_k \Psi_f = \frac{\partial}{\partial q_k} S\Psi_f$

(2c) $\qquad P_k \Psi_f = -\frac{\partial}{\partial Q_k} S\Psi_f$

The partial differential operators are understood to act on everything to their right. That is our postulate, and we must allow ourselves no others if logical economy is to be honored. The whole story of mechanics from A to Z must be contained in those three relations; if it turns out otherwise, we have chosen the wrong form to preserve.

What evidence is there that no further postulation is needed for physical descriptive purposes? The rest of this paper will be concerned with answering that. We begin by formulating a purely mathematical taxonomy of solution classes of Eq. (2):

Class 1. $\qquad\qquad \Psi_f = constant.$

In this trivial case we recover H-J mechanics as an exact solution class, since a constant cancels from each of the three parts of Eq. (2), leaving Eq. (1) as the residue. So we recognise that classical mechanics is an exact, not an approximate, solution of the candidate generalisation of mechanics. (The status of classical mechanics relative to other "higher" forms of mechanics is drastically altered by this circumstance).

Class 2. $\qquad\qquad S = \frac{\hbar}{i} = constant.$

By giving this particular constant value to the formal analog of Hamilton's principal function we recover accepted quantum mechanics. That is, by substituting $S = \hbar/i$ into Eq. (2), we reduce its three parts to

(3a) $\qquad H\Psi_f = -\frac{\hbar}{i}\frac{\partial}{\partial t}\Psi_f$

(3b) $\qquad p_k \Psi_f = \frac{\hbar}{i}\frac{\partial}{\partial q_k}\Psi_f$

(3c) $\qquad P_k \Psi_f = -\frac{\hbar}{i}\frac{\partial}{\partial Q_k}\Psi_f$

On making the substitution

(4) $\qquad \Psi_f = e^{-\frac{i}{\hbar}\Sigma_k Q_k P_k}\Phi(t, q_k)$

where Φ is an undetermined function, we see that Eq. (3c) is satisfied identically, and Eqs. (3a), (3b) are reduced to the Schrödinger-Dirac equations

(5a) $\qquad H\Phi = -\frac{\hbar}{i}\frac{\partial}{\partial t}\Phi$

(5b) $\qquad p_k \Phi = \frac{\hbar}{i}\frac{\partial}{\partial q_k}\Phi$

Thomas E. Phipps

This reduction occurs because we preserve the classical interpretation of the (Q_k, P_k) as constants, so that the exponential expression in Eq. (4) is just a constant phase factor that cancels out. If these quantities were not at all sise scales constant, it would be necessary, as above, to say precisely where in the descriptive transition from large to small they turned into variables ... and there is no answer to such a question, just as there is no answer (in the ordinary quantum "Correspondence" argument) to where it is, on the physical world-scale, that the integral number of mechanical descriptive parameters changes from $12m+1$ (old plus new canonical variables plus time) to $6m+1$ (old canonical variables only, plus time).

It is clear that the Class-2 solutions of Eq. (2) recapitulate ordinary quantum mechanics, aside from a constant phase-factor $\exp(-i\alpha)$, where $\alpha = \hbar^{-1}\sum_k Q_k P_k$, attached to the wave function Φ. This phase factor affects nothing directly observable, since it can be absorbed into the wave-function normalisation factor. It is thus just a sort of electromagnetic "gauge" analog.

Class 3. $\qquad\qquad S \neq constant, \Psi_f \neq constant.$

The most general solutions of Eq. (2), wherein S and Ψ_f appear as simultaneous unknowns, fall into this category, which may be supposed physically to describe nuclear bound states of electron-positrons. An example of such a solution, based on a Dirac-type Hamiltonian, has been given elsewhere [5,10] and need not detain us here. We merely remark on a few points of mathematical interest. The reason light particles can exist stably as constituents of heavier aggregates on a nuclear scale of dimensions is simply that the Heisenberg postulate, which prohibits such things in ordinary quantum theory, is violated by the Class-3 solutions locally, near a massive center of Coulombic (and, if you will, nuclear) force. This possibility follows from the fact that the Heisenberg postulate is generalised to

$$(6) \qquad p_k q_j - q_j p_k = \frac{\partial}{\partial q_k} S q_j - q_j \frac{\partial}{\partial q_k} S = S\delta_{jk}$$

as follows directly from Eq. (2b). The Heisenberg postulate is the special case, $S = \hbar/i$ of the Class-2 solutions. In the Class-3 solutions, however, the p, q commutator can be a more general function of the distance from a force-center. S is not a postulated function, since we have long finished with postulation. By contrast, it and Ψ_f are solved for as simultaneous unknowns of the three simultaneous equations (2). This new degree of mathematical generality gives rise to a technical question regarding the Hermitean property of operators.

If we write $S = (\hbar/i)\, s$, where $s = s(t, q_k, Q_k)$ is some real scalar function, we see that the classical-analog operators for energy and momentum in Eq. (2) become non-Hermitean. For instance, $p_k = (\hbar/i)(\partial/\partial q_k)s$ is seen to be the product of two Hermitean operators, which, by a standard theorem, is non-Hermitean. The Hermitean property, a generalised "realness," is needed for physics. Luckily, new Hermitean operators can be introduced by the simple "reification" transformations

$$(7) \qquad \mathfrak{H} = Hs^{-1} \qquad \mathfrak{p}_k = p_k s^{-1} \qquad \Psi = s\Psi_f$$

These new operators, $\mathfrak{H}$ and $\mathfrak{p}_k$, together with the new operand Ψ, yield a reversion to the standard Hermitean formalism,

$$(8) \qquad \mathfrak{H}\Psi = -\frac{\hbar}{i}\frac{\partial}{\partial t}\Psi \qquad\qquad \mathfrak{p}_k\Psi = \frac{\hbar}{i}\frac{\partial}{\partial q_k}\Psi$$

etc., where for known classical-analog operators the transformed operators $\mathfrak{H}$ and $\mathfrak{p}_k$ are in all cases found to be Hermitean. For example, in a non-relativistic one-body problem the new "reified" Hamiltonian becomes

$$(9) \qquad \mathfrak{H} = Hs^{-1} = \left(\frac{\mathbf{p}\cdot\mathbf{p}}{2m} + V\right)s^{-1} = -\frac{\hbar^2}{2m}\nabla s\cdot\nabla + V\, s^{-1}$$

which is seen to be Hermitean, since s is real.

The recovery of familiar forms through a reification transformation has caused mathematicians to greet this formalism with monumental ennui. Physicists, however, can hardly avoid admitting that these reified operators are different from the classical-analog ones they have always worked with. Since all the physics is in the Hamiltonian, and we deal with an altered Hamiltonian never seen before, interest would manifestly be aroused *if* there were any physicists. Since 1960 I have amassed the evidence of 36 years [5] that there are indeed no physicists. This will perhaps be more surprising to philosophers of science than to would-be innovators in the hard sciences: Ever-changing in the winds of fashion that blow along their frontiers, the hard sciences are adamant against change in their mathematical foundations, although these be known by every child to rest on quicksand. By that invariant signature may be recognised the dead hand of expertise.

3. Measurement Theory Reappraised

Today's quantum measurement theory (or theories) constitutes one of the most vigorous exercises of the human imagination in the long annals of casuistry (defined as "application of general moral rules to particular cases"). The general moral rule in this case is that **thou shallt not** by a hair's breadth alter the sacred mathematics of quantum mechanics: *Interpret thou mayest; alter thou mayest not.* Naturally, the game-playing instincts of the experts are aroused by such a challenge, and the result has been a century of truly Olympian performances in the pilpul arena.

Thomas E. Phipps

To date, the highest vault or broadest jump has been performed by the discoverers of the Many Worlds interpretation. Their commendable aim is to minimise the postulational excesses embodied in a Projection Postulate or equivalent postulational means of *getting something to happen* locally in the external world. Ordinary quantum mechanics based on Eq. (5) lacks any means of severing phase connections - hence it has no way of ending the problem or of allowing the famous Einsteinian point-event to occur. But why an inability to end the problem in one universe is supposed to be cured by extending that inability to many universes is one of those subtle points of pilpul into which we need not delve here. Suffice it, from this example, to say that the innocent world is allowed to be bent all out of shape, but the guilty mathematics is protected from even evolutionary changes.

Such willingness of the human intellect to mold a defenseless world into any form needed to match its self-created mathematics must surely provide part of the explanation for that perennial marvel, on which profound intellects are always commenting, viz., the ability of mathematics to describe an external world. If one-tenth of the intellectual horsepower devoted to justifying the mathematics of quantum mechanics had been devoted to improving it, the virtue of a rigorised formal Correspondence, giving rise to a covering theory of existing quantum mechanics, might have been recognised long ago.

The inevitable consequence would have been a more widespread recognition of the "incompleteness" of the existing quantum formalism and of the possibility of doing with extra parameters what extra postulates cannot legitimately be called upon to do. For the Projection Postulate and its like directly contradict the already-postulated equations of motion, viz. Eq. (5). One does not build a consistent set of postulates by allowing postulates to contradict one another. It is surprising that the mathematicians who have largely taken over theoretical physics have not been quick to recognise that for themselves. But many surprising things can be expected when expediency is allowed to dictate the moral rules of casuistry.

The idea behind a rigorised Correspondence is that if equations of motion suffice for physical description, as they do on the Newtonian side, they must suffice on the other side of the Correspondence transition as well. For, again, the reasoning is that if on one side a flock of extra postulates is needed and on the other side it is not, then we have to be able, physically, to say where within the continuum of system sises this discontinuity occurs ... and that is obvious nonsense. To get out of this logical forked stick the simplest escape is to reject the mathematics that got us into it; specifically, to

Thomas E. Phipps

use the extra parameters provided by Correspondence rigorisation to do the job of wave-function phase-connection severance that the extra postulates were unable to accomplish. This turns out to be trivially easy to do.

Let us go back to the Class-2 solutions discussed above; specifically, to Eq. (4), which shows the system formal wave function as the product of a Schrödinger wave function and a phase factor, namely $\Psi_f = e^{-i\alpha}\Phi$, where $\alpha = \hbar^{-1}\sum_k Q_k P_k$ is a constant. The numerical value of α is not an observable; so we are free to make hypotheses. Since it derives on the classical side from "constants of the motion", we may suppose that a feature of such constants endures, viz., that they stay constant during, and only during, a particular descriptive problem. That is, these constants are what particularise physical description and distinguish one "problem" from another.

Note that Einstein's relativity principle depends on the distinction between "laws of nature" (equations of motion) and particular realisations, which do not obey the principle: measured numerical values of particle energies are different in different inertial frames because initial conditions are different, although the "laws" be the same. This distinction has been dropped from quantum theory because the (Q_k, P_k) have been unjustifiably dropped.

If α is a dynamical constant, its numerical value, whatever it may be, may be thought to "jump" in an unpredictable and unaccountable manner whenever the "problem" changes. In the same way, classically, when a mechanical problem described by one set of initial-condition constants is terminated and a new problem is initiated, the new constants of the motion owe no debt to the old ones and constitute an entirely independent set of numbers, even if the same physical particles are under description.

We infer in the quantum case that (a) if our initial problem of describing some given portion P of the physical world involves a wave function with phase factor $exp(-i\alpha^{(1)})$; (b) if a point event occurs physically within P (process completion); then (c) that event may be assigned particular numerical values of the (Q_k, P_k) that furnish a new phase factor $exp(-i\alpha^{(2)})$, where $\alpha^{(1)}$ is unrelated to $\alpha^{(2)}$, either numerically or conceptually.

Such an unknowable phase jump is mathematically discontinuous and, in terms of probability, leaves no grounds for inference from system before to system after. We thus exploit the existence of a parametric mechanism - newly provided by our postulated equations of motion, Eq. (2) - for phase-connection severance of the system wave function whenever a localised event occurs (independently, of course, of human volition) in the portion of the world being described by that wave function.

Thomas E. Phipps

4. Time Irreversibility

This simple result paves the way for an epistemological advance. The conception that $\alpha^{(2)}$ describes some definite fact that "really happened" at some definite time and place in the world provides the basis for assuming the describability of that fact and the feasibility of a qualified retrodiction - as, in order to retrodict the past, one must have experienced, and remembered, it. Prediction remains impossible-in-principle on the micro scale since a wave function still governs ($\alpha^{(1)}$ or $\alpha^{(2)}$ being entirely useless for prediction).

Thus history, conceived as a lattice of irrevocable localised events, is real and the idea of it is (for the first time since 1925) admissible to physics. We no longer have to live with the strange doctrine [12] that "besides physics there is history". The past differs from the future through the attribute of "knowability". One may encapsulate all this in the assertion that *objectivity* is restored to physics but not *determinacy*. This and more are accomplished by a simple reform of the parametrisation of quantum physics, in a word, through exercising the common sense required not to discard parameters that were there in mechanics to start with. The onus of "justification" or proof should rest on those who claim that the discarding constitutes physics.

It will be noticed that "the mind of the observer" loses whatever physical-process "enabling powers" it may have had under the Copenhagen regime, as interpreted by such authorities as Wigner. Now that we have parameters, we no longer need observers. The physical world, of course, never needed either. Given parameters, physics (the discipline) subsides into its old rôle as description of nature, and observers either evaporate or else subside into mindless detectors that force local process completions.

What has time irreversibility to do with phase factors? Let us review: When a quantum descriptive problem is undertaken, a formal wave function is introduced to do the job, viz. a Class-2 solution of Eq. (2). This can be represented as a Schrödinger wave function to which is attached a constant phase factor $exp(- i\alpha^{(1)})$. The value of $\alpha^{(1)}$ is unknowable and unimportant, since the phase factor, *as long as it stays constant*, is absorbed into the wave-function normalisation factor and is unobservable. How long is it constant? Well, until something observable happens in the system under description. That may be forever in the ideal case of an isolated hydrogen atom.

Eventually, we may suppose, something happens in the system at some specifiable time and place. This is different from ordinary quantum mechanics (without extra postulates) in which nothing definite ever happens, as the equations of motion contain no parameter descriptive of happenings.

Thomas E. Phipps

Given that something has happened, we can assign to the new canonical variable parameters (either the Q_k alone or these in conjunction with the P_k) contained in $\alpha^{(1)}$ new values descriptive of the phase-space location of the event(s) that happened. This causes a discontinuous "jump" $\Delta\alpha = \alpha^{(2)} - \alpha^{(1)}$ of the α-value and hence of the wave-function phase factor. That terminates the quantum descriptive problem - and *does so in an irreversible way.*

One could say that phase knowledge has been destroyed in an irrevocable way. But there are two dubious aspects of such a way of speaking. In the first place, this "knowledge" never existed in any literal sense, because $\alpha^{(1)}$, $\alpha^{(2)}$ and $\Delta\alpha$ are all unknowable numerically and, if "known", could never be verified by observation. Secondly, introducing what amounts to information-theoretical ways of thinking and speaking transmogrifies and perpetuates the Wignerian fallacy that what is going on in our heads has some "enabling" influence upon the functioning of the world.

The fact that we have acquired parameters usable to describe irreversible events in the external world is not the cause of irreversibility. Whatever makes time flow irreversibly, whatever causes the event to happen in the world, is the world's own business and we shall never be let in on it. Our rôle under the Class-2 solutions has shrunk back to even less than what it was classically - to a mere description of whatever happened in the past, and this is a purely *post factum* description (whereas classically, *via* the Class-1 solutions, we can predict as well as retrodict).

But at least the mystery of asymmetry of "time flow" is cleared up in the quantum-descriptive world. It is mirrored in the mathematical descriptive asymmetry we have been discussing. The parametric capacity to "end the problem" via an unknowable quantum jump of the phase factor, leading to a "severance of the von Neumann chain" of phase connections, establishes an irreversible distinction between "the problem before" and "the problem after". The "Dedekind cut" that lies between these two is the event occurring at that "now" which separates the knowable past from the unknowable future.

It is out there - in the world itself - that true irreversibility is hidden. All we have done is to provide ourselves with the parameters necessary for a *post factum* description of this important aspect of the world. The problem of time irreversibility, originating with classical mechanics, was already largely solved by the advent of ordinary quantum mechanics except for one glaring omission: the parameters to describe local events at all. With that incapacity corrected, there is certainly no further motivation to look for the "cause" of time irreversibility in more remote or peripheral aspects of physics.

Thomas E. Phipps

5. All Physical Description is Approximation.

In the foregoing I have, deliberately, adopted a "naïve realist view" of what I call "the world". This is standard among physicists, and I do not apologise for it, even to philosphers, who know much more about such things than physicists do. In these concluding paragraphs I should like to offer an "insight" of my own regarding the relationship of description to the described. The view, though a trivial consequence of the rigorised Correspondence we have carried out, leading to Eq. (2) as the postulated basis for a new universal mechanics, is nevertheless heretical from the standpoint of quantum physics supposed to be complete and final by today's authorities.

The experts, teachers and their pupils, all tend to view established quantum mechanics as embodying the exact physical truth (recall the moral ground-rule of measurement theory). Classical mechanics, then, is just an approximation (mediated by wave packets, etc.) to this underlying exact truth. No matter how massive an object may be, or how short its de Broglie wavelength, the real truth (however well-hidden from laymen's eyes) is that it is a quantum object. Quantum mechanics rules the waves, and the waves rule all. Such is the conventional wisdom of our day.

That view is incompatible with Eq. (2) as the basis for mechanics. We were at pains to point out that the Class-1 solutions are exact solutions of our proposed equations of motion. Now, exacter than exact one cannot get. That is an ineluctable mathematical fact. If you insist on having something better than an exact solution of your assumed equations, you are going to have to assume some other equations. If you cannot tolerate classical mechanical states of motion as the most nearly exact descriptions of the motions of "sufficiently massive" objects attainable by mathematical physics, you will have to follow some other path than the one here recommended.

My view is this: On one hand we have the "external world," a seamless whole, sufficient unto itself. On the other we have Eq. (2) and its three classes of mathematically exact solutions. This, also, is sufficient unto itself. If there is any relation between these quite disparate "selves", the world and the math, it must (on the face of it) be some relationship of approximation. To make it more than that - e.g. to allege identity on a level of deeper truth - is to indulge in arrant mysticism. That theoretical physicists, since Einstein, have been tempted to indulge in bad metaphysics, is only one of a long bill of particulars that could be brought against poor old Einstein.

Thomas E. Phipps

Finally, then, what is being said is that an aspect of dynamics, that of massive objects, is best approximated by the Class-1 solutions; another aspect, that of atomic systems, is best approximated by the Class-2 solutions; and yet another aspect, that of nuclei, is best approximated by the Class-3 solutions. At the joints between these different world-aspects there may be room for negotiation, but never for dogmatism.

So much for the mechanical aspects of the world. Newton, with his customary perspicacity, suggested that it would be nice to be able to do the whole job of physical description by employing solely mechanical themes. Three hundred years later, we still do not know how to do this. But I suggest we should keep looking, trying, poking at every pebble. Strange, is it not - and a commentary on our times - that this could be a radical agenda?

References

1. Graneau, P., 1994: *Ampère-Neumann Electrodynamics of Metals*,
    2nd ed., Hadronic Press, Palm Harbor, FL.
2. Graneau, P. & N., 1996: *Newtonian Electrodynamics*,
    World Scientific, Singapore.
3. Gray, R.I., 1995: *Phys. Essays* 8, p. 285.
4. Graneau, Roscoe, and Phipps:
    An Experimental Confirmation of Longitudinal Electrodynamic Forces
    in submission, variously.
5. Phipps, Jr.,T.E., 1960: *Phys.Rev.* 118, p. 1653.
6. idem, 1969: *Dialectica* 23, p. 189.
7. idem, 1973: *Found.Phys.* 3, 435.
8. idem, 1975: *Found.Phys.* 5, p. 45; 1976: 6, p. 7; 1976: 6, p. 263.
9. idem, 1979: 'Do Quantum 'Events' Occur?'
    International Conference on Cybernetics and Society,
    IEEE publication CH1424-1, Oct., p.630.
10. idem, 1987: *Heretical Verities: Mathematical themes in physical description*
    Classic Non-fiction Library, Urbana, IL.
11. Goldstein, H., 1950: *Classical Mechanics*,
    Addison-Wesley, Cambridge, MA.
12. Süssmann, G., 1957, in: *Observation and Interpretation*,
    S. Körner, ed., Butterworth's, London, p. 145.

Thomas E. Phipps

J. R. LUCAS

A NOTE ON TIME AND TENSE

McTaggart argued that time is unreal because time involves tense and tense is unreal.[1] More recently Mellor has argued that tense is unreal, but time does not really involve tense, so that time itself is real, tense being only a perspective we need to have on time, but not the essence of time itself. I agree with McTaggart that time involves tense and with Mellor that time is real, but I contest the view they hold in common: that tense is unreal.

McTaggart argued that tensed language (*the A-series*, as he called it) is inherently inconsistent, as every event has to be past, present and future, but these are incompatible predicates. Although McTaggart and his followers disallow it, we often use a mixture of tensed and tenseless language.

We would all agree that:
every event is at some time future (F):

(1) $\quad\quad\quad\quad (\forall e)(\exists t)\, F_t e$

every event is at some time present (N):

(2) $\quad\quad\quad\quad (\forall e)(\exists t)\, N_t e$

every event is at some time past (P):

(3) $\quad\quad\quad\quad (\forall e)(\exists t)\, P_t e$

Hence we agree that every event is at some time future (F), at some time present (N), and at some time past (P):

(4) $\quad\quad\quad\quad (\forall e)(\exists t)\, F_t e \wedge (\forall e)(\exists t)\, N_t e \wedge (\forall e)(\exists t)\, P_t e$

But from this follows only that:

(5) $\quad\quad\quad\quad (\forall e)(\exists t,t',t'')\, [F_t e \wedge N_{t'} e \wedge P_{t''} e]$

It certainly does not follow that:

$\quad\quad\quad\quad (\forall e)(\exists t)\, [F_t e \wedge N_t e \wedge P_t e]$

McTaggart does not allow a mixed language. A supporter of tenses (let us call him: a *tenser*) can reasonably object that he never claimed that the tenseless language of dates (*the B-series*, as McTaggart termed it) is *verboten*. What he claims is merely that tenses are essential, not that they suffice for temporal talk. McTaggart demands his thesis that every event has to be past, present and future to be expressed in tensed terms exclusively; then he seeks to fault the tensed expression, and keeps on faulting any revision designed to meet his previous objection (so, in this sense, he is a *detenser*).

In ordinary tensed language we would agree that every event is either future or present or past:

(6) $(\forall e) [Fe \lor Ne \lor Pe]$

We would also agree that if it is future, then it will first be present and later be past; and that if it is present, it was future and will subsequently be past; and that if it is past, it was first future and then present, and it will forever be past; and we can put these together in various ways, and say, for instance:

(7) $(\forall e) [(e$ is $F \land e$ will be $N \land e$ will be $P)$
                     $\lor (e$ was $F \land e$ is $N \land e$ will be $P)$
                     $\lor (e$ was $F) \land e$ was $N \land e$ is $P)]$,

or, equivalently:

(7') $(\forall e) [(e$ is $F \lor e$ was $F)$
                     $\land (e$ will be $N \lor e$ is $N \lor e$ was $N)$
                     $\land (e$ will be $P \lor e$ is $P)]$.

What McTaggart wants us to say is that every event is both future, present and past; but all we need concede is, in tenseless language, that every event *be* both at some time future, at some time present, and at some time past; or, in tensed language, that every event both either was or is or will be future, and either was or is or will be present, and either was or is or will be past.

McTaggart maintains that on the tensed account every event is both future, present and past, hence that the tensed account is self-contradictory. Tenses are therefore, he argues, unreal; and since time, he admits, involves tense, time must needs be unreal too. Met with the obvious retort that these ascriptions of futurity, presentness and pastness are made at different times, so that no contradiction is involved, McTaggart claims that this is naive. My writing the present paper was future, is present, and will be past, true: but, McTaggart and Mellor would argue, these complex tenses likewise involve a contradiction, in as much as each event has to have incompatible tenses.

Once again the same retort is made, that the incompatible ascriptions are made at different dates, so that no contradiction is generated, and once again the resolution is reconstrued in terms of yet more complex tenses, held to give rise to a further contradiction. The critics of tense claim this as a victory, and that they have found a vicious regress in the concept of tense; but it does not look like that to their opponents, who accuse them of being needlessly muddled at each stage, and when their muddle is pointed out to them, deliberately getting further muddled about the reply. In such a stand-off it is clear that deeper issues are at stake, and that the two parties are being moved by metaphysical assumptions which we need to make explicit.

J.R. Lucas

Mellor recognises that McTaggart's argument may not convince, and he therefore articulates a deeper argument based on token-reflexives.[2] Tenses are essentially token-reflexive. The present tense is used of events contemporary with the time of speaking, the past is used of events that happened before the time of speaking, and the future is used of events expected to take place after the time of speaking. No pure non-token-reflexive translations of tensed utterances can be given, nor can their truth conditions be expressed in pure non-token-reflexive terms. Rather, the truth conditions of tensed utterances are functions of the time of their utterance as well as of the tenseless facts of the case. And so, Mellor concludes, tense is unreal.

But it does not follow. The argument does not show that tensed language is inherently self-contradictory, but merely that it is token-reflexive. Further argument is needed. Plato would give it. He thought the philosopher should disengage himself from the transitory flux of the now and instead be a spectator of all time.[3] Token-reflexives (or indexicals as they are also called) were bad, for the reason that Russell's term, "egocentric particulars", suggests: they depend on the self, when *I* speak, where *I* am situated, and who *I* am. Plato was against the self which is arbitrary, fickle and unreliable, making judgements based on sensation rather than rational consideration.

But this is too quick a condemnation. Tenses are not so much *ego*-centric as they are *nos*-centric. I talk to *you*, and use the present of what is happening as *you* listen, the past of what happened before, and the future of what will happen after *our* conversation. It is not the arbitrary choice of *my* selfish self, but the necessary framework of *our* dialogue, in which you and I communicate with each other, pool information and share rationality.

Plato's prejudice against token-reflexives was clearly misconceived, but arguments from invariance can also be adduced in support of his view that the real world, the world of the Forms, is timeless, spaceless, and impersonal. So too, in the early church, religious truths were, according to the Valentian canon, those that were accepted *semper*, *ubique* and *ab omnibus*. These are, indeed, important marks of reality, but not the only ones.

Only if it tells us about us - or me about me - can a proposition have any bearing on our - or my - concerns. A message without any bearing on our concerns tells us no news. A completely subjective report may be in-communicable, and is likely to be of no interest to others; an account devoid of experience will be devoid of interest, and perhaps meaning, for everyone. An adequate account must save appearances in order to seem significant to us. The real and persisting problem with Platonism is that it appears irrelevant.

J.R. Lucas

Extreme non-indexical accounts are defective. A tenseless account of time is likely to be as useful as a map which does not enable us to locate on it where we are, or a list of guests at a party with no means of discovering to whom one is talking. Language needs to conjugate over tenses as it needs to conjugate over the first- and second-person. Otherwise it has no anchor in experience and fails to address us in our actual situation.

Once experience is accepted as relevant to reality, the near-universal experience of the passage of time must be taken into account. Admittedly, the accounts given are often metaphorical. But widely used metaphors are not to be rubbished. When we speak of time having gone fast we may be unable to answer the question "How many seconds a second?", but this should be a spur to think more deeply rather than to dismiss the locution as meaningless.

In the present century physics had been cited in support of a tenseless view of time. In particular, the Special Theory of Relativity (SR) is thought to give support to the idea of a "block-universe" and hence to tenseless time as an analogue to tenseless space. But this is a mistake. Minkowskian spacetime is not simply a space with four dimensions, but one having $3 + 1$ dimensions with a sign distinguishing time-like separations from space-like ones.

Putnam and Rietdijk have argued that there is no absolute distinction between present, past and future, so we must take a tenseless view of time.[4] Two observers moving with uniform velocity relative to each other, each one at rest in his co-moving frame of reference, will have different hyperplanes of simultaneity. So one event may be simultaneous with another which is itself simultaneous with a third that is a causal antecedent of the first; hence, they argue, it is simultaneous with an event absolutely earlier than itself.

But this is a sophism depending on our not noticing that simultaneity in SR is, like other equivalence relations, a triadic relation, in which things are equivalent to each other with respect to a feature that must be specified, in this case the reference frame. Simultaneity with respect to different reference frames does not constitute an equivalence relation at all. If I was at the same school as you, and you were at the same school as James, then the conclusion that I was at the same school as James depends on which school you shared with me and which with James. If you were at the same nursery school as I, and were at the same secondary school as James, nothing follows about my having been at the same school as James.

But an argument free from that fallacy can be adduced. An event which is future in one frame of reference may be past with respect to another. Whether an event is future or past depends on our choice of reference frame.

J.R. Lucas

Hence it cannot be anything absolute. Nevertheless that argument also fails. The hyperplane of simultaneity for a frame of reference does not determine what is currently going on at distant places, but only what dates should be ascribed to them in order to make electromagnetic phenomena coherent. As far as electromagnetic phenomena are concerned, we have no means of telling exactly when a distant event takes place; but for any given frame of reference, *if* we ascribe the same date to all events on a particular hyperplane, the laws of electromagnetism apply neatly and yield harmonious results.

So far as *SR* goes, simultaneity is a rather superficial and frame-dependent property which we find useful for assigning dates to different events in different places, but which is not of any fundamental importance in accounting for the propagation of causal influence. The ascription of pastness, presentness, or futurity, to events outside the light cone is nominal rather than real, and has no bearing on their ontological status.[5]

Many physicists are persuaded by this argument. But it is to lay too much weight on one physical theory. Once, perhaps, *SR* seemed to be the last word in physics, and its principles were taken to have universal sway. But physicists' views of time have always been tenseless - unsurprisingly, since physicists view the world through non-token-reflexive spectacles.

Newtonian mechanics makes no distinction between past and future, and though it allows hyperplanes of simultaneity, it does not distinguish any particular one as the world-wide present. Newton believed in absolute space, although Newtonian mechanics was unable, alone and unaided, to identify any frame of reference as being at rest rather than being in uniform motion. But Newtonian mechanics, though by itself relativistic as regards rest and uniform motion, did not rule out there being an absolute frame of reference - thus, if the Michelson-Morley experiment had yielded a positive result, we should have identified the rest frame of the ether as being absolutely at rest. In the same way *SR*, though not itself picking out a preferred frame giving a world-wide hyperplane of absolute simultaneity, does not rule it out either.

And in fact, other physical theories rule it in. Most cosmologists use a version of the General Theory of Relativity (*GR*) with boundary conditions yielding a world-wide cosmic time. More fundamentally, quantum mechanics, when interpreted in a realistic way, distinguishes a probabilistic future of superimposed *eigen*-states from an unalterable past in which each dynamical variable is in a definite *eigen*-state, with the present being the moment at which - to change the metaphor - the indeterminate ripples of multitudinous wave-functions collapse into a single definite wave.

J.R. Lucas

Admittedly, many of those who think about quantum mechanics are not realists, and admittedly again, there are horrendous difficulties in the way of constructing a coherent account of the collapse of the wave-function. But an obstinate realism, as well as a slight sympathy for our feline friends, precludes my envisaging any long period in which Schrödinger's cat could be half-dead and half alive, and this whether she be in a laboratory in Europe or on some planet circling Betelgeuse. There is a definite fact of the matter, there as much as here, whether or not we are dealing with a superposition of wave-functions or a definite *eigen*-function. So there is a unique hyperplane advancing throughout the whole universe of collapse into *eigen*-ness.

We can understand why philosophers and scientists have been led to espouse a tenseless view of time, and also why they are wrong to do so. The austere intimations of reality allowed by Plato are too austere: we cannot, on pain of ultimate irrelevance, discount the evidence of human experience. Moreover, the conditions in which we are able to pool information and share rationality are such that ought to enter into any adequate account of reality.

The view of science, important and illuminating though it is, is only a partial view, and the features it ignores do not on that account fail to exist. It is too soon to suppose that quantum mechanics is the last word in physics, or that the way it is interpreted by me is the way it ought to be interpreted. But at the present time it looks as if a tensed view of time is in fact a view required by physics as well as by our ordinary untutored experience.

References

1.   J.M.E. McTaggart, 1927: *The Nature of Existence*, Cambridge.
2.   D.H. Mellor, 1987: *Real Time*, Cambridge.
3.   R. Sorabji, 1980: *Necessity, Cause and Blame*, London.
4.   R. Torretti, 1983: *Relativity and Geometry*, Oxford.

J.R. Lucas

[1] J.McT.E. McTaggart, 1908: *Mind* 18, pp. 457-84; and:
    1927: *The Nature of Existence*, vol.2, Cambridge.
[2] D.H. Mellor, 1981: *Real Time*, Cambridge, pp. 98-102
[3] Plato: *Republic VI*, 486a8
[4]   H. Putnam, 1967:
'Time and Physical Geometry', *Jour.Phil.* 64, pp. 240-47; reprinted in:
1979: *Mathematics, Matter & Method. Philosophical Papers*, Cambr., pp. 198-205
    C.W.Rietdijk, 1966:
'A Rigorous Proof of Determinism ..', *Phil.Sc.* 33, pp. 341-44, and 1976:
'Special Relativity and Determinism', *Phil.Sc.* 43, pp. 598-609;
    John W. Lango, 1969:
'The Logic of Simultaneity', *Jour.Phil.* 66, pp. 340-50.
[5] For further discussion of these arguments, see
    Howard Stein, 1968:
'On Einstein-Minkowski space-time', *Jour.Phil.* 65, pp. 5-23; and, 1970:
'A Note on Time and Relativity Theory', *Jour.Phil.* 67, pp. 289-94;
    R.Sorabji, 1980:
Necessity, Cause and Blame, London, pp. 114-19; and:
    R.Torretti, 1983:
Relativity and Geometry, Oxford, pp. 249-51.

J.R. Lucas

WILLIAM LANE CRAIG

THE PRESENTNESS OF EXPERIENCE

Introduction

We experience the reality of tense in a variety of ways which are so evident and pervasive that the belief in the objective reality of past, present, and future is a universal feature of all human experience. Phenomenological analyses af temporal consciousness carried out by philosophers have emphasised the importance of what McTaggart called 'A-determinations' to our experience of time. In his classic phenomology of time consiousness, Edmund Husserl very aptly described our human experience of time.

Following Husserl, we experience on the one hand a sort of "flowing away" (*Ablaufsphänomene*) consisting of the recession of experience from the 'now' into the past: "This now apprehension is, as it were, the nucleus of a comet's tail of retentions referring to the earlier now-points of the motion".[1] But we also protend the future in that we anticipate and live toward that which is to come. The transformation of now-consiousness to consiousness of the past, and its replacement by a new now-consciousness, says Husserl, "is part of the essence of time consciousness".[2]

Thus, our differing attitudes towards past and future, as well as our apprehension of temporal becoming, are constitutive of time consciousness: "The immanent contents are what they are only so far as, during their 'actual' duration, they refer ahead to something futural and back to something past .. In each phase which .. constitutes the immanent content we have retentions of the preceding and protentions of the coming phases of precisely this content."[3] Though Husserl, in line with his phenomenological practice of *epoché*, made no judgement concerning what he called "objective flow of time" or "world-time" or "real-time",[4] he accurately described how we experience temporality.

Psychologist William Friedmann, who has made a career of the study of time consciousness, reports: "Like (temporal) order and the causal priority principle, the division between past, present, and future so deeply permeates our experience that it is hard to imagine its absence."[5] We have, he writes, "an irresistible tendency to believe in a present. Most of us find quite startling the claim of some physicists and philosophers that the present has no special status in the physical world, that there is only a sequence of times, that the past, present, and future are only distinguishable in human consciousness."[6]

As a result, virtually all philosophers of space and time, including the so-called B-theorists of time, admit that the view of the common man is that time involves a past, present, and future which are objectively real and that things or events really do come to be and pass away in time. For example, Horwich muses that "the quintessential property of time, it may seem, is the difference between past and future".[7] As Coburn confesses, "if the existence of A-facts is an illusion it is one of our most stubborn ones".[8] The depth and pervasiveness of the commonsense belief in A-determinations lead A-theorist W. Godfrey-Smith to state flatly that, "anyone who rejects the notions of past, present, and future has got a lot of explaining to do".[9] Mellor admits this: "the experienced presence of experience is the crux of the tensed view of time", he acknowledges, "and the tenseless camp must somehow explain it away".[10]

An A-theorist could argue plausibly, I think, that the objective reality of tense is the best explanation of our tensed experience and that the proffered B-theoretical alternatives are either demonstrably inadequate or speculative. But it seems to me that our belief in objective tense is more fundamental than such an argument would suggest. Our belief in past, present, and future is not an inference drawn from experience by way of providing an explanation of that experience; rather it is what Plantinga in his critique of foundationalist epistemology has called a "properly basic belief".[11]

We do not, I think, adopt a belief in past, present, and future in an attempt to explain our experience of the temporal world; we simply form such a belief automatically in the context of our experience of the world. And, I should argue, we do so properly. Indeed, I should say that belief in the reality of tense enjoys such powerful epistemic status for us that not only can we be said to know that tense and temporal becoming are real, but also that this belief constitutes an intrinsic 'defeater-defeater' which simply overwhelms all defeaters brought against it. However, the truth of the claim is not essential to the A-theorist's case. All he needs to do is to show the proper basicality of our belief in tense and refute the B-theoretical defeaters brought against it.

If our universally held belief in tense is properly basic, then anyone who denies this belief, and whose defeaters of that belief have themselves been defeated, and who is apprised of these refutations, is irrational in the sense of not fulfilling his epistemic duties or having a flawed noetic structure. For such an individual fails to hold - or rather denies that he holds - a belief which is for him properly basic. Far from being controversial, this is an objective assessment of our epistemic situation with which, according to my impression, many B-theorists would be in agreement.

William Lane Craig

Mellor, for example, frankly admits that "tense is so striking an aspect of reality that only the most compelling argument justifies denying it: viz., that the tensed view of time is self-contradictory and so cannot be true".[12] It is for this reason that McTaggart's Paradox constitutes, in Mellor's own words, "the lynchpin of my book".[13] If this *prima facie* defeater of our belief in tense is itself defeated, then the remaining potential defeaters of the tensed view of time seem paltry in comparison with the enormous warrant enjoyed by our belief in tense. I have elsewhere considered McTaggart's Paradox,[14] and cannot repeat my arguments given there. In this paper I shall restrict myself to refuting defeaters aimed specifically at our experience of tense.

Our Experience of the Present

We all experience events as happening presently. Everyone of us lives in the present, which we often refer to indexically as 'now'. Moreover, we most decidedly do not experience events merely as tenselessly occurring simultaneously with some linguistic or psychological token nor on some given date at a given clock-time. Rather we experience events as irreducibly present. Moreover, it is clear that we do not infer the presentness of events from our experience of them; we just are appeared to presently.

Our unconscious use of the verbal present-tense wholly in the absence of temporal indexicals like 'today' or 'now' shows that our vantage point in the present is not a self-conscious inference drawn from experience, but is just the way we experience events happening.[15] Our belief that they are happening presently is really no different than our belief that they are happening - and that they are happening is a basic belief grounded in part in the circumstances that we "are appeared to" in just that way. Hence, if beliefs like 'I see a tree' are properly basic, so is also 'I am presently seeing a tree', since the former is a tensed belief identical with the latter.

Mellor goes to great lengths to try to explain away our experience of the present. Since, in his view, there can be no present, we cannot, despite appearances, be experiencing it. Hence, he argues first that we do not really observe the tenses of events.[16] According to Mellor, if tenses, especially the present tense, were properties which we can directly observe events to have, it would dispose of the B-theory at once.[16] As "a good empiricist, I will not waste time arguing against the deliverances of my senses", he says.[16]

An examination of Mellor's ensuing arguments reveals that we should not press his language too strictly. For example, Mellor's reasoning is not aimed at some imagined claim that presentness is a property which we can

William Lane Craig

observe by means of our senses. His own examples of our purported observations of presentness are not examples of our observing a sensible property.
For example, we are tempted to think, he says, "that all observation, of all
events, itself occurs in the present. That is, our own experiences, of seeing and
hearing things are given to us in experience as being present tense events".[16]
Here we have an example of what Mellor calls the presence of experience;
even if what we see and hear is not present, our experiences of seeing and
hearing are observed as present. But our experiences of seeing and hearing are
not themselves seen and heard.

Again, he writes: "Even our knowledge of past events seems to be
given to us by our present tense experiences. In the simplest case, we know
about past events because we now remember having seen or heard them
happen. Our present memory tells us that the experience of seeing or hearing
them, when they were present, is itself a past event."[16] Memory beliefs about
events as past are obviously not cases in which we observe a sensible property
'pastness' of said events or a sensible property 'presentness' of our memories of
those events. Mellor's argument is not even directed against the more limited
claim that presentness of events in the external world is a sensible property.
Not only would this be to attack a straw man (since no one, to my knowledge,
has made such a claim), but it would leave Mellor open to the retort that the
presentness of external events is a non-sensible property.[17] Mellor's remark
about not arguing against the deliverances of one's senses expresses his refusal
to dispute beliefs which are properly basic. If our belief in the tenses of events
is properly basic, then, Mellor thinks, the B-theory is finished.

The comparison of our observation of tenses with sense perception
shows that by 'observing that' Mellor does not mean something akin to 'seeing
that' plus some propositional content, an operator that is necessarily veridical,
like 'knowing that'. The deliverances of our senses are properly basic, but
defeasible, beliefs, and Mellor says that if our observation of tenses is like
that, then there is no use arguing against the A-theory. This is an impressive
concession, for it implies that, since Mellor accepts McTaggart's argument
against objective tenses, the warrant enjoyed by our observation of the tenses
of events exceeds that attending the premisses of McTaggart's argument.
Thus Mellor indirectly concedes that our belief in tense is an intrinsic defeater
not only of McTaggart's Paradox but of all arguments aiming at the A-theory.

It would also be a mistake to press Mellor's language concerning our
directly observing the tenses of events. If Mellor were arguing that we can
have no direct observation of tenses, he would leave himself open to the reply

William Lane Craig

that we indirectly observe presentness in our direct observations of events.[18] What Mellor wants to prove is that we do not at all observe the presentness of events in the external world. Finally, it would be a mistake to press Mellor on his characterisation of tenses as properties, since many A-theorists deny the ontological identification of tenses with properties, thinking of them instead as tense logical operators, and Mellor's argument is intended as a refutation of such A-theorists, too, since he will not allow any belief of the form 'S is presently ϕ-ing' to be properly basic.

It might be rejoined that on my interpretation, Mellor has expressed himself so poorly that he did not mean to say almost everything that he said, which seems unlikely. But I think that a sympathetic reading of his argument bears out my interpretation; in any case, if he did mean to prove only that presentness is not a sensible property of events in the external world that we observe directly and indefeasibly, then he has proven very little, indeed.

When Mellor says that we do not observe the tenses of events, he is talking about events in the external world. Mellor agrees that by introspection we do observe our experiences to be present, though such observations will be seen to be non-veridical. Mellor's contention is that, while we do experience our inner experiences as being present, we do not experience external events as present. In the terminology I am employing Mellor contends that, while we have a basic belief in the presentness of experience - a belief which is ultimately defeated, and thus not properly basic - we have no such belief at all in the presentness of events in the external world. Now such a claim *prima facie* seems outrageous; how can Mellor think such a contention plausible?

His answer is that our phenomenology of temporal consciousness is mistaken. We have confused our observing the events to be present with the events themselves being present. We do not observe events to be present, but only our experience of observing them to be present. To prove this, Mellor appeals to our observations of celestial events through a telescope:

I observe a number af events, and I observe the temporal order in which they occur: which is earlier, which later. I do not observe their tense. What I see through the telescope does not tell me how long ago those events occurred. That is a question for whatever theory tells me how far off the events are, and how long it takes light to travel that distance .. So, depending on our theory, we might place the events we see anywhere in the A-series from a few minutes ago to millions of years ago. Yet they would look exactly the same. What we see tells us nothing about the A-series positions of these events.[19]

William Lane Craig

I think it is obvious that this argument is completely ineffectual against the case for our experience of tense as I have framed it. In the first place, I clearly do not form my belief that, say, 'The train is presently pulling into the station' by inference from my belief that 'I am presently experiencing observations of the train pulling into the station', since I typically have no such belief as the latter at all. Mellor's analysis of the phenomenology of our temporal consciousness is plainly unrealistic and contrived.

What then of his telescope illustration? All this proves is that our belief that certain events are presently occurring is defeasible and sometimes defeated. One might as well argue that the deliverances of our senses are not properly basic because when we look through a microscope things appear to be larger than they are. Nor does anything in these illustrations depend on the use of instruments: just as to the unaided eye a star which has in fact ceased to exist appears to be present, so the proverbial stick in the water appears bent. In both cases, physical theory defeats and corrects erroneous basic beliefs. But just as Mellor is not therefore ready to abandon the general veracity and proper basicality of our senses, neither should he abandon the general veracity and proper basicality of our observations of events being present.

As a result of physics and neurology, we have realised that nothing we sense is instantaneously simultaneous with our experience of it as present. But in most cases, the events we observe are contained within a brief temporal interval which is present, for example, the so-called 'specious present', and our basic belief that 'E is presently occurring' makes no reference to instants, so that such a belief remains properly basic even for scientifically educated persons like ourselves. The fact that under extraordinary circumstances our basic belief in the presentness of some event should turn out to be false is no proof at all either that we have no basic beliefs concerning the presentness of events in the external world or that such beliefs are not properly basic. Mellor is therefore simply wrong when he asserts that we do not observe (defeasibly) the tenses of events. If he is nevertheless correct that such observation of tenses intrinsically defeats all B-theoretical objections brought against it, then the debate is over.

So as not to end this paper too abruptly, however, let us proceed to consider Mellor's arguments against the veridicality of our basic belief in the presentness of our experiences. Mellor admits that we do observe our experiences to be present. With respect to our celestial observations, for example, even if the observed super-nova is not occurring presently, nonetheless my observing the super-nova is, if I reflect on it, observed by me as present.

William Lane Craig

In response to the question whether we do not surely observe our own seeings and hearings as present, Mellor gives the paradoxical reply that, "although we observe our experience to be present, it really isn't".[20]

This is a curious reply, for if it be true that our observations of external events as present would disqualify the B-theory, why wouldn't observations of inner, mental events as present do the same? If a basic belief in the presentness of external events would be an intrinsic defeater of even McTaggart's Paradox, why wouldn't a basic belief in the presentness of experience intrinsically defeat the philosophical arguments brought against it? Mellor never addresses these questions, but takes it for granted that his argument against the veridicality of our observation of our experiences as present has more warrant for us than do those observations themselves.

The question we need to ask ourselves is whether Mellor's argument successfully defeats our basic belief in the presentness of our experiences. Mellor begins by noting that there is a difference between our experiences of presentness and our conscious judgement about such experiences. This is a valid and important distinction: typically we have experiences of presentness without self-reflectively judging that our experiences are themselves present.[21] But sometimes we do reflect on our experiences themselves and observe them to be present. In fact, the judgement that our experience is present is, Mellor recognises, one in which we cannot be mistaken. He concludes:

So my judging my experience to be present is much like my judging it to be painless. On the one hand, the judgement is not one I have to make: I can perfectly well have experience without being conscious of its temporal aspects. But on the other hand, if I do make [a judgement], I am bound to be right, just as when I judge my experience to be painless. The presence of experience, like some at least of its other attributes, is something of which one's awareness is infallible .. No matter who I am or whenever I judge my experience to be present, that judgement will be true. That is the inescapable, experientially given presence of experience.[22]

This analysis only heightens the oddity of Mellor's paradoxical reply. For through the comparison of our observation of the presentness of our experience with pain reports, not only is the proper basicality of our belief in the presentness of our experiences underlined, but such experience is said to be incorrigible. But if I am bound to be right in judging that my experience is present, how can it be that, as Mellor says, "it really isn't" ? If, unlike my belief that some external event is present, my belief that my experience of the event is present is indefeasible, how can that experience not be present?

William Lane Craig

By allowing our belief in the presentness of our experiences to be not only basic but incorrigible, Mellor seems to have painted himself into a corner. Mellor's strategy, as he describes it,[23] is to contend that the belief that one's experience is present is a tautologous truth and, tautologies being trivial, so is this belief. He notes that not all one's experiences are judged to be present, but only the experiences which one is having now. But while the belief (1) *The experiences which I am now having possess the property of being present* may not be a tautology on a tensed theory of language, it is on Mellor's New B-Theory of Language. For the tenseless, token-reflexive truth conditions of (1) are given by (2) *The experiences which S has at the time of the tokening of* (1) *possess the property of existing at the time of the tokening of* (1). Therefore, (1) is true, but trivial. - But this strategy is multiply ineffectual:

First, the belief in question is not a belief like (1), but rather like (1'), *My experience of seeing the supernova is present*, which is not tautologous. Mellor creates his tautology by stipulating that it is present experiences which are experienced as present. But there is no need to identify experiences in this way; definite descriptions or proper names of experiences will do.

Second, even (1) is not tautologous if taken as a *de re* description rather than *de dicto*. Granted that *The experiences which I am now having* picks out certain experiences *de re*, the ascription of presentness to those experiences out of all one's experiences across time is not trivial.

Third, even if (1) is tautologous, it does not follow that the presentness of experience is trivial. Consider by way of analogy a misguided philosopher who denies that anyone has any experiences at all. We might now point out to him that we have a basic belief that we have experiences, and perhaps he will admit that this belief is incorrigible. What value, then, would his reply have that (3) *My experiences are my experiences* is tautologous and therefore the belief that one has experiences is trivial? None at all, for the fact that one has experiences is not denied by (3). Similarly, it may be tautologous to assert that (4) *My present experiences are present*, but (4) does nothing to deny or explain away the presentness of my experience. The fact that one can state a tautology like (1) or even (5) *My present experiences are experiences*, does nothing to undercut the belief in the presentness of experience.

Fourth, the stating of tenseless truth conditions for a belief in the presentness of one's experiences does not constitute even a *prima facie* defeater of that belief. Even if we suppose that Mellor's tenseless, token-reflexive account of the truth-conditions of tensed sentence tokens or beliefs

William Lane Craig

were correct, the mere statement of such conditions for the belief that one's experiences are present is just irrelevant to the proper basicality of that belief.

One does not believe what the tenseless truth conditions of one's belief state; rather one believes that one's experience has the present tense. Supplying tenseless truth conditions for that belief does nothing to show that the belief is false or even *prima facie* defeated. Neither is one's belief shown to be trivially true by the provision of tenseless truth conditions. In order for that to be the case, (1) would have to be shown to mean the same as (2), which would be to collapse into the Old B-Theory of Language, which Mellor wishes assiduously to avoid. If (1) and (2) are not synonymous, the triviality of (2) in no way undermines the significance of (1). No incompatibility has so far been alleged or demonstrated between the beliefs' having tenseless truth conditions and one's experiences' having the property of being present.

Mellor more or less admits this by affirming that merely supplying tenseless truth conditions for tensed sentences does not show that the tensed view is wrong. To accomplish that, he must turn to McTaggart's Paradox. This clearly puts Mellor in an inconsistent position, since he earlier admitted that McTaggart's Paradox could not defeat a properly basic belief in the presentness of events, and he also admitted that we do have an infallibly true belief in the presentness of our own mental events. In any case, the reliance on McTaggart shows that the belief in the presentness of our experience is not defeated merely by the stating of its tenseless truth conditions, but remains properly basic unless and until some further defeater is proposed.[24]

Fifth, Mellor's token-reflexive account of the tenseless truth conditions of tensed sentences is in any case inadequate and incoherent, as I have argued elsewhere.[25] Thus, Mellor has not even succeeded in supplying a plausible alternative to our basic belief in the presentness of our experiences.

In Mellor's amended account of the presence of experience, given in response to MacBeath,[26] Mellor makes no advance in the argument for a defeater of our basic belief in the presentness of our experiences. So far I can see, he merely adjusts his account to make the belief cognitively significant while remaining in content a tautology. But he gives no further reason to distrust our basic belief in the presentness of our inner experiences, and so his proposed defeater remains vitiated by the five considerations above. It seems to me, therefore, that Mellor's account of our observation of events as present, whether in the external world or in one's inner, mental life, completely fails to defeat our properly basic belief in the present tense.

William Lane Craig

What other reasons might be given to doubt our experience of the present? Clifford Williams tries to enlist the B-theorist's *tu quoque* argument regarding spatial 'tenses' in order to defeat our basic belief in the presentness of events.[27] He claims that our experience of presentness is like our experience of 'here-ness' and that since no objective property of events, or things, corresponds to the latter, neither is it the case with the former.

Williams attempts to show that the same phenomena which characterise our experience of presentness, such as inexorability, privilegedness, movement, and so on, are also phenomena of our experience of 'hereness'. He contends that if our experience of presentness is alone said to require a mind-independent property then the A-theorist must show how our experience of presentness differs in a crucial way from our experience of 'hereness.'

Not only does Williams err, however, in conflating 'our experience of here and now'[28] with our experience of here and the present but, because of this inadequate exploration of the nature of indexical reference, he fails to see that, as I have argued elsewhere,[29] the indexical 'here' may be plausibly analyzed in A-theoretical terms as the spatial location of 'I-now.' Williams consistently overlooks the tense implicit in his own characterisations of 'here'. Thus when stating "When we experience an object being here .. we experience the object being in the proximity of the place we occupy",[30] he fails to notice that 'occupy' is tensed. Again, when he says that our experience of an object's being here "consists of our awareness of the object's being in the proximity of our location",[31] the present tense of the participle 'being' escapes his notice.

Once an A-theoretical analysis of spatial indexicals is provided in terms of tense and the self, it is hardly surprising that our experience of being 'here' should share certain features with our experience of tense, since 'being here' is itself a tensed notion. So long as a reductive analysis of 'here' in terms of the location of I-now is just coherent, it constitutes an undercutting defeater of Williams's defeater of our experience of presentness. The B-theoretical *tu quoque* argument provides no grounds at all for doubting the proper basicality or veridicality of our experience of events (or things) as present.[32]

I know of no other putative undercutting defeaters for our basic belief in the presentness of events (or things). Since those offered are themselves either rebutted or undercut, we may conclude that that belief is properly basic.

William Lane Craig

Conclusion

I have argued that our belief in the reality of tense is a basic belief grounded in our temporal experience. Whether that belief is properly basic will depend upon whether there are defeaters for any defeater of that belief which the detractor of tense might propose. Thus far, I think it can be safely said that no successful defeater of our belief in the objectivity of tense has presented itself. Our belief has been neither rebutted nor undercut and therefore remains properly basic.

But a further point might well be made appropriately at this juncture. I have alluded to the fact that there is such a thing as an intrinsic defeater-defeater, a belief which enjoys such warrant for us that it simply overwhelms the defeaters brought against it without specifically rebutting or undercutting them. It deserves to be asked whether our belief in the reality of tense is not itself precisely such a superlatively warranted belief.

Here our analysis of temporal consciousness takes front and center. It is hard to imagine how any belief could be more powerfully warranted for us than our belief in the presentness of experience. What argument for the unreality of tense or temporal becoming could possibly be based on premises more evident than our belief in that reality? McTaggart's Paradox? Hardly. Even in the absence of a resolution of that puzzle, McTaggart's Paradox, as compared to our basic belief in the reality of tense and temporal becoming, must take on the air of Zeno's Paradoxes of motion: an engaging and recalcitrant brain-teaser whose conclusion nobody really takes seriously.[33] I am far more certain of the reality of tense that I am of McTaggart's argument that the belief in tensed facts is inconsistent. Tensed beliefs are so strongly held that no one can successfully divest himself of them - their abandonment would generate repercussions throughout one's entire noetic structure.

This leads to one final point: unlike many properly basic beliefs, such as perceptual or memory beliefs or beliefs grounded in testimony, the belief in the reality of tense is universal. We all experience the presentness of our inner experiences. Therefore, belief in the reality of tense is a belief which is basic to all persons. If I am right that this belief is an intrinsic defeater which overwhelms all B-theoretical philosophical arguments brought against it, then it follows that belief in tense and temporal becoming is properly basic and thus rational not only for A-theorists, but for all persons, yes, that insofar as B-theorists reject this belief in favor of a tenseless view of time, they have a flawed noetic structure and are, therefore, in that respect irrational.

William Lane Craig

Notes

1. Edmund Husserl: *Phenomenology of Internal Time-Consciousness*, ed. Martin Heidegger, Indiana Univ.Press 1964, p.52.

2. Ibid., p.86.

3. Ibid., p.110.

4. Ibid., p.23.

5. William Friedmann: *About Time*, MIT Press, 1990, p.92

6. Ibid., p.2.

7. Paul Horwich: *Asymmetries in Time*, MIT Press 1987, p.15.

8. Robert C. Coburn: *The Strangeness of the Ordinary*, Rowman & Littlefield 1990, p.118.

9. W. Godfrey-Smith, critical notice of D.H. Mellor, *Real Time*, *Aust.Jour.Phil.* 61, 1983, p.109.

10. D.H. Mellor: *Real Time* Cambridge 1981, p.6.

11. Those who are unfamiliar with the notion of properly basic beliefs should consult A. Plantinga: 'Reason and Belief in God', in *Faith and Rationality*, eds. A. Plantinga & N. Wolterstorff, Univ. of Notre Dame Press, 1983, pp.16-93. Space does not permit an exposition of his views here. For further development of Plantinga's views on the conditions requisite for knowledge, as well as his critique of the competing theories of deontologism, coherentism, and reliabilism, see Plantinga: *Warrant: the Current Debate*, Oxford 1992 and: *Warrant and Proper Function*, Oxford 1992. My argument in this paper is independent of one's specific construal of warrant and should be acceptable to advocates of all camps.

12. Mellor: *Real Time*, pp.4-5

13. Ibid., p.3.

14. W.L. Craig: 'McTaggart's Paradox & the Problem af Temporary Intrinsics', *Analysis*, forthc.

15. I take this phenomenological fact to dispose at once of Grünbaum's claim that what qualifies a physical event at time t as occurring now is that some mind-possessing organism M experiences the event at t in such a way that at t M is conceptually aware that his having the experience of the event is simultaneous with an awareness of the fact that he has that experience at all. - See for instance A. Grünbaum: 'The Status of Temporal Becoming', in *Modern Science and Zeno's Paradoxes*, Wesleyan Univ. Press, 1967, p.17. Grünbaum here confuses 'presentness' with 'nowness', which are not the same, the latter alone being arguably ego-centric; otherwise his making 'nowness' mind-dependent would not eliminate presentness as an objective feature of reality. But as analysis of presentness, his explication is phenomenologically untenable, since a belief that something is present typically involves no such self-reflective activity.

16. Mellor: *Real Time*, p.25.

17. See Gilbert Plumer, 'Detecting Temporalities', *Philosophy & Phenom.Res.* 47, 1987, p.453. In the Aristotelian tradition unity, number and existence were thought of as transcendentals because they are entailed by the predication of a property in any of the ten categories. The concept of presentness as a transcendental, non-sensible property is especially plausible if we adopt an A-theoretical, presentist ontology in which presentness is just existence. For discussion, see Quentin Smith, *The Felt Meanings of the World*, Univ. of Indiana, 1986, pp.168-175. Contra Plumer, the best argument for presentness's not being a sensible property is that mental events can be observed via introspection to be present and that in a way indistinguisable from the presentness of external events.

William Lane Craig

18. See H. Scott Hestevold, 'Passage and the Presence of Experience', *Phil. & Phenom.Res.*50, 1990, pp.542-44, who argues that presentness is not a phenomenal property, but that a person's mental experience is necessarily such that it can be known to be present. The value of Hestevold's analysis, it seems to me, lies not in his ultimately unsuccesful refutation of phenomenalism, but in the intimation that presentness could be indirectly apprehended by us in our direct apprehension of things/events. Nothing in Mellor's argument depends on whether our observation of tense is said to be direct or indirect.

19. Mellor: *Real Time*, p.26. Ironically, Mellor's argument, if succesful, would undermine not only our observation of tense, but also our observation of B-relations between events, which Mellor defends. A very well-known problem with using magnitude of luminosity to calculate distances to galaxies is that a more distant galaxy may have the same apparent magnitude as a nearer one because it is larger; in such a case one would not know that the events observed in the larger galaxy are actually earlier than, rather than simultaneous with, the events observed in the smaller galaxy.

20. Mellor: *Real Time*, p.26

21. Unfortunately, Mellor's account of the distinction is skewed by his peculiar view that we do not form the basic belief that external events are present. Mellor confuses our experience of presentness, which involves external events with the presentness of our experience, the self-reflective awareness of the presentness of one's mental states. When we observe an external event, we are not enjoying the presentness of our experience, but experiencing the event as present. When we experience the presentness of our inner experience itself, that is just the presentness of experience. The distinction which Mellor wishes to draw does not obtain within the mental realm, but only between experiences of the external world and the inner realm.

22. Mellor: *Real Time*, p.53.

23. In D.H. Mellor, 'MacBeath's Soluble Aspirin', *Ratio* 25, 1983, p 92.

24. Mellor does argue that the A-theorist can provide no alternative explanation of the presentness of our experience: "If events can in reality have a range of tense, I see no good reason for experience to be confined as it is to present events", Mellor: *Real Time*, p.54. But Mellor's demand for an explanation of the presentness of experience is not at all clear. As Hestevold observes, how could an experience be anything but presently experienced? Even memories and precognitions are themselves experienced as present, Hestevold, 'Presence of Experience', p. 549. Perhaps Mellor is demanding why on the A-theory only present experiences are experienced as present, rather than past and future experiences. But the obvious A-theoretical answer is that only present events exist, and so one cannot be having past and future experiences. Mellor grudgingly accepts this explanation, but complains that such an explanation fails to tell us why external events which we experience as present may really be past, whereas our experiences alone are restricted to the present. Perhaps I am missing something here, but the obvious answer seems to be that sensory information about external events is transmitted to us at finite velocities so that, when we see the supernova or hear the gunshot, the event itself is past. Through their traces we can experience events which are no longer present. Future events, because they have no traces, cannot be experienced until they occur. Since the apprehension of mental events through introspection involves no transmission of signals, there is no delay involved in the presentness of experience. Indeed, Mellor's argument seems to turn against him. For all he has provided is a putative solution to why our present experiences are present.

William Lane Craig

Taken *de dicto* that is a tautology. But if we take the reference to our present experiences to be *de re*, Mellor has provided no answer why these mental events are being experienced by us as present rather than other, equally real, mental events elsewhere in the B-series.

25. See W. Lane Craig: 'Tense and the New B-theory of Language', *Philosophy* 71, 1996: 5-26.

26. See Mellor: 'MacBeath's Soluble Aspirin', in response to Murray MacBeath, 'Mellor's Emeritus Headache', *Ratio* 25, 1983, p.84.

27. C. Williams: 'Phenomenology of B-Time', *Southern Jour.Phil.* 30, 1992, pp.127-33.

28. Ibid., p.127.

29. W. Lane Craig: 'The New B-Theory's *Tu Quoque* Argument', *Synthese* 107, 1996, 249-69.

30. Williams: 'Phenomenology of B-Time', p.127.

31. Ibid., p.133.

32. See also Quentin Smith: 'Williams's Defense of the New Tenseless Theory of Time', in *The New Theory of Time*, ed. Q. Smith and L. Oaklander, Yale Univ. Press 1994, pp.112-13.

33. On behalf of the B-theorist, Schlesinger argues that Zeno's Paradoxes and McTaggart's Paradox are not analogous, since the B-theorist denies that it is in fact now t_1 and subsequently t_2, so that he does not assert anything contrary to experience, whereas Zeno fails to offer any new interpretation of our observations which entail that in fact no movement has taken place, Georg Schlesinger, 'How Time Flies', *Mind* 91, 1982, p.503. If I understand him correctly, Schlesinger's claim seems to be that Zeno admits that an object is at location l_1 at t_1 and then at l_1 at t_2. Zeno admits the facts, but says they lead to incoherence, whereas the B-theorist does not admit the tensed facts at all. But this seems to be a misinterpretation of Zeno. Zeno admits our experience of movement, but, as a Parmenidean who held that all is one, he denied the facts of movement and multiplicity, entertaining them only for the purpose of a *reductio ad absurdum*. Movement and multiplicity are shown to be illusory. Similarly, the B-theorist denies the facts of tense and temporal becoming, while admitting our experience of the same. He employs McTaggart's reasoning as a *reductio argument* against tensed facts. The situation thus seem quite parallel, and in both cases the veridicality of our experience overwhelms the effete philosophical arguments lodged against it.

William Lane Craig

NIELS VIGGO HANSEN

MODERN PHYSICS & THE PASSAGE OF TIME

For us believing physicists, the distinction between past, present and future is only an illusion, even if a stubborn one.[1]   *A. Einstein*

1.   Process Metaphysics and the Passage of Time

Apparently modern science has taught us that the passage of time doesn't really fit into physical reality. In the world of our experience there is an obvious and vast difference between the facts of the past, the acuteness of the present and the possibilities of the future. But in the universe disclosed by modern physics the notion of a 'now' seems to be inconsistent, let alone the 'passage' of this now through the continuum of time.

Since the time of experience thus seems to be at odds with modern scientific concepts of space and time, some have drawn the conclusion that our everyday notions of change and becoming are illusory. Others have taken this inconsistency to show that scientific abstraction blocks the understanding of the depth of fundamental questions of existence and temporality. Others again have claimed that a coherent understanding of time is a metaphysical chimera which should not be expected or sought after.

This paper is the first step[2] to outlining a different and, I hope, more adequate kind of response. It points to a way of overcoming the contradiction by realising that it depends on tacit assumptions in the interpretation of physical continua of space and time and of the temporal aspects of experience. Without these assumptions even strong notions of dynamism and becoming can be reconciled with the special theory of relativity. The suggested solution to the problem is a radically processual and relationist interpretation based on Whitehead's process metaphysics. It involves a reading of special relativity as a source of new and deeper (radicalised rather than weakened) understanding of temporality in technical as well as existential horizons.

The idea that there is a conflict between a systematic understanding of time and the intuitive or experienced sense of change and becoming is not new of course, in fact it has very ancient roots - it can be traced back at least to the origins of Western philosophy, e.g. in Zeno and Parmenides. But in the context of 20th century physics there is a specific and acute version of the classical problem which seems more immune to classical solution models.

The modern Whitehead-inspired solution suggested in this series of papers does in fact involve a reconstruction of some ideas central to Western thinking about time. I will even suggest that the deeper reason why process metaphysics has not, in general, been considered seriously yet, although it offers an attractive solution to a problem much more frequently discussed, has to do with the power still exerted in our secularised culture by a certain theological framework for our ideas of time.

In order to cope with these problems I conclude with a discussion of some relevant aspects of the alternative theological understanding suggested by Whitehead in close connection with the development of his process metaphysics of experience, science and nature. The suggested solution to the problem of relativity and becoming does not require the assumption of any theological framework. Whether or not the reader shares my sympathy for the Whiteheadian God, I believe the contemplation of the proposed modification of the idea of divinity can be helpful as an illustration of the radical nature of the Whiteheadian re-interpretation of temporality.

2.   Special Relativity and the Problem of Simultaneity

One of the fundamental theories of modern physics has particularly fascinating consequences when compared with concepts of time reflecting our ordinary experience of human life, viz. the Special Theory of Relativity (*SR*). The way *SR* is at odds with the classical idea of dynamic time or passage of time is not implying that ideas of change or passage are by themselves self-contradictory, as in the classical atemporalist[3] arguments from Zeno to McTaggart. Rather, *SR* dissolves a necessary condition for the classical idea of passage: the existence of a unique order of the events of the universe, the allocation of every event to a point or interval on one axis of time over which the passage of the now might take place.[4]

In *SR*'s reorganised grammar of spatio-temporal relations, events can no longer be said to be placed in such a 1-dimensional continuum of time and in a separate, independent 3-dimensional continuum of space, rather they are placed in a 4-dimensional continuum of "space-time" which allows for a multiplicity of equally valid formulations of timelike and spacelike orderings. This reorganisation seems to complete what Bergson has aptly phrased: the "spatialisation" of time. As a consequence the passing of the 'now' not only becomes foreign and irrelevant to the physical universe but cannot even be formulated coherently in the context of current physical theory.

Niels Viggo Hansen

Apparently this results in an outright contradiction between our systematic knowledge of time as part of the structure of the physical universe and our intuitive notions of time, based on whatever nonsystematic and perspective-dependent view of a fraction of the physical universe our immediate experience covers. Let me briefly outline the contradiction technically:

The classical idea of dynamic time or passage involves that there is, at each moment, an ontological state of affairs of all events in the universe in which it is the case, for each event, either that it has already happened, or that it is now happening, or that it has not yet happened. In this way all events, regardless of spatial position, are required to be divided into the basic ontological or modal regions of past, present and future. This implies the existence of a relation of simultaneity determining, for a given present event X_{now} and a given sequence of spatially distant events $Y_n .. Y_m$, a division of the Y-series into a past subsequence followed by a future subsequence, with at most one event Y_{now} being situated on the border, copresent with X_{now}.

However, in SR, this unique relation of simultaneity is replaced by a multiplicity of simultaneity relations depending on our own choice of inertial frame, i.e. on the arbitrary choice of a particular point of view. In SR many members of the spatially distant Y-series may thus have equally valid claims to simultaneity with our own local X_{now}. This implies that a coherent division of a set of events into regions of past, present and future is only possible in the degenerate case where the set considered is limited by the light cones of X_{now}. In the general case the attempt to formulate the classical modal state of affairs is faced with the dilemma of either overriding any reasonable construal of temporal modality by accepting that an event is co-present with events in its own causal past and future, or overriding SR by arbitrarily claiming a basic ontological privilege for one of the many inertial systems without any corresponding physical mark of distinction.

The argument is unfolded with slight variations and in greater detail by several authors of a scientific realist bent, including Adolf Grünbaum and the early Hilary Putnam. For our discussion here it is sufficient to notice that, due to SR, it is no longer possible to assume an unique natural temporal ordering of events separated by spatial distances.

Excurse:

The ambiguity of the simultaneity relation happens to be small enough to be negligible in most practical matters, because of the limited distances and durations involved. Thus, between two persons on the same planet the maximal size of the ambiguity would be a few tens of milliseconds, and a

Niels Viggo Hansen

serial ordering of all the words spoken and all the acts performed by human beings on Earth therefore remains precise for all practical purposes.

Thus, if I speak a word now, every word spoken and act performed by other human beings can be nicely ordered into the past, present, or future, of this event, simply because the light cones encompass the entire history of the earth except for an intermediate zone whose temporal "thickness", even at the remotest point of the earth, is small compared to the time it takes to pronounce the word "now". But there are practical issues related to modern technology in which technicians have to handle the ambiguity: one example would be the parallel programming of networked computers. The ambiguity might even be argued to be perceptible in the short time lags experienced when phone calls, TV interviews etc. are transmitted via satellite.[5]

Further, the essential nonexistence of a unique temporal order of events entailed by *SR* implies only a natural limit to ordering, but not total arbitrariness. Events capable of being causally connected lie by definition within each other's light cones and hence conserve their sequence, and the limitation of sequential ordering is, in most practical cases, insignificant compared with the limits which are anyway imposed by practical problems of delimiting and timing events. In other words, certain groups of events form "island universes" where an unique sequential ordering is virtually possible, and our own social-practical world is such an "island".

Generally, however, the ambiguity of sequential orderings is large - and even if it was not , its very existence would still undermine the unique universal time sequence required by the idea of time's passage.

3.   Anti-Metaphysical Attitudes to the Problem

The traditions of philosophy of science contain several conflicting standard attitudes to the problem of simultaneity. First, some will shrug their "mental shoulders" at this kind of apparent contradiction. They will claim that commonsense conceptual structures of time and tense[6] work well enough in their practical sphere, and that the terminology of *SR* works well enough in a completely different set of contexts of very technical character, and that finally the apparent problem only arises because these concepts are applied and compared beyond their native language games. Accordingly they can reassure us that the problem will dissolve through a Wittgenstein-inspired criticism of metaphysics which will eliminate the idea that there has to be any overarching coherent object, *time*, referred to by commonsense notions of time and tense as well as physical theory.

Niels Viggo Hansen

Our Wittgensteinian critic might even admit that there are certain "family likenesses" between any two language games using the word 'time' and related terms, but still maintain that metaphysical problems like the one outlined occur exactly whenever we have gone too far in our metaphysical emphasis on the similarities, taking them to commit the concepts to mutually cohere more than they simply happen to do. From this the anti-metaphysician might conclude that any attempt to speculatively construct solutions to such problems is bound to fail, or to produce even more metaphysical cramps of language, until we simply realise that the question is meaningless because each of the concepts of time we were trying to compare is meaningful only by virtue of a local context of use.

However, even if we follow the Wittgensteinian insight that concepts and language games are rooted in particular concrete uses, it is hard to see that we could or should avoid the very common tendency of phrases, concepts and specialised languages to extend beyond their native use by metaphors, analogies etc. For example, the Wittgensteinian herself will be using certain terminologies and metaphors ("practice", "use", "language games") which are extended beyond their native use in order to account for what other sections of language do and mean. Further, questions of time, change and process seem too difficult to be coherently deconstructivist or anti-metaphysical about. Many people who have aired a general critical attitude towards overarching metaphysical concepts have in fact been emphatic defenders of particular metaphysical views on this issue, favouring the primacy of either extension or passage as in the two classical responses to this problem. Metaphysics, like ideology, tends to be identified with platforms different from one's own.

Even if anti-metaphysics is unable to produce the non-metaphysical platform from which our problem could be dissolved once and for all, the anti-metaphysical tradition contains an insight for dealing with the problem constructively. Whenever particular concepts and language games are taken to be automatically valid and powerful beyond their sphere of concrete use, problematic and useless metaphysics is likely to be produced.

But if we avoid fundamentalist assumptions about the simple given and coherent objects of temporal language, we may find more humble ways to explicitly participate in the metaphysical attempt of producing coherence and relevance, which is already latent or present in the ordinary use of language. We may then accept the unavoidable metaphysical activity as constituting a philosophical project rather than a philosophical problem.

Niels Viggo Hansen

4.   Taking Sides: The Scientistic Atemporalist Response

Among those who have found the passage / relativity contradiction significant and found that some coherent understanding must be produced, we recognise two classical positions, each of them taking one of the mutually contradictory notions of time for true and concluding that the other must somehow be flawed, illusory, or only approximately valid.

The *scientistic* response is the one that insists, explicitly or implicitly, on a kind of strong scientific realism about the most fundamental physical theories, including *SR*, and their representation of time. On this basis the contradiction is taken to imply that the passage of time is an illusion, a *myth*. This is the view expressed by Einstein in the introductory quote, and it is the conclusion drawn by several philosophers of science such as Grünbaum and the early Putnam who base their argument on expositions of the contradiction. Scientistic atemporalism based solely or partly on this type of argument has also been advocated by more popular science writers such as Davies.[7]

The project of bringing about a coherent understanding here takes the form of the challenge of explaining what Einstein called the "stubborn" appearance of passage and ontological difference, given a spatio-temporal continuum in which all events are assumed to possess the same kind of reality. Various resources of physical, psychological / neurological and linguistic / logical theory have been applied in such reconstructions in order to show it redundant to assume the reality of the apparent dynamism - to assume that there is 'a mysterious Mr. X out there doing "The Shift"'.[8]

Some aspects of the apparent passage or flow of time yield relatively easily to such a program of reconstruction. This is the case with statements containing pure temporal references to now, to past or future, or to other points of time specified relative to the present ("last year", etc.). If any such reference is considered in isolation from the contexts of utterance - social, practical, linguistic - it can be reconstructed in terms of the classical time continuum or *SR*-spacetime as implicit self-reference regarding the (spatio-) temporal position of the utterance, so that "last year" is equivalent to "the year before" this utterance is pronounced or otherwise expressed (i.e. tenselessly). This reconstructing move can be formulated as indifferent to the further physical or mathematical elaboration of concepts of (spatio-)temporal position or their semantics; particularly it can be made indifferent to the constraints *SR* may be taken to impose on the semantics of "now".[9]

Niels Viggo Hansen

Obviously any event - at least any event of a suitable type, say a speech act - regardless of its time and place, may point to itself and claim to be *now*, as well as *here*, just as you may while reading this. If temporalism is construed as the claim that this particular "now" of yours is privileged over all other similar "nows" in the universe it is easy to dismiss any such attribution of significance to *now* beyond simple indexicality as subjectivism or solipsism. The atemporalist seems to fulfill the task of reconstructing the sense of "now-ness" as an effect of the particular perspectives of certain complexes of events: those which speak and think of themselves and other events as past, present and future, basically events of consciousness.

In Grünbaum's view, the sense of "now" depends on consciousness and is not physically real, consequently the sense of time's passage must be an effect of the structure of this particular kind of self-referential events. Davies, for example, identifies the sense of passage with a temporal analogue of "dizziness" - "the 'whirling vortex of self-reference' that produces what we call consciousness and self-awareness, and I strongly believe that it is this very vortex which drives the psychological time-flux". It is hard to escape the conclusion that nowness, understood as a mere position of a *present* now-point of time, may be thus reconstructed in terms of self-reference. However, the intuitive notion of passage contains not just the singular moment of pointlike presence but also its movement: *the passage from past to future*.

Thus we can no longer avoid the difficult question: what exactly is the content of the intuitive temporalist notion of becoming, and how much of it should the scientistic atemporalist be committed to account for. Atemporalist hardliners may hold that no further explanation is needed since anything beyond indexicality is derivative; it may be analyzed psychologically but has no bearing on the question of the nature of time. Further, since there is no generally agreed explanation of the intuitive notion of becoming, the atemporalist seems justified in focusing his criticism on what appears to be a minimal equipment for the general use of notions of change and becoming.

Within the tradition of analytical philosophy, temporalists as well as atemporalists have developed a broad consensus about analyzing the problem of time in terms of a particular model, McTaggart's *A*-series and *B*-series.[10] This model may be represented as a classical time axis (the *B*-series) to which a hypothetical now-point (the *A*-series) may or may not need to be added. However, McTaggart's model is further minimalised as regards metaphysical furniture in order to be indifferent to questions of the construal of physical time as relational or absolute, continuous or quantised.

Niels Viggo Hansen

It is clear that McTaggart developed this canonical minimal model exactly in order for his argument for the untenability of temporalism to be independent of the discussions of assumptions of a more technical character. But even McTaggart's minimalised model retains the construal of 'nowness' and 'passage' strictly in terms of sequential position, which implies a suppression of other aspects of the temporalist intuition of becoming.

In other words, it must be asked whether experience and language of temporality is adequately captured in terms of such pure positional references. There are some very important characteristics of experiences and expressions of temporality which do not quite fit into the *A*-series/*B*-series distinction, and these may be summed up in the categories of modality and causation. Time as experienced is characterised - at least outside of McTaggart's framing of the discussion - not just by *position*: the sense of presence of a particular event and the sense of absence and distance of events at other points of time, but also very much by *orientation*: the sense of difference between past events (remembered to some variable extent, traceable through causal effects on later states of affairs, and considered as given or *necessary* facts) and future events (never remembered, not traceable, and considered as open *possibilities*).

Accordingly, explicit references to time as well as implicit temporal expressions (omnipresent in tensed language) do not just refer to temporal position, but carries connotations of modality. Now, since the atemporalist claims all perspectival "nows" to enjoy the same ontological status, clearly he must deny the reality of the modal asymmetry as such and claim it to be produced, along with the "now-feeling", by perspectival effects. Thus the account of apparent modal asymmetry would be based on this subjective "now-feeling" combined with a difference in our abilities of knowing past and present events. But then an account of this apparent difference is required.

At first this seems as simple as the reduction of pure *A*-references: it seems that all we need is to appeal to ordinary causality. A given event is causally influenced by a number of other events situated in its relativistic past (backward lightcone), and such causal chains leading to a present conscious event from its past exist in a number of varieties corresponding to immediate sensation, retention, short term and long term memory. Again, some present event can causally affect events in the future (forward lightcone), and some of the ways conscious events do so involve such patterns as desires, beliefs, decisions and volitions. The physicalist atemporalist seems justified in leaving further details of these patterns of perception, memory and decision making to be investigated by psychology and neuroscience *if* the key point is granted.

Niels Viggo Hansen

Similarly the sense of openness of the future must be accounted for as springing from an informational asymmetry in causal relations, so that "backwards" conservation is incomplete - i.e., the future is not remembered. A full account should probably invoke a complex of such relations involving remembered experiences of having causally affected what was then future. Regardless of such details, the key point of the physicalist account of apparent modal asymmetry is that it is rooted in the unidirectionality of causation.

However, this raises an interesting problem on the physicalist's own premises, because on the level of physical laws describing the basic forces there is no unidirectionality of causation. It is clear that in a deterministic physical system governed by laws invariant to time reversal, the *present* state of a system at time t contains all information about the *future* state at $t + \Delta t$ in the same sense as it contains all information about the *past* state at $t - \Delta t$. This symmetry with regard to the preservation of information by causal chains is not affected by the lack of invariance ascribed to the weak nuclear force,[11] just as it is not affected by the shift from classical to quantum mechanics.[12]

Of course in practical cases of applied physics, the unidirectionality of causation is generally obvious. But such an appeal to obvious facts of the world of applied physics would be very problematic here, as it would be analogous to the temporalist's appeal to the obviousness of time's passage in the concrete world, no matter whether it has a correlate in the equations of mathematical physics. Hence, the force of the claim that an apparent past/ future difference can be explained on physicalist grounds via unidirectional causation depends on the possibility of giving a physical reason for the asymmetric loss and preservation of informational content in causal connections.

Two aspects of physical theory have been discussed, by Davies, Fraser, and others, as more or less independent candidates for such a reason:

1) thermodynamical increase of entropy, and
2) quantum mechanical wave function collapse.

1)   A thermodynamical account of experienced temporal modality and apparent unidirectional causality is based on the claim that both are effects of a huge entropy gradient rendering very different the practical conditions for prediction and retrodiction, i.e., for making inferences from a given state of affairs to states at a temporal distance from this in both directions of time. Some information on past states of affairs would then be conserved along causal connections as low-entropy traces because a low-entropy state has a very low probability of arising spontaneously, but a low-entropy state is not a trace of its own future as it has a high probability of decaying spontaneously.

Niels Viggo Hansen

So the entropic account of unidirectional causation means that although, at the elementary level, causality is symmetrical, in practice the entropy gradient constrains the identification of ordered states and their causal connections in such a way that only causation in one temporal direction can be found. However, this entropic account of the temporal asymmetry of the well known world of human experience and action leaves two other problems.

Firstly, it is not established that states of affairs which are recognised as "traces" of the past are adequately characterised as states of low entropy. Denbigh illustrates this with Earman's dramatic example of a bomb crater in a city which is obviously a clear and serious trace of a past event but cannot in any reasonable sense be described as more ordered than its surroundings.[13] He concludes that .. *most records and traces are not distinguished as such in any objective or physical sense, it is rather what we read into them that constitutes them as records or traces. Indeed there are very few physical objects which do not function in this way ..* Thus, a broken window as well as an intact window are traces of certain events in the past if we know the kinds of projects and contexts they take part in. It is indeed questionable whether one can coherently formulate a theory of traces from the past and not from the future, and of asymmetric information loss, without regress to the kind of project for which the states in question are traces or information. Surely, this regress can be expressed in terms minimalised, de-contextualised and objectified in many respects, but hardly without the temporal content of directedness which was exactly what was to be reconstructed.

Secondly, the move of invoking thermodynamics as the basis of a physicalist reconstruction of the experienced difference between past and future also invokes metaphysical questions regarding the interpretation of the second law of thermodynamics. It is often claimed, particularly by defenders of physicalist atemporalism, that truly basic physical reality shows no sign of an "arrow of time", and that the second law's "arrow" is itself a derivative phenomenon rooted some way or other in subjectivity - either because the definition of entropy expresses ignorance of the precise microphysical states (Gibbs / Einstein) or because some version of the Anthropic Principle is implied in order to account for an extremely abnormal border condition amounting to the entropy slope of an inhabitable universe. I have discussed these and other interpretations of the second law elsewhere.[14] For the present discussion it is sufficient to note that the main issue in debates over the interpretation of thermodynamics is between:

Niels Viggo Hansen

a) *moderate positions* which allow for a realistic interpretation of temporally asymmetric laws as well as branching, stochastic events and commonsense asymmetric causality - i.e. interpretations which do not attempt to reconstruct intuitive temporality as mind-dependent because that phenomenon is openly assumed to be part of the physical world - and

b) *extremist positions* which accept a realistic interpretation for only the most basic level of theoretical physics, so that large portions of physical reality must be regarded as derivative on a par with mind-dependent phenomena, or even as being constituted by mind.

The universe open to observation is a temporally asymmetric portion of physical reality because asymmetry is a necessary condition of observation. But, just like the aspects of nowness and passage discussed above, the pure fact of observation which is here referred to as the basis of the physicalist reconstruction of the asymmetric features of lived and experienced dynamic time has in itself no physical correlate. This points back to subjectivity as the ultimate source of temporal irreversibility in the physical world. Paradoxically the attempt of deriving the elements of experienced time from fundamental atemporal physics seems to lead to just the reverse: the grounding of large portions of physical reality on the temporal constraints of human subjectivity.

What is interesting about this is not that it may seem to challenge the explanatory power of thermodynamics or other physical theories, or seem to support classical idealist notions of observing subjectivity affecting nature. The interesting observation is that when thermodynamics is invoked as an element in the atemporalist reconstruction of temporality, what is depended on is precisely those aspects that press the theory to the limits of its domains of ordinary objective use where discussions of subjectivist interpretation have traditionally been raised by the physicalists themselves.

2)   A closely related observation can be made with regard to quantum mechanics, which is the other branch of physics frequently invoked in attempts of the physicalist reconstruction of consciousness and temporality as a possible source of the apparent modal asymmetry between past and future. The strength and nature of such a support depends very much on the preferred interpretation of quantum mechanics. A thorough discussion of the interesting structures of physical and metaphysical assumptions built by the various schools of interpretation is beyond the scope of this article. For our present purpose it is sufficient to note one of the central questions regarding the common central issue of events having the nature of quantum measurements.

Niels Viggo Hansen

The events referred to are those involving a "breakdown" of the wave function. This is the kind of event in which a complete quantum mechanical description of the dynamics of the system in question (the wave function) does not yield a full determination of its behaviour in some particular observable respect, but only a probability distribution over several possible outcomes. The actual observation, of course, is a particular and determinate one. One of the questions disputed between the schools of interpretation is what amounts to an act or event capable of effecting such a "breakdown", but we can accept for the sake of argument that it may not strictly require an observing physicist and a laboratory but may happen frequently enough (and in relevant places such as the human brain) to be a plausible candidate for the source of something explaining the ongoing sense of passage and modality.

The question we need to ask now is: How is the temporal aspect of the "breakdown" to be understood? In some interpretations the breakdown is taken to *happen* in time in a commonsense way. This means that the kind of process exemplified in the quantum measurement is taken to be a real change in which outcomes are not fully determined by even a complete description of physical laws and previous states. When the quantum event is seen as a real addition or emergence of information contained in the state of the system, and when the indeterminacy is understood in a direct, ontological way, as in the Copenhagen interpretation, quantum mechanics seems to be just what we need in the role of a spring of temporality.

Many have argued, on the basis of such commonsense understanding of quantum indeterminism, that various mechanisms in certain special types of complex systems could amplify the microscopic quantum processes to become macroscopic effects of truly unpredictable behaviour and emergence. It has even been argued that such amplified quantum effects could play a major role in the ordinary brain processes underlying human consciousness.[15] This interpretation involves the re-introduction of temporal modality as an element in basic physics. It implies the claim that every quantum event in the world belongs to one or the other of the classical ontological regions of time: either the quantum "breakdown" has happened (past), or it has not (future). The "breakdown" itself becomes a kind of passage, events being transitions from an undetermined future to a determined past. This takes us back to the problem we started with: how to conceive becoming under *SR*'s dissolution of the classical temporal ordering of events. This difficulty of reconciling the 'now' of the quantum wave function "breakdown" into relativistic spacetime is sometimes seen as a serious problem for the Copenhagen interpretation.[16]

Niels Viggo Hansen

It is recently claimed that the "Bell's Inequality" type of experimental evidence brought forth by Alain Aspect and others has shown that quantum phenomena override *SR* in a sense which implies a supraluminous influence from one act of measurement to another. Comparing certain measurements of pairs of particles which have previously interacted, these experiments have demonstrated correlations which were expected according to Bohrian notions of indivisibility of quantum phenomenon and quantum measurement setup, and which fail to satisfy requirements of local realism made notably by Einstein, Podolsky and Rosen. A treatment of the full scope of metaphysical implications of these experiments is postponed to another paper; however, it is essential to observe that there is no indication of any supraluminous or instantaneous causal influence in these results. In particular, they carry no evidence of a classical, non-relativistic time for such influence to happen in.

Take any one of the ingenious experimental setups successful in making measurements on sets [17] of pairs of particles (or whatever previously interacting entities for that matter) exhibit the kind of correlation in question. The *SR*-overriding interpretation then goes like this: Since the outcome of one member *B* of the pair is correlated with conditions involved in the process of measurement of the other member *A*, *B* must be influenced by those conditions at *A*. Therefore, if the setup is constructed in such a way that there is not time enough for a light pulse or anything slower than that to travel from *A* to *B*, then they must be connected by some kind of influence transferred at a greater speed or perhaps instantaneously.

In order to show that this is a misinterpretation it is sufficient to consider that the experimental setup could be modified through a series of slight displacements, with event *A* being placed anywhere, early and late, in the time between B's lightcones. This series of displacements will not reveal a hyperplane of true simultaneity at which the influence from *A* to *B* sets in, as of course it should if the idea is that *A* happens first and then influences *B*. It makes no difference which one happens first. Hence these phenomena offer no support for the notion that there must be an absolute sequence of events. In fact there is also another important sense in which this type of correlation is not an influence at all: its statistical form is precisely of such a nature as to prohibit its use to transfer a particular message or controlling signal from one part of the experimental set-up to the other. Whatever these interesting quantum mechanical phenomena may amount to,[18] they have nothing to do with "supraluminous" or "instantaneous" influences.

Niels Viggo Hansen

Some of the alternatives to the Copenhagen interpretation seem to avoid the problem of the temporal status of the breakdown, because the breakdown is not viewed as a real passage in time, from potentiality to reality. In one school of interpretation the breakdown would be unreal because a complete description would contain additional "hidden variables" selecting one of the multiplicity of apparently possible outcomes as real and rendering the others impossible, so that future events are just as determined as are past ones. In short, this would relieve us of the problem of the temporal structure of the "breakdown", but in the same move it would destroy the possibility of seeing quantum events as a source of non-classical, temporally asymmetric, causality.

The famous "many worlds" interpretation (*MWI*) of quantum physics, due to Everett and de Witt, appears more metaphysically daring. According to the *MWI*, the breakdown is unreal because only the quantum wave functions are real objects; this implies that all of the potential future outcomes, and even the entire branching family of further events dependent on them, and also all of the apparently determinate past events already observed, have equally valid claims to partial or, rather, "perspective-dependent" reality. In some versions of the many-worlds interpretation, the splitting of these branching worlds is understood as producing two or more entire parallel universes in the instant of the quantum event, and such branchings would be understood as happening only in the future direction. Hence, the temporal aspect of these (popular) versions of *MWI* is analogous to that of the Copenhagen interpretation: they share with it the problem of defining a cosmic instant to accommodate a quantum change (here, the split into future branches) in the face of *SR*.[19]

However, a more esoteric and abstract version of *MWI* escapes this problem which stems from the need of a *meta*-time in which splits "happen". Instead, the splits are taken to happen locally and to split faraway regions of the universe only as effects of the splitting event reach them. This, in effect, overcomes the need of assuming an ontologically privileged inertial system contradicting *SR*. Also in the esoteric *MWI*, the preference of world branching in the future direction is not taken as a metaphysical assumption implying an ontologically privileged "arrow" of time defined as the direction of splitting. Instead, the arrow of splitting is derived from the arrow of entropy as a consequence of the required temporal structure of events corresponding to the "quantum decoherence" giving rise to a world split. Since entropy is here taken in the sense of statistical mechanics, world splits in the "backwards" direction of time are not strictly excluded, the present state of the universe just happens to make them exceedingly less probable than "forward" splits.

Niels Viggo Hansen

Consequently the ultimate source of temporal asymmetry is, again, assumed to be an extremely special border condition: the contingent existence of a low-entropy initial state in one of the temporal directions, as viewed from "now", an entropy slope defining this direction as pointing towards the past.

It should now be clear that if quantum mechanics is invoked as a source of the temporal asymmetry needed for a physicalist reconstruction of temporality, the aspects depended on are really on the border of the theory or rather just outside it. They are interpretative additions which fall, for our purpose, in only three categories. In some interpretations they involve a re-introduction of modality and hence seem to require a unique order of events thereby producing the clash with *SR* that we started out with. In other interpretations, what is relied on is the thermodynamic asymmetry just discussed. Finally, some interpretations refer directly to the subjectivity involved in the observer effect as the source of broken temporal symmetry.

Again my implication is not that quantum mechanics does not meet all reasonable standards of objectivity or that it supports mysterious claims such as the alleged mysterious observer effect, nor is it meant to disqualify the *MWI*'s or the Copenhagen interpretation (which I support). The point is not even a criticism of more or less metaphysical attempts such as Penrose's to extend the theoretical structures of quantum mechanics in order to construct possible connections to neurology and consciousness.

However, I have argued that the invocation of thermodynamics, or quantum mechanics, as resources for a physicalist atemporalist account of temporality either breaks down by simply resting on implicit assumptions of temporalism, or depends on some version of an anthropic or transcendental argument which does not only construe temporal nowness, orientation and passage as *mind-dependent* and as having *no physical correlate*, but does also throw, along with these aspects of experienced temporality, the larger part of physics' explanatory power into the abyss of mind-dependence.

In conclusion, it does not seem plausible that a workable model for coherent physicalist atemporalist reconstruction of the structure of apparent temporality has been found. This by no means proves classical temporalism which is connected with equally serious problems. But it weakens the idea that a coherent understanding can be achieved on the basis of physicalist atemporalism, and it pushes us either back into the anti-metaphysical idea that we should renounce on requirements of coherence beyond local language games, or forward to the construction of new models of temporalist accounts.

Niels Viggo Hansen

Notes

1. Letter from Albert Einstein to the widow of his friend Michel Besso, cited in Griffin (ed.), 1986: *Physics and the ultimate significance of time*, p.x.

2. The present paper is the first of a larger essay split into three separately readable papers. At the time of writing no separate arrangements are made for the publication of parts 2 and 3, but an appendix to this paper offers a synopsis.
Write e-mail <filvig@hum.aau.dk> for preprints or ref.s.

3. *Temporalism* in the following, is used to denote the notion that time is something more than a kind of extension or a series, whether this something is expressed in terms of passage, ontological or modal difference between past and future, emergence or becoming. Conversely, what *atemporalism* denies is not the existence of a continuum or series but this *something more*.

4. Or, with the equivalent inverted metaphoric of passage preferred by some, what is dissolved is the sequence of 3-dimensional "pictures" constituting a universal movie which might pass across the "projector" point of temporal presence.

5. The graveness of the problem of ambiguity can be grossly expressed in terms of the relative size of the intermediary zone which is simply proportional to the product of the clock rate of the processes involved and the maximal physical distance involved.

6. Verbal tense: the phenomenon that utterances in natural language (at least in the indo-european and several other language groups) generally involve temporal references to past, present and future, even when no explicit mention of time is made, through the inflections of verbs.

7. Paul Davies: *God and the New Physics*, 1984 & *About Time, Einstein's un-finished revolution*, 1994. Davies proposes a physicalist reconstruction of experienced time, describing our sense of the passage of time as a kind of *dizziness*, but in his latest books the tendency is that further scientific evidence is needed to tell if our ideas of ultimate reality should be purged of time.

8. Gale, G: 'Time', in Audi (ed.): *The Cambridge Dictionary of Philosophy*, 1995.

9. The atemporalist reconstruction is the claim that in whatever approximate way *now*-references, including references to points of time specified in relation to now, can make sense in physical time, this sense can be reconstructed as a reference to the time of the utterance. The temporalist making the *now*-statement can choose whether this is to be understood in a context of classical or relativistic time, in an absolute or relationist account of the continuum, whether the scope of the reference is only in local terms *A before B & A one day before B*; or global in terms of a relationistically constructed clock system or even an absolute (space-) time system. In any case the sense is reconstructed as a reference to the time of the utterance in ths sense. It is only that with *SR*, unfortunately for the temporalist, the now-utterances cannot refer to a cosmic now, but this applies whether the utterances are reconstructed in this way or taken to refer to an ontologically privileged event. The atemporalist reconstruction's indifference with regard to the underlying topological and metrical characteristics of time is a main theme in one of the classical formulations of the reconstruction: D.C. Williams: 'The Myth of Passage', *Jour.Phil.* 48 no.15, 1951, pp.457-72.

Niels Viggo Hansen

10. McTaggart gave a classical formulation of the question of passage, in his definit-ion of the two series: The B-series referring to the *content* of time so to speak, the chain of events ordered only relatively (before-after), and the A-series referring to the *modalities*, to pastness, nowness, futurity, as abstracted from the specific events which happen to be past, present or future. McTaggart's series became a standard framework for the discussion of time, particularly in the Anglo-Saxon tradition. McTaggart's classical definition and argument concerning the two series is presented systematically in the opening sections of McTaggart: *The Nature of Existence*, 1927.

11. The equations describing the fundamental forces of nature are temporally sym-metric, just as classical mechanics was - except for the *small* anisotropy ascribed to the weak nuclear force, in the sense that these interactions can only be time reversed if some properties of some particles are reversed. The existence of deterministic trajectories forward as well as backward in time is unaffected by this. See R.G. Sachs: *The Physics of Time Reversal*, Oxford 1980, p.8-12.

12. In the sense that the object in quantum mechanical description is a wave function satisfying the Hamilton equation, the complete conservation of information in both temporal directions is just as in classical mechanics. In the sense that the object includes the *breakdown* of wave functions into statistical distributions for singular outcomes there is some level of indeterminism in the sense of underdeterminedness of events at times later than a known state, but it is at least not clear that this does not apply in backward direction as well.

13. Earman J., *Phil.Sci.* 41,1974,15, quot. in Denbigh, K: *Three concepts of time*, Springer 1981, p.127. Denbigh gives an extensive discussion of the relations between a number of *arrows*: causality, predictability, memory, cosmology and thermodynamics.

14. Hansen, N.V.: *Process Thought, Teleology and Thermodynamics*, presented at the conference on *'Time, Heat and Order'*, Aarhus 1997.

15. A recent argument of this type is R. Penrose: *Shadows of the mind*, 1994.

16. If my argument holds, this is not a valid objection to the Copenhagen Interpretation.

17. The correlations are not exhibited by any one pair of measurements, the correlation is of a statistical character so that it is only discernible when many pairs are compared.

18. I think they are primarily strong manifestations of the Bohrian point that quantum measurements and quantum measurement set-ups are not ultimately separable. This means that what counts as a particle and a state is dependent on this kind of context. But once there is a context in which states and particles are defined, these are constrained by SR as the grammar of time and space. The shift from one context to another cannot be construed coherently as a process in which specific particles do things prohibited by that grammar. Therefore there is no reason to consider this a reduction of the universal validity of SR, and I am sure Bohr did not.

19. The popular version of the many-worlds interpretation is not necessarily com-mitted to temporalism. It would allow an atemporalist interpretation of the entire branching tree of worlds - but then of course the Copenhagen interpretation need not be committed to temporalism either. If branching doesn't require real passing time, neither does the random selection of one branch.

Niels Viggo Hansen

Appendix

A brief summary of the two papers to follow this one, cf. note 2:

Temporalist accounts take change and becoming for an ultimate fact, available in immediate experience and participation in life. Many defenders of this view simply state this fact in terms of classical notions of time and simultaneity. But this obviously leads directly to the clash we discuss. As long as the classical notion of time is taken to be necessarily enfolded in this metaphysical ultimate, the clash can be escaped only by requiring the form of physical theory to be modified in accordance with it. I argue that this aprioristic metaphysical strategy is not as promising as the radical approach of formulating temporality independently of classical or relativistic notions of spatial and temporal continua. The more radical tradition of temporalism has made ground-breaking contributions towards such reformulations. However, the most successful and influential radical temporalist approaches (the article discusses those of Bergson and Heidegger in some detail) still fail in solving the puzzle of relativity and becoming, either because they fail to be radical enough and relapse into a version of classical temporalism, or because the radical intention leads them to simply accept the clash with physics rather than unfolding and applying the potentials of their succesfully reformulated notion of becoming. Indeed they tend to agree with the atemporalist physicalist response that temporality belongs in the sphere of subjectivity and not in nature at all.

The proposed alternative to the traditional responses is a form of radical temporalism which begins with a thorough explicitation of the concept of process. This approach is developed in particular depth and clarity in the late philosophical works of Whitehead. Classical categories like time, substance, causality and space are constructed as patterns of process rather than implicitly assumed to underlie processes. This is the case for matter and experience as well, so that temporality is construed as equally fundamental to nature and mind. Whitehead very explicitly shows how such a radicalised notion of becoming is not dependent on absolute simultaneity. Thus, temporality is characterised by local temporal facts rather than global ones. I argue that such local temporality is perfectly able to capture and express the intuitive and experiential evidence temporalists hold to be fundamental. Whitehead succeeded in interpreting *SR*'s clash with simultaneity as an expression of a metaphysical principle of much wider scope than theoretical physics, a priniciple of radical and local processuality. Finally I argue that this shift in the understanding of time is resonant with a process theology abandoning classical notions of omniscience and omnipotence and associating divinity with participation, immanence and wisdom, and I suggest that the reason for our difficulty in imagining temporality without global time is that a particular tradition of theology still implicitly active in spite of our self-understanding as secularised moderns. Apparently the Whiteheadian modifications of divinity are too radical to be acceptable to even the school of process theologians, but to a non-theologian it is very attractive, also because it encourages reasonable traffic across the well guarded modern borders between the religions and the spheres of sciences, humanities and political fora.

Niels Viggo Hansen

PER F.V. HASLE

THE PROBLEM OF PREDESTINATION
A PRELUDE TO A.N. PRIOR'S TENSE LOGIC

Introduction

In his memorial paper on the founder of temporal logic A.N. Prior (1914-69), A.J.P. Kenny summed up his life and work with these words:

Prior's greatest scholarly achievement was undoubtedly the creation and development of tense-logic. But his research and reflection on this topic led him to elaborate, piece by piece, a whole metaphysical system of an individual and characteristic stamp. He had many different interests at different periods of his life, but from different angles he constantly returned to the same central and unchanging themes. Throughout his life, for instance, he worked away at the knot of problems surrounding determinism: first as a predestinarian theologian, then as a moral philosopher, finally as a metaphysician and logician. (Kenny 1970, p. 348)

It is by now recognised that, with the construction of tense logic, Prior made a highly original and lasting contribution to philosophy and logic. In honesty, nothing similar can be said for his early theological work. Nevertheless, the above lines clearly grasp a continuity within Prior's work as regards some of its themes. Considerable changes in approach notwithstanding, one can indeed trace motivations and considerations of a theological nature underlying later formal and philosophical achievements.

So far, however, little has been done in order to investigate the relation between his theological work and his later work on tense logic. One reason for this is the simple fact that much of the early work is all but inaccessible, a significant part of it indeed unpublished. Moreover, there is the plain observation, already suggested above, that his later work is much more far-reaching than his early writings. But apart from sheer historical interest it seems to me that philosophical logic - as well as theology - will be well served by spelling out this relation in somewhat greater detail.

The aim of my paper is to disclose some major points of this relation. For that purpose I shall make use of some still unpublished work by Prior. Almost immediately after the death of Arthur Norman Prior, 6 October 1969, his widow Dr. Mary Prior, aided by Peter Geach, went through his papers, notes, correspondence, etc. They were suitably grouped and deposited in the Bodleian Library, now holding the material in 21 boxes. This material bears significantly on the subject, as I hope to make clear.[1] As for Prior's published papers I shall refer to them by their entries in the *Øhrstrøm/Flo Bibliography* - e.g.: [1942a]; please see *Introductory Remarks* to the *References*.

1. The Problem of Predestination

Prior was brought up as a Methodist, but during his first year as a Philosophy student at Otago University, aged 18, he became a Presbyterian. The reason for this shift was his dissatisfaction with the lack of systematicity in Methodist theology - especially, a dissatisfaction with its strong emphasis on having a personal conversion experience. Prior had not had, and never was to have, any such experience himself. During his B.A. studies in Philosophy, he attended courses at the Presbyterian Knox Hall with a view to entering the Presbyterian ministry. This intention was never realised, but he was for many years to come a practising member of the Presbyterian denomination.

The Presbyterian denomination is Calvinist. Now the central insight of the Reformation was that man could not save himself through his deeds, but rather salvation was pure grace, a gift from God, demanding only faith. However, this immediately raises the question whether faith is something man is free to accept or reject, or whether some are 'elected' to be believers - receiving passively the gift of faith - while others are not accorded that gift. The reformers differed on this point, but Calvin, at any rate, took a firm and consequent stand: indeed that there is no such thing as a free choice with respect to faith; every person is predestined either to belief or disbelief, and thus to salvation or damnation. The most marked feature of Presbyterianism, then, is its teaching concerning predestination. The *Westminster Confession*, a fundamental statement of the Presbyterian Christian creed formulated by the Westminster Assembly, London 1643, states on predestination these articles:[2]

III. By the decree of God, for the manifestation of his glory, some men and angels are predestinated unto everlasting life, and others foreordained to everlasting death. - IV. These angels and men, thus predestinated and fore-ordained, are particularly and unchangeably designed; and their number is so certain and definite, that it cannot be either increased or diminished.

The understanding of these articles in turn depend upon the relationship between some other major decrees by God, especially the decrees:
1) to create the world and man - 2) to permit the Fall - 3) to redeem the world - 4) to elect Christ to redeem the world - 5) to elect some to believe in Christ, i.e. to salvation, and to pass others by, i.e. leave them to damnation.

Per F.V. Hasle

The order among the above decrees can in no way be taken for granted, but on the contrary it determines how predestination should be understood. One crucial concomitant question is whether Christ died for all men, or for 'the Elect' only. We shall come back to these issues below.

It is rather a striking fact that even though Prior had become a Presbyterian by his own choice, he was from a very early point concerned about the doctrine of predestination. He quickly took up the "revisionist" Calvinist theology of Karl Barth, who was a leading theologian at that time (in fact Barth remains one of the most important theologians of this century). After completing his M.A. thesis, Prior spent the years 1937-40 in Europe, where he hoped to make a living out of religious journalism. In 1938 he attended the 4th International Congress of Calvinists in Edinburgh, writing up its proceedings for various journals. In 1939 he took part in the World Conference of Christian Youth, Amsterdam, recording his impressions for various journals (and praising the Barthian Calvinist resistance to nazism). Back in London he wrote on a proposed revision of the *Westminster Confession*. His concern about predestination is evident [NWC p.1]:

There would be almost universal agreement that the original Calvinist doctrine of predestination requires revision ... The cue to the revision that is necessary is already given in the original confession itself, when it takes over the Biblical description of the Church as "the fulness of him that filleth all in all." The Calvinist doctrine of predestination should be criticised in the light of what is here cited as its own proof-text, Ephesians 1.

These remarks are followed up in another unpublished paper, [LC]: *The Logic of Calvinism*. Here he criticises 'The Orthodox Calvinist doctrine' of predestination for maintaining *that men are created saved men or damned men; what then becomes the necessity of a "new creation"? We seem to have moved a long way from the original premise of the doctrine of predestination, which is that men have nothing to hope for in themselves, and everything to hope for in Christ, in whom God has seen them from all eternity.* [LC p.17]

These remarks are indicative not only of his concern, but they also anticipate his (Barthian) answer to such worries. This answer is elaborated in *Robert Barclay: Quaker or Calvinist?* [RB].[3] The paper takes its starting point in a discussion of the different attitudes towards mission exhibited by Quakers as compared to Calvinists. The Quakers eagerly endorsed mission, whereas Calvinists were reluctant - a difference which stems from a difference in opinion as regards whether Christ died for all men or for the Elect only. That, in turn, leads back to the interpretation of predestination.

Per F.V. Hasle

In RB (p.8), the distinction between the Elect and the Reprobate (those predestined to damnation), drawn by the leading 17th century Scottish Presbyterian John Knox, is determined as essentially a distinction between what men are in Christ and what they are in themselves or "in Adam". This is refined by reference to Karl Barth's discussion of Election in his Gifford lectures (Edinburgh 1939), where Barth ... *unites the doctrine of Predestination with that of Christ's Person and Work so intimately that neither has any meaning without the other. Predestination - the doctrine that God "chooses" men for himself no matter what they themselves may be or do - means that from all eternity God sees us, not as we are in ourselves, lost men and reprobates, but as we are in His Son Who came to take our place.* [RB p. 12]

One might say - somewhat crudely - that on such an interpretation the division introduced by the doctrine of predestination is not so much a division between different individuals as a division within each individual. Prior concludes that *Calvinists have increasingly succumbed to the temptation to replace the distinction between what men are in Christ and what they are in themselves, by one between different groups of men.* [RB p. 13]

In *The Reformers Reformed: Knox on Predestination*, [1946b], these considerations are dealt with in greater depth. The paper opens with a quote from George Every,[4] stating inter alia: *Where the logic of Calvin is pressed to a conclusion, the struggle between the self and God is gone, for either the self has been by decree united to God, or left to build a life of its own ... And the difficulty must lie not with predestination, but with the individualistic, atomic way of thinking about predestination* which, according to Every, was a heritage from Hellenistic thinking. Clearly these passages condense the task which Prior takes up in this paper. He does so through a discussion of John Knox's *Treatise on Predestination*, which he immediately declares to be *a useful starting point for those of us who would like to see a further "reformation" of the Church's teaching about it.* [1946b, p. 19]

The main distinction drawn in the paper is that between an election of individual men, a notion which stands in danger of imparting upon the elected ones a quality of having received special grace - almost as if deserving this - and election "in Christ", where men are united solely on grounds of what Christ has done for them, which is also directed towards unbelievers. Prior points out that while Knox insists on predestination to damnation, he usually takes this as a prelude to praising the mercy and grace of God - in fact, that the doctrine of predestination is important because it stresses that while we are in ourselves lost men, our hope in Christ is boundless. [5]

Per F.V. Hasle

A main point in the same paper is that insight into predestination to damnation should not lead the Elect to feel any superiority towards the "reprobate", but on the contrary to realise that they, and all men, are lost in themselves, but have everything given to them in Christ: *In Knox the doctrine of reprobation, emphatically as he always affirms it to begin with, continually dissolves into an assertion of the free and undeserved character of election* [1946b, p.20] - which is exactly seen to be free and undeserved in Christ.

Nevertheless, Prior admits that in spite of such attempts to draw positive conclusions from the idea of predestination, Knox accepted its harshest conclusions, and Prior explicitly wants to "reform" Knox (and Calvinism) on this point, by reinterpreting predestination along the lines already sketched. But interestingly, he praises Knox for consequent thinking: *But it is not enough to deplore his willing acceptance of horrifying beliefs, which in part shows an admirable and even scientific determination to bow to the truth as he sees it and hide nothing and tone nothing down.* [1946b, p. 21]

The paper proceeds to deliver a "criticism in the light of the Bible", very much along the lines suggested above - stressing that the essence of predestination is really an idea of election in Christ. The latter notion in some sense comprises all mankind, for *Salvation is not salvation if we are saved alone* and *election into Christ means election into a living body, whose Head is the Head of the Elect because he is the Head of Mankind.* [1946b, p. 23] These observations are related to the discussion on whether Christ died for all Mankind or for the Elect only; this theme was already touched on in RB.

In the paper *Supralapsarianism* (1947d) this issue is discussed with greater systematicity. As said at the beginning, God's 'decrees' - and the internal order among them - bear upon the understanding of predestination. In *Supralapsarianism* some major lines of interpretation concerning the doctrine of predestination (as determined by the order of decrees) are analysed with a special view to the theology of Karl Barth.

In the 17th century there were three major 'schools' within Calvinism as regards the interpretation of these questions. It should be noted that the order among the decrees was *not a time-order but a logical one* [1947d, p. 20], as was realised by all parties. Now the supralapsarians, in brief, held that, "first", God decreed to manifest his own Glory by his attributes of mercy and justice, this being the purpose of creation; "second", God decreed to elect some for mercy and others for justice for the purpose just stated; "third", God permitted man to fall in order to have objects for this election; "fourth", God decreed the salvation of the Elect through the death of Christ.

Per F.V. Hasle

The obvious consequence is that Christ did not die for all men, but for the Elect only. The infralapsarians, by contrast, saw it as morally troubling that men should be created with the purpose of visiting mercy on some and justice on others. They held that God "first", for reasons unknown, permitted the Fall, leaving all men as deserving justice (punishment), and then decided to visit mercy on some and pass others by. However, they agreed with their counterpart that the decree to elect Christ to redeem the world was a means to implement the salvation of the Elect, hence, that Christ died for those only.

Even so, the latter position seems more morally understandable than the former (at least as seen from our day and age). But one school, the post-redemptionists, went one step further. The post-redemptionists held that the decree of permitting the Fall preceded the election - such that God, seeing man as fallen, decreed to redeem the world through Christ; but contemplating that man was unable even to lay hold on this redemption, He decreed to elect some to receive the gift of faith, and hence, to be saved. The consequence is that Christ did indeed die for all mankind, viz. mankind as fallen, election "taking place" logically speaking after the sacrifice of Christ.

Having described these differences or, as Prior himself calls them, "somewhat ethereal disputes", the paper examines the position of Karl Barth. In brief, Barth emphasised that Christ died for all men, but (at least on Prior's reading) also appeared to hold that the world was created in order to be redeemed. In this manner Barth combined Post-redemptionism with Supra-lapsarianism; but it becomes clear that Prior would like a still more radical re-interpretation of predestination, for he then concludes the paper[6] by saying:

Although his Post-redemptionism removes some of the more object-ionable features of 17th century Calvinism, his Supralapsarianism seems to be still open to what was even then the principal objection to the doctrine, namely that the redemption of a world created for the very purpose of being redeemed has a certain moral artificiality about it, as it seems to involve the artificial engineering of the need for redemption. It still seems a too incaut-ious application to the ways of God of the category of means and end.

We have seen how Prior struggled, intellectually as well as morally, with the doctrine of predestination. This struggle began no later than at the end of the thirties, and at least lasted towards the end of the fourties. For most of this period, Prior was nonetheless a committed Presbyterian.

Per F.V. Hasle

2. A Crisis of Belief

The most quoted and referred theological paper by Prior is without doubt *Can Religion be Discussed?* [1942a]. Written in 1942, it does express, one can safely say, deep worries about the tenability of Christian belief.[7] Kenny [1970 p.326] describes how, at this time, *Prior passed through a crisis of belief, which gave rise to his first philosophical article which is still remembered.* Prior became strongly influenced by Freud, and clearly the most serious doubt is induced by a psychoanalytic explanation of religious belief.

The paper is built as a discussion between five invented characters, namely Barthian Protestant, Modernist Protestant, Catholic, Logician and Psychoanalyst. The Barthian Protestant represents the Calvinist-Barthian conviction that religion cannot be discussed since the faith itself is a miracle.[8] An atheist account of religion is an intellectual possibility, but no rational decision can be made between belief and unbelief, only a religious leap. Catholic, on the other hand, stands on Scholastic ground, arguing that God is a 'necessary being', and hence, that the creed is intelligible - implying, of course, that it must be able to answer intellectual criticism. Both of these positions seem to be fairly demolished by Logician and Psychoanalyst.

The fideism of the Barthian is rejected by Logician by observing that there is no choice or rational decision between belief and unbelief, based on an argument that religious belief consists of meaningless statements - hence there is not "anything" of this sort to believe at all: "Unbelief is inevitable".[9] As for the Catholic, Logician destroys his notion of "a necessary being" by an argument in the positivist vein (existence is not a predicate; further, Catholic is equivocal between using 'God' as an abstract and as a concrete noun).[10] Psychoanalyst agrees with the criticisms made by Logician - clearly, the two share a modern scientific spirit - but he goes one step deeper by explaining the roots of religious belief in terms of the Oedipal Complex, concluding that:

These 'irresistible' illusions are things we all suffer from ... they cannot be cured by the methods we are using just now [referring to Logic and Psychoanalysis]. But a time may come... when in the painful process of their own analysis they will see for themselves the roots of their urge to believe. Only in this way are genuine atheists made. [1942a, pp. 10-11]

This concludes the discussion, save for the Barthian's final cry of 'Lord, I believe; help Thou my unbelief'. As for the Modernist Theologian, he isn't given much of a hearing - he is allowed just one (slightly ridiculous) remark, and Psychoanalyst can be said to dispatch of this kind of position by stating that it tries to satisfy the urge to believe *by inventing milk-and-water religions like that of Modernist here, using religious language to describe any-thing they find impressive or moving or mysterious.* [1942a, p. 11] But, as Kenny observes: *The atheism of 'Can Religion be Discussed?' does not seem to have lasted very long ... After a very brief pause he resumed the writing of Presbyterian articles.* [Kenny 1970 p. 326] However, the influence of Freud is spelled out even more clearly in two later (unpublished) papers (ca. 1942):

In *The Case of Edward Irving* [EI], Prior discusses this 19th century minister of the Scottish Established Church. Irving preached that idolatry en-compassed not only *outward homage to a material image*, but also worship of ideas or values cherished by us, e.g. Mammon-worship. In doing so he was not unusual; but he further contended that parents are the objects of idolatry by their infants in early childhood. He thereby anticipated a Freudian insight - accepted by Prior - which could not be tolerated by the church,[11] especially since it is a model of our wider motives for being religious. The paper seems to embrace Freudian theory to a degree where it must lead to atheism.

The same can be said of *Children of the damned* [CD], which exam-ines the cases of four persons directly or indirectly influenced by a perception that they themselves, or one of their parents, were irretrievably damned. The persons in question are Frederick Denison Maurice, a Victorian theologian, Søren Kierkegaard, 19th century Danish Christian philosopher, "Rabbi" John Duncan, 19th century Scottish Presbyterian minister and missionary to the Jews, and James Joyce. In each case a Freudian analysis is offered as an explanation of their preoccupation with damnation, especially with reference to the Oedipus-complex.[12] The analyses offered appear sharp and inventive. Also this paper is Freudian to the point of a psychoanalytically motivated atheism. It is obvious that in *Children of the damned*, Prior's worries about predestination merge with his doubts induced by Freudian psychoanalysis.

However, around 1944 the influence of Freud was diminishing. Kenny thus records that, in October 1944, Prior wrote: *God "dwelleth not in temples made with hands"... not even in the strange structures erected by psychoanalysts in the mental depths they have discovered'.* His Christianity had always had a strong political content, and Freudian analyses of religion were inadequate to account for this. [Kenny 1970 p. 328]

An interesting unpublished paper, *Faith, Unbelief and Evil*, [FUE], forms a striking counterpart to *Can Religion be Discussed?*. Like the latter, it is built as a dialogue, this time between Historian, (Barthian) Theologian, and (atheist) Humanist. The paper opens with a quotation from Karl Barth, the fourth of his "main theses" on God's Election of Grace in his *Dogmatic*:

Per F.V. Hasle

... that the choice of the Godless is null and void, that he belongs to Jesus Christ from eternity and thus is not rejected, but rather chosen by God in Jesus Christ, that the reprobation which he deserves on the basis of his wrong choice is borne and removed by Jesus Christ ... [FUE p. 1]

This being a significant prelude, given Prior's constant preoccupation with the problems of predestination and determinism, the paper proceeds as a discussion among the three on the subjects of (i) Our Knowledge and Our Ignorance of God, (ii) The Paradox of Evil, (iii) Atheism and Evil, (iv) The Two Edged Sword, (v) God's Strategic Retreat. In good Priorean style, central themes are quickly identified and lucidly debated, but I content myself with a significant quote about predestination, put forth by 'Theologian' [FUE p. 17]:

We are not called upon to do the really crucial acting here - we are not called upon to "take damnation lovingly" [as Christ did on the Cross], and we couldn't do it if we were; but we are called upon to live as those for whom God himself has done this. And that is the whole of the negative side of predestination - the whole meaning of "predestination to damnation". And the positive side, too. It is the Gospel. - This, especially when taken together with the Barth-quote above, may well be Prior's reply to his own worries about the Calvinist doctrine of predestination.

It is interesting to compare FUE with *Can Religion Be Discussed?*. Both are cameos built as dialogues between invented persons typifying certain positions. But here, in FUE, the implicit answer to the question: Can Religion Be Discussed? is a (qualified) affirmation. In the course of the discussion, Humanist at times seems to be on the point of saying that further discussion is not possible - venting reservations that have no doubt troubled Prior himself:

It seems to me frankly, that the central affirmations of Christianity are self-contradictory and absurd, and Barth even seems at times to be saying as much himself ... One cannot even discuss Christianity then, for if it is self-contradictory, then its statements just cancel out one another and there's nothing to discuss. [FUE p. 3-4]

These remarks are obviously very much like Logician's objections in 1942a. Actually, Theologian and Historian - who is also a Christian, as his statements in the long run make it clear - are on the point of concurring that further discussion is meaningless; but the discussion does carry on, obviously in a meaningful way. If this paper is later than 1942a,[13] it may well be seen as reflecting Prior's overcoming his personal religious crisis vented in 1942a. In *Faith, Unbelief and Evil*, Theologian is given the last word:

Per F.V. Hasle

Faith may be awakened in men by their seeing how near they have brought us to the loss of it - as we all brought God near to loss of faith in Himself [Jesus on the Cross] - or it may not; but to this degree at all events, "as was the master, so must the servant be". [FUE p.19]

3. From Predestination to Indeterminism: the 'invention' of tense logic

One remarkable defence of predestination, respectively determinism, is given in *Determinism in Philosophy and Theology* [DPT]. This paper is difficult to date, but it was probably written in the mid-fourties.[14] In contrast to Prior's other "theological papers" from the fourties (and earlier), this paper thematically compares the doctrine of predestination with philosophical determinism, respectively, indeterminism. The paper opens by observing that in "modern discussions", determinism is often associated with a "scientific creed" as opposed to the idea of free will, which is considered to be religious. But this perception is immediately countered [DPT p.1]:

It is exceedingly rare for philosophers to pay any great attention to the fact that a whole line of Christian thinkers, running from Augustine (to trace it back no further) through Luther and Calvin and Pascal to Barth and Brunner in our own day, have attacked freewill in the name of religion.

The paper then proceeds in four major steps:

First, it is emphasised that philosophical or scientific determinism is in part different from the idea of predestination: the Calvinism expounded by Barth and Brunner is not pure determinism, but a paradoxical mixture of determinism and free will [DPT p. 1]. They wish to replace the "secular mystery of determinism", respectively, indeterminism, by the "holy and real mystery of Jesus Christ." Man is seen as unable to perform by himself an act of faith, but when, by the grace of God, he does perform it, that is an act of real freedom,"free will for the first time".

Second, it is argued (with reference to arguments put forward by the contemporary philosopher C.D. Broad) that the ordinary ideas of free will, when understood as moral accountability and general indeterminism, are at least as absurd as the idea of predestination:

We are guilty of that which we are totally helpless to alter; and to God alone belongs the glory of what we do when we are truly free. - Absurd as these doctrines appear, they are in the end no more so than the ordinary non-Augustinian concept of "moral accountability" ... [DPT p. 2]

Thirdly, Prior goes on to describe how certain human experiences actually are compatible with the notion of predestination, observing that:

Per F.V. Hasle

Even those of us who accept a straightforward determinism have to give some account of men's feeling of freedom, and their feeling of guilt; and it is at least conceiveable that the "absurdities" of Augustinianism contain a more accurate psychological description of the state of mind concerned, than does the "absurdity" of the ordinary non-Augustinian concept of "moral accountability". [DPT p. 3]

Various - quite convincing - arguments are offered to underpin the plausibility of Augustinianism in the face of ordinary human experience. Up to this point, the paper - even if brief in its analysis - is a vivid and convincing defence of predestination, or determinism in an Augustinian sense. But this perception is modified in the final step of the analysis. In the fourth and concluding part, Freudian psychoanalysis is thus brought into the picture. It is argued that religious determinism is concerned with "particular inward compulsions and dependences", from which we can be released through (psycho) analysis [DPT p. 4].

Following Freud,[15] the doctrine of sin and salvation in St. Paul and Augustine is seen as a partial psychoanalysis, leading to the conclusion that *The theological doctrine of predestination is a "Theory of Obsessions", prefaced to the analysis of a particular case.* [DPT p. 4] Nevertheless, it is not quite clear whether this means that Christianity, and especially the doctrine of predestination, are "subjected" to a psychoanalytical viewpoint, or whether it rather implies that evidence from psychoanalysis corroborates the idea of predestination within (Prebyterian) Christianity. The final remarks point in the former direction, the overall context rather points in the latter direction. This has nothing to do with inconsistency, of course, but there is a tension here which may well reflect Prior's own state of mind at the time of writing.

As is probably known to most students of tense logic, Prior's stance on determinism was to change from the early fifties and onwards. Throughout the fourties, he was interested in logic - mainly classical and non-symbolic logic - but apparently even more interested in philosophical and historical issues within theology. In 1949, he was in the process of writing a history of Scottish Calvinist theology. However, the Priors' house was burnt in March 1949, the loss including parts of the draft for this history. That was a turning point, he gave up the project, and increasingly turned his attention to logic. His first interest in modal logic was aroused in 1951, leading to publication of *The Ethical Copula* (1951a). At this time he also developed into an adherent of indeterminism, and indeed, of free will. Jack Copeland describes how

Per F.V. Hasle

... Aristotle speaks of some propositions about the future - namely, those about such events as are not already predetermined - as being neither true nor false when they are uttered ... This appealed to Prior, once a Barthian Calvinist but now [1950/51] on the side of indeterminism and free will. There can be no doubt that Prior's interest in tense logic was bound up with his belief in the existence of real freedom.[16] [Copeland 1996 p. 16]

But in one respect this perhaps says too much, for Prior was still an active Presbyterian, becoming an elder of the Presbyterian Church in 1951. Clearly, he must have been revising his former attempts to understand and defend the doctrine of predestination, but apparently this did not at that time shake his fundamental Christian belief. In 1956, when the Priors went to Oxford, they also joined the local Presbyterian community there.

At any rate, Prior's first hint at the possibility of a logic of time-distinctions is found in the unpublished manuscript *The Craft of Logic* 1951 (cf. Copeland 1996 p. 15). In 1953, when he was reading a paper of Findlay *Time: A Treatment of Some Puzzles*,[17] he decided to take up Findlay's challenge of working out a calculus of tenses (cf. Øhrstrøm and Hasle 1993 p. 25). Major sources for him were also Lukasiewicz' discussion of future contingents,[18] which was inspired by Aristotle's *De Interpretatione*, and the Diodorean "Master Argument", which he came to study via a paper by Benson Mates on *Diodorean Implication*.[19] In both of these problem sets - future contingents, and the Master Argument - the logic of time is strongly interwoven with a discussion of determinism versus indeterminism.

Thus from the very outset of Prior's development of tense logic, the problem of determinism was dealt with parallel with the logic of time. (Here I shall ignore the richness of details, but see [Øhrstrøm and Hasle 1995] for a discussion of these and related subjects).[20] Moreover, it is clear that the determinism-issue has roots in the problem of predestination, and that Prior's dealing with it was a natural continuation of his earlier preoccupation with predestination. At the same time, however, there also is a breach in the very approach to these problems. The emphasis on time and change is itself a marked departure from the peculiarly atemporal spirit of the Calvinist teaching on predestination, as witnessed by the *Westminster Confession* in general, and in particular by the articles III and IV quoted earlier.

Prior's early work on the logic of time led to the papers *Three-valued Logic and Future Contingents* (1953d) and *Diodorean Modalities* (1955d).[21] In the second half of the fifties, he increasingly took up the notion of (Divine) 'foreknowledge', which is obviously related to the issues of determinism and predestination. His studies led him to consider the classical Christian belief in Divine Foreknowledge as untenable (except perhaps in a very restricted form). In *Some Free Thinking About Time*,[22] he stated his belief in indeterminism as well as the limitations to Divine Foreknowledge very clearly [SFTT pp. 1-3]:

I believe that what we see as a progress of events is a progress of events, a coming to pass of one thing after another, and not just a timeless tapestry with everything stuck there for good and all ...

This belief of mine ... is bound up with a belief in real freedom. One of the big differences between the past and the future is that once something has become past, it is, as it were, out of our reach - once a thing has happened, nothing we can do can make it not to have happened. But the future is to some extent, even though it is only to a very small extent, something we can make for ourselves ... if something is the work of a free agent, then it wasn't going to be the case until that agent decided that it was ...

I would go further than Duns Scotus and say that there are things about the future that God doesn't yet know because they're not yet to be known, and to talk about knowing them is like saying that we can know falsehoods.

In December 1958 the Priors left New Zealand for good, Arthur Prior taking up a professorship at the University of Manchester. This time he refrained from joining the local Presbyterian community. His logical studies had increasingly led him away from what he regarded as indispensable parts of the Christian faith. He had become an agnostic, although not an atheist. He remained respectful in his treatment of Christian belief as an intellectual possibility, but at least one sharp remark in *Creation in science and theology* on Karl Barth reveals how Barth's theology, acknowledged as a pinnacle of theological thought in our century, had ceased to be of any aid for him:

One silly thing it's only too easy to do... is to talk as if "nothing" were the name of some kind of stuff out of which the world was made. I've even read a theologian (Barth) who [in his Dogmatics in Outline, 1949] talks as if "nothing" were a sort of hostile power from which God rescued the world in giving it being. [1959d, p. 89]

In *The Formalities of Omniscience* (1962e), he further investigated the problems of determinism and foreknowledge. The paper examines the idea of omniscience, especially in the form of statements such as:

- *God is omniscient*, and some putative consequences of it, such as:
- *It is, always has been, and always will be the case that for all p, if p then God knows that p* ('7' p. 117), and:

Per F.V. Hasle

- For all p, if (it is the case that) p, God has always known that it would be the case that p ('8' p. 117).

Various interpretations of such statements are discussed, especially with reference to St. Thomas Aquinas, Ockham, and Peirce. It is argued that, for logical reasons, future contingents cannot be 'known' at all, leading to the observation: *I don't think we get my proposition '8'... except in the weak sense that He [God] knows whatever is knowable, this being no longer co-extensive with what is true* (1962e, p. 122). Prior concludes with the following statement (which may be indicating not an atheist, but rather an agnostic position):

I agree with the negative admission of Thomas... that God doesn't know future contingencies literally... But (and this is what Thomas himself says) this is only because there is not then any truth of the form 'It will be the case that p' (or 'It will be the case that not p') with respect to this future contingency p, for Him to know; and nihil potest sciri nisi verum (nothing can be known except (what is) true) [1962e, p. 129]

For completeness' sake it should be mentioned that, in a number of papers, Prior also dealt with the ideas of *Creation out of Nothing* and personal identity (both issues bearing, directly and indirectly, on beliefs in individual immortality).[23] Noteworthy in this connection is also his unpublished paper *The fable of the four preachers* [FFP], which in an allegorical form discusses ideas of immortality. It is clear from the discussion that problems concerning temporal and 'trans-world' identity are on his mind here.[24] At the same time, the Calvinist background is also traceable in the paper.

4. The Freedom of Inquiry

Already in the late thirties, Prior combined his Christian faith with a strong commitment to the cause of the poor and oppressed. The Barthian resistance to Nazism was for him a welcome confirmation of the values of his chosen denomination. Indeed, socialism was for him an integral part of Christianity; in 1940 he remarked that *Christian socialism is neither a sugaring of the socialist pill with Christianity, nor a sugaring of the Christian pill with socialism. It is just sound Bible Prebyterianism properly understood.*[25] Prior was to remain left wing, even though he gave up Christian faith.

Although "conservative" in his theological outlook as a Christian, he was never a "fundamentalist". This is made clear already in the unpublished *A Modernist Stocktaking* [AMS] (ca. 1940), which warns against taking for granted the gains of "Modernism", especially the right to free critical inquiry. The paper deals with the position of Christianity in the face of Modernism.

Per F.V. Hasle

It rejects fundamentalism, but otherwise embraces Christianity - warning, however, against a "bringing-up-to-date" of Christianity such as the one taking place in Nazi Germany at the time. The example from Germany may well have contributed to that obvious suspicion against any manipulative modernisations of Christianity, which is also evident in *Can Religion be Discussed*. On the other hand it is observed that scientists, being men, need to be defended from making a religion out of science, a defence which is a duty of Christian thinkers.[26] Finally, the modernist spirit is endorsed:

... the Modernist spirit, the spirit of free and critical inquiry and hard and courageous thinking, is as unpopular as ever it was, and will need our militant defence for a very long time to come. [AMS, p. 6]

At that time, and for many years to come, Prior saw no conflict between his faith and his insistence on the freedom of inquiry and criticism. But as we have seen, he gradually came to doubt the dogmas of Christianity. One is tempted to formulate a "trilemma":

• the doctrines of predestination and foreknowledge are integral parts of the Christian faith,

• the doctrine of foreknowledge is untenable for intrinsic logical reasons, and the doctrine of predestination is incompatible with a belief in indeterminism and free will,

• any convenient 'abbreviation' of Christianity is dishonest and untrustworthy.

The last paper, wherein Prior seems to be endorsing Christian faith, if only vaguely, is *The good life and religious faith* (1958c). This is a discussion between Prior and a few other philosophers on religion - among them John Mackie.[27] Prior seems at this point to be still "defending" religion (Christianity) in replies to Das and Mackie. However, a statement by Mackie seems to anticipate one essential reason why Prior became an agnostic.[28] The statement Mackie makes is this:

In fact I think it [religion] hostile to the good life, because of the value it always puts upon firm belief for inadequate reasons. It blocks inquiry, which is a principal ingredient of the good life. [1958c, p. 10]

Conclusion

On the face of things, Prior became agnostic because he came to see Christianity as an obstacle to the freedom of inquiry. According to Mary Prior, he felt that as a logician it was his job to (freely) investigate the consequences of any assumptions, which we may make, and:

Per F.V. Hasle

He found having a total commitment to any particular set of theological beliefs made it difficult to follow the logical consequences of a system with complete freedom, and this made him agnostic. [Mary Prior]

At the same time, it should be remembered that even as a young and devout Christian he insisted on this very same freedom of inquiry - cf. *A Modernist Stocktaking* (1946). His problem, then, seems to have been a discovery that Christian doctrine, as he saw it, leads to unacceptable conclusions. What worried him were first and foremost the doctrine of predestination, and the related doctrine of foreknowledge.

Of course, to become an agnostic on these grounds presupposes that an honest and consistent believer must actually accept these doctrines as inherent in Christianity. We have seen Prior praising Knox for his honesty and "almost scientific mind" in the matter of predestination. At that time (1946) Prior attempted a Barthian solution to avoid the "horrifying beliefs" imparted by the doctrine of predestination to damnation, but obviously this approach became unsatisfactory to him in the course of the fifties. In parallel with his development of tense logic he became a firm believer in indeterminism and free will, tenets incompatible with Calvinism (even in its Barthian version). Moreover, on strictly logical grounds he came to consider the ideas of omniscience and foreknowledge as untenable. It is worth noting, though, that agnosticism was for Prior a position different from atheism:

.. agnosticism was for him not an alternative belief but a neutral basis from which inquiry could be made - he was not so much an *agnostic as 'agnostic'* [Mary Prior (b)]

Even so, a modernist-liberal "milk-and-water" Christianity was not an option which lay open to Prior; he obviously saw such an approach as an almost dishonest and at any rate inconsequential way of thinking. It is perhaps not too hard to follow Prior in this on a general level, but maybe there is also a paradox here. Prior gave up Methodism in favour of Presbyterianism, finding the former "unruly", but the latter consistent and well worked out. An even more important reason for this shift was his lack of any 'conversion experience', an ingredient of Christian faith which is strongly emphasized in Methodist theology.[29] But at least as regards that troublesome point of predestination, Methodism is more congenial with the spirit of Prior's later indeterministic conviction. Methodism traces its roots to Jacob Arminius (1560-1609), a Calvinist who sought to modify the reformed faith exactly on the points appertaining to predestination: in particular he taught that men were free to choose to believe. [30]

Per F.V. Hasle

At any rate, the founder of Methodism, John Wesley (1703-91), was strongly influenced by Arminius, not least on this point. Thus, in a sense, Prior of his own accord left one interpretation of Christianity in favour of another whose most distinctive feature was that doctrine of predestination which appears to have been a main motive for his later becoming an agnostic.

Such observations can, of course, in no way detract from A.N. Prior's arguments. He has, perhaps more clearly than any other thinker, pointed out the *logical* limitations of foreknowledge. Likewise, he has shown and developed the logical possibilities for indeterminism. Theology is challenged - as well as enriched - as much as logic and philosophy by those insights.

In the wider perspective of our cultural history this is not the least significant among Prior's achievements.

Acknowledgements

The work on Prior's papers is supported by a grant from the Aarhus University Research Foundation.

I also wish to thank the staff at Bodleian Library in the Department for Western Manuscripts, especially in the Modern Papers Reading Room, for being always helpful when I have been working with Prior's papers there.

Thanks must also go to Balliol College for a gracious offer of accomodation while working in Oxford on Prior's papers.

I am indebted to Jack Copeland for answering various questions, and to Peter Øhrstrøm for carefully reading and commenting this paper.

Finally, and above all, I wish to thank Mary Prior for her forthcoming and helpful answers to questions on Arthur N. Prior's work and life, and her kind support in every respect.

References

Introductory Remarks

The references are divided into three sections: i) General references, ii) Published papers by A.N. Prior, iii) Unpublished papers by A.N. Prior.

The papers by Prior are mainly or at least significantly concerned with theological problems. As for the published papers, I follow the numbering used in the Prior bibliography by Øhrstrøm & Flo (in: Copeland 1996). The unpublished papers are kept in 21 boxes at the Bodleian Library, Oxford. I indicate for each paper its length, whether it is typed or hand-written, and the box in which it is kept. Moreover, I add a dating wherever possible.

Per F.V. Hasle

The Øhrstrøm/Flo bibliography and further information on Prior's unpublished papers in the Bodleian Library can be found at the following WWW-site: http://www.hum.auc.dk/~poe/prior.html.

i) General references

1. Copeland, J. (ed.): *Logic and Reality: Essays in the Legacy of Arthur Prior*, Oxford University Press /Clarendon Press, Oxford 1996.
2. Kenny, Anthony: *Arthur Normann Prior (1914-1969)*, Proceedings of the British Academy, Vol. LVI, 1970, pp. 321-49.
3. Kenny, Anthony: *A Path from Rome*, Sidgwick and Jackson, London 1985.
4. Prior, Mary: Letters to the author, 31 July 1996 (a) and 9 Febr. 1997 (b).
5. Øhrstrøm, P.: *Prior's Ideas of Temporal Realism*, in: Copeland 1996.
6. Øhrstrøm, P. & Hasle, P.: *A.N. Prior's Rediscovery of Tense Logic*, Erkenntnis 39, 1993, pp. 23-50.
7. Øhrstrøm, P. & Hasle, P.: *Temporal Logic - from Ancient Ideas to Artificial Intelligence,* Kluwer Academic Publishers, Dordrecht 1995.

ii) Published papers by A.N. Prior

Published papers by Prior with a significant theological content:

1942a. *Can Religion be Discussed?*
Australasian Jour. of Psychology & Philosophy 15, 1937, pp. 141-51.
Reprinted in Flew, Antony; MacIntyre, Alasdair (eds.):
New Essays in Philosophical Theology, S.C.M., London.1955, pp. 1-11

1946b. *The Reformers Reformed: Knox on Predestination,*
The Presbyter, vol.4, 1946, pp. 19-23

1947d. *Supralapsarianism*, The Presbyter 5, 1947, pp. 19-22.

1955g. *Is necessary existence possible?*
Philosophy and Phenomenological Research 15, pp. 545-47.

1958c. *The good life and religious faith*
(East-West meeting at Canberra Dec. 1957),
Australasian Journal of Philosophy 36, 1958, pp. 1-13.

1959d. *Creation in science and theology,*
Southern Stars 18, 1959, pp. 82-89.

1962e. *The Formalities of Omniscience,*
Philosophy 37, 1962, pp. 114-29.

1996a. *Some Free Thinking About Time.*
First published in Copeland 1996; for its original dating, see note 20.
I quote from the original 'SFTT', kept in the Bodleian Library, box 7.

Per F.V. Hasle

iii) Unpublished papers by A.N. Prior

Unpublished papers by Prior with a significant theological content:

[EI]. Ca.1942. *The Case of Edward Irving*, 5p. typed. Box 6

[CD]. Ca.1942. *Children of the damned*, 10p. typed, + 2p. hand-written. Box 6

[DPT]. Ca.1943? Cf. note 6. *Determinism in philosophy & theology*, 4p. Box 6

[FFP]. Ca.1962. *The fable of the four preachers*, 5p. typed. Box 6

[RB]. Ca.1942. *Robert Barclay: Quaker or Calvinist?*, 15p. typed. Box 7

[NWC]. 1940. *Notes on the Westminster Confession (and proposed revision)*,
      2p. typed. + 3p. hand-written. Box 7

[LC]. Ca.1940. *The Logic of Calvinism*, 26p. hand-written. Box 7

[FUE]. Ca.1943. *Faith, Unbelief and Evil*, 19p. typed. Box 7

[AMS]. Ca.1940. *A Modernist Stocktaking*, 6p. typed. Box 7

iv) Appendix

Further papers by A.N. Prior with a significant theological content:

1938a. *Review of Etienne Gilson, The Philosophy of St. Bonaventure.*
      The Criterion 18, 1938, pp. 141-43.

1940a. *Makers of Modern Thought (1): Kierkegaard,*
      The Student Movement, March 1940, pp. 131-32.

1940b. *A Scot Seeks God*, The Churchman, 1940, pp. 34-42.

1940c. *A Calvinist Romantic*, Purpose 12, no.1, 1940, pp. 15-21.

1948a. *Adam Gib and the Philosophers,*
      Australasian Journal of Psychology & Philosophy 26, 1948, pp. 73-93.

1948c. *Disruption*, Landfall 2, 1948, pp. 8-18.

1957b. *Is it possible that one and the same individual object should cease to
      exist and later on start to exist again*, Analysis 17, pp. 121-23.

1957d. *Opposite number*, The Review of Metaphysics 11, 1957, pp. 196-201.

1960c. *Identifiable individuals*, Review of Metaphysics 13, 1960, pp. 684-96.

1962f. *Limited indeterminism*, Review of Metaphysics 16, 1962, pp. 55-61.

1965f. *Time, existence and identity,*
      Proceedings of the Aristotelian Society 66, 1965-1966, pp. 183-92.

1976b. *On Some Proofs of the Existence of God*, in:
      Geach, P.T.; Kenny, A.J.P. (eds.): *Papers in Logic and Ethics*.
      University of Massachusett Press, Amherst, 1976. pp. 56-63.

Per F.V. Hasle

Notes

1 It must be said that one cannot entirely exclude that some of it has been published in lesser-known journals. Peter Øhrstrøm and the author are in the process of investigating in detail the material in the Bodleian Library. The aim is to provide a systematical and annotated present-ation of this material, including the dating of it as exactly as possible. One further aim is to try to establish more conclusively whether some of the 'unpublished papers' are in fact published.

2 Chapter iii, *Of God's eternal Decree.*

3 The paper was at first entitled *Ut omnes unum sint*, That they may all be one (i.e., in Christ), John 17. (This was the chapter which the Scottish Presbyterian John Knox asked to have read on his deathbed, cf. Prior 1946b, p. 20). The paper was obviously written around 1941-42, when Prior was in London. Whether it was submitted while Prior was in London is not clear; but by all evidence it was submitted late in 1942, briefly after he returned to New Zealand (unfortunately, it is not known to which journal). The problems dealt with as well as references to the Westminster Confession suggest that it is a follow-up to Prior's work in 1940 on the proposed revision of the Westminster Confession.

4 Every, George: *On Some Speculations of T.E. Hulme*,
The Student Movement, January 1936.

5 It must be admitted that to anybody not well versed in reformed thought, this distinction may seem to explain little, indeed to be spurious; and in the long run it would also prove to be unsatisfactory for Prior.

6 1947, p. 22.

7 In 1955, when it was reprinted in Antony Flew and Alasdair MacIntyre (eds.), *New Essays in Philosophical Theology*, London, Prior had added a footnote (p.1): *This dialogue was written over a decade ago, and no character in it represents the present opinions of the author.*

8 A positio n involved in the Calvinist teaching on predestination.

9 1942, p. 8.

10 Kenny [1985 p. 143] stresses the importance of this paper with respect to the notion of God as a necessary being: "The most decisive intervention in the debate came from A.N. Prior, who could be said to have started the whole discussion in a 1948 [sic] dia-logue in the Australasian Journal of Philosophy entitled *Can Religion be Discussed?*". Kenny points out that Prior followed up on the topic in *Is Necessary Existence Possible?* (1955g), which however makes a breach with the implicit positivism of Logician in *Can Religion be Discussed?*

11 Edward Irving was dismissed from his ministry - formally, on grounds of his understanding of the Incarnation.

12 It seems that Prior retained throughout his life an interest in the plight of persons believing themselves predestined to damnation.

13 I think it is - as Kenny [1970 p.24] writes, "it looks forward to
Logic and the Basis of Ethics" (1949a).

14 Dating: ca. 1943? - The clear defence of the doctrine of predestination would suggest that the paper is written after Prior's religious crisis (1942). However, the influence of Freud, diminishing from 1944 onwards, is also strong in this paper. (Even though I think that around 1943 is the most likely dating, it might also be later than that. One notable feature is that the issue determinism/predestination is discussed more in philosophical than in theological terms. This is a difference from Prior's other papers dealing with predestination, and might put the paper even later than *The Reformers Reformed* (1946b) and *Supralapsarianism* (1947d), viz. in the late fourties, before Prior began to give up his determinist stance in the early fifties).

15 In his *Moses and Monotheism*. Freud, Sigmund: The standard edition of the complete psychological works of Sigmund Freud, transl. from the German under the general editorship of James Strachey. Vol. 23 (1937-1939).

16 Copeland further refers to the two essays *Some Free Thinking About Time* and

Per F.V. Hasle

A Statement of Temporal Realism by Prior, first published in Copeland 1996.

[17] Findlay, J.N.: *Time: A Treatment of Some Puzzles*, in:
Australasian Journal of Psychology and Philosophy, vol. 19, 1941.

[18] Lukasiewicz, Jan: 1920, *On Three-Valued Logic*, and: 1930,
Philosophical Remarks on Many-Valued Systems of Propositional Logic
in: Borkowski, L. (ed.): *Jan Lukasiewicz: Selected Works*, Amsterdam 1970.

[19] Mates, Benson: 'Diodorean Implication', *Philosophical Review 58*, 1949, pp. 234-44.

[20] In [Øhrstrøm & Hasle 1995], there are accounts of *The Master Argument* (ch.1.2),
Human Freedom & Divine Foreknowledge (ch.1.9), *Lukasiewicz on De Interpretatione* (ch.2.3),
Indeterministic Tense Logic (ch.3.2) and *Leibnizian Tense Logic* (ch.3.3);
in all cases Prior's contributions are discussed.

[21] Prior 1953d: 'Three-valued Logic and Future Contingents',
The Philosophical Quarterly 3, 1953, pp. 317-26,
and Prior 1955d: 'Diodorean Modalities',
The Philosophical Quarterly 5, 1955, pp. 205-213.

[22] In [Copeland 1996]. Original dating: ca. 1958-59? - Peter Øhrstrøm [1996] has scrutinised the possible dating of *Some Free Thinking About Time* (SFTT), observing that "there is an obvious textual overlap with *The syntax of time-distinctions* (1958 d)", which was based on a talk given by Prior in 1954. However, "with respect to the treatment of relativity, STD [i.e. 1958d.] seems premature when compared with SFTT ... [this and a few other] observations make it natural to assume that SFTT was written some years after STD". It must be added that Mary Prior (letter b) dates SFTT (first version) to 1953. The paper was inspired by the Prior's daughter Ann, then aged 4, who was sorry about something. When Arthur Prior tried to comfort her, she vehemently declared that nothing could now make it 'not to have happened'. - Even so, the manuscript in the Bodleian library could be a later and refined version, which would account for its comparatively sophisticated treatment of relativity.

[23] I hope to deal with these questions at a later time. The most relevant papers are:
Is it possible that one and the same individual object should cease to exist and later on start to exist again (1957b), *Opposite number* (1957d), *Creation in science and theology* (1959d), *Identifiable individuals* (1960c), *Time, existence and identity* (1965f).

[24] Hence, this paper is probably relatively late; Mary Prior (letter b) dates it between 1961 and 1964, with 1962 as the most probable year.

[25] Quoted from Kenny 1970 p. 325.

[26] A thought often stressed by Brunner, another theologian who influenced Prior.

[27] Prior and Mackie first met at a conference in Sydney 1951, cf. [Kenny 1970 p. 332]. Prior often discussed philosophy with Mackie, and maintained an impressive corre-spondence with him (now kept at the Bodleian Library).

[28] It has already been told how soon after, on arriving in Britain, Prior was to refrain from join-ing the local Presbyterian Community, a breach with previous practice throughout his adult life.

[29] At a more *personal* level, this lack of conversion experience was according to Mary Prior [b] a very important factor in setting Arthur Prior on a path leading to agnosticism. But of course, such a 'lack' does not by itself raise any intellectual doubts about Christianity. (In fact, the very idea of a conversion experience is not seen as vital in the major Christian denominations). For that reason I do not attribute crucial significance to this point when discussing the *intellectual* development of Prior's attitude towards Christianity, as attested by his writings.

[30] He also taught, though, that God elected persons on the basis of his fore-knowledge of their (free) choice. His theology therefore still leaves us with the problem of foreknowledge.

Per F.V. Hasle

PETER ØHRSTRØM

THE CONTINGENCY OF THE FUTURE
A DISCUSSION OF A MEDIEVAL ANALYSIS

During the Middle Ages logicians related their science to theology. Clearly they felt that they had something important to offer with regard to solving fundamental logical questions in theology.

One of the most important questions of that kind was the problem of the contingency of the future. This problem has come to be regarded as one of the most important problems in the logic of time and modality. In our own days, the problem of the contingency of the future is no longer primarily seen as a theological problem; but intellectuals of the Middle Ages saw it as closely connected with the relationship between two fundamental Christian dogmas, viz. the dogma of human freedom and the dogma of divine foreknowledge.

According to the dominant Christian tradition, divine foreknowledge is taken to comprise total knowledge of all future choices to be made by men. This apparently yields a straightforward argument from divine foreknowledge to necessity of the future: if God knows the decision I will make tomorrow, then a now-unpreventable truth about my choice tomorrow is already given! Therefore there seems to be no basis for the claim that I am able to choose freely, a conclusion which violates the doctrine of human freedom.

The problem of a contingent future was often discussed in connection with the text of Aristotle in *De interpretatione* about the sea-battle tomorrow. Another piece of classical text that was occasionally taken into consideration was Cicero's *De Fato* which among its subject matters treats the Diodorean Master Argument. There is a very extensive literature about the problem of the contingent future, and any attempt to produce a detailed exposition of the subject seems hopeless.[1] On the other hand it is possible to give a systematical overview of some of the more basic approaches to the problem.

Such a survey is found in the writings of the medieval logician and philosopher Richard Lavenham in his treatise *De eventu futurorum* (c.1380). Lavenham's central idea is clear: If two dogmas appear to be contradictory, then one can solve the problem either by accepting or by rejecting the reality of the contradiction. If the contradiction is accepted then solving the problem implies the denial of at least one of the dogmas. If the contradiction is rejected it must be proved that the contradiction is only apparent and not real.

Denial of the dogma of human freedom means fatalism (1. solution). Denial of the dogma of divine foreknowledge can be based either on the claim that God does not know the whole truth about the future (2. solution), or on the assumption that no truth about the contingent future has yet been decided (3. solution). Rejection of the contradiction between the two dogmas must be based on the formulation of a system according to which the two dogmas, rightly understood, can be united in a consistent way (4. solution).

Lavenham rejected the 1. and 2. solution as being contrary to the Christian faith. It should, however, be noticed that the opinion of St. Thomas Aquinas can be read as a version of the 2. solution, since Thomas held that divine knowledge abstracts from differences between past, present and future. According to his position, all truth is always present to God in an atemporal sense of 'always'. For this reason one may say that such knowledge is not really *fore*knowledge. The problem clearly bears on the theological task of clarifying questions such as: 'In which way can God know the future?'

It seems that Lavenham, like Ockham, saw the Aristotelian approach to the question of future contingents as being equivalent to the 3. solution. Some of Ockham's contemporaries favoured this possibility. Peter Aureolus (1280-1322), for example, held that neither the statement *Antichrist will come* nor the statement *Antichrist will not come* is true whereas the disjunction of these statements is necessarily true now. From that point of view one can naturally claim that the dogma of divine foreknowledge is still tenable even if God does not know whether Antichrist will come or not. God knows whatever is true, and if he does not know that Antichrist will come, the reason must be that there is as yet no truth value for the statement *Antichrist will come*.

Lavenham held that on Aristotle's account some propositions about future contingent facts are neither determinately true nor determinately false. Whether he had in mind a third truth-value corresponding to indeterminate, or he held that no truth-value is as yet defined for future contingent propositions, is not clear; what is clear is merely that Lavenham rejected the 3. solution as contrary to the Christian faith. This is quite sensible since such understanding of the doctrine of God's foreknowledge seems somewhat clobbered. According to the 3. solution, a Christian must accept that God's complete knowledge two days ago did not necessarily cover all that happened yesterday.

It is worth noting that a related version of the 3. solution has been defended by important later philosophers such as C.S. Peirce and A.N. Prior. According to their view, contingent facts are not real facts yet, therefore all propositions concerning future contingent "facts" should be regarded as false.

Peter Øhrstrøm

According to this view, all propositions about the contingent future should be regarded as false now, since there *are* no facts about the contingent future.

Lavenham himself clearly preferred the 4. solution. Though some of its elements are found in Anselm of Canterbury (1033-1109), the full solution was first formulated by William of Ockham (1275-1349). It is interesting that Leibniz (1646-1711) much later invented a similar system as a part of his metaphysical considerations, cf. Øhrstrøm (1984). The characteristic feature of their theories is the idea of "the true future".

The ordinary interpretation of Christian faith claims that God knows in advance not merely the necessary future, but also the contingent future. This means that one particular future is privileged among all possible futures, since it is that course of events which is going to be actualised in the future; that this particular future is privileged, however, does not make it necessary. This line of thinking may be called *the medieval solution*, even though other approaches were known. The justification for that is partly that the concept of "the true future" is the outstanding medieval contribution to the problem, and partly that most medieval logicians regarded this solution as the best one. Lavenham called it *opinio modernorum*, the opinion of the modern.

Ockham discussed the relation of divine foreknowledge to human freedom in his *Tractatus de praedestinatione et de futuris contingentibus*. Here he claimed that God knows all future contingents, but at the same time he insisted that human beings can choose freely between alternative possibilities, i.e., he argued that divine foreknowledge and human freedom are compatible. In his writings Lavenham later made a considerable effort to capture and clearly present the features of the 4. solution (i.e. the system of Ockham) as opposed to the 3. solution (i.e. the system of Aristotle).

Lavenham considered an argument from God's foreknowledge to the necessity of the future and the lack of human freedom. The main structure of this is close to what is believed to have been the core of the Master Argument of Diodorus Kronos. We know from Lavenham's text that he was acquainted to this old Stoic or Megaric argument through his reading of Cicero's *De Fato*. In the following I am going to present an elaborated version of this medieval argument making use of an extension of metric tense logic with

$F(x)$ *"in x time units it will be the case that ..."*
$P(x)$ *"x time units ago it was the case that ..."*
N *"it is necessary that ..."*
D *"God knows that ..."*

A formal analysis of Lavenham's argument discloses that it is based on these five principles (A being an arbitrary well formed statement, q being an atomic statement and $F(y)q$ being a statement about the contingent future):

(P1)   Divine foreknowledge:
$$F(y)A \supset P(x)DF(x)F(y)A$$

(P2)   The infallibility of God's foreknowledge:
$$N(P(x)DF(x)A \supset A)$$

(P3)   The necessity of the past:
$$P(x)A \supset NP(x)A$$

(P4)   Assumption about modality:
$$(N(A \supset B) \wedge N(A)) \supset N(B)$$

(P5)   The determinateness of the future:
$$F(x)A \vee F(x)\sim A$$

Here A represents an arbitrary well formed statement within the logic. Let q stand for some atomic statement so that $F(x)q$ is a statement about the contingent future. The argument proceeds in two phases: first from divine foreknowledge to necessity of the future, and then from that to the result that there can be no real human freedom of choice. Formally it goes as follows:

(1) $F(y)q$ (assumption)
(2) $P(x)DF(x)F(y)q$ (from 1 & P1)
(3) $NP(x)DF(x)F(y)q$ (from 2 & P3)
(4) $N(P(x)DF(x)F(y)q \supset F(y)q)$ (from P2)
(5) $NF(y)q$ (from 3, 4, P4)

In this way we have proved

(6) $F(y)q \supset NF(y)q$

Similarly it is possible to prove

(7) $F(y)\sim q \supset NF(y)\sim q$

The second part of the main proof is carried out as follows:

(8) $F(y)q \vee F(y)\sim q$ (from P5)
(9) $NF(y)q \vee NF(y)\sim q$ (from 6, 7, 8)

Here (9) is equivalent to a denial of the doctrine of human freedom.

Peter Øhrstrøm

To save this doctrine and escape fatalism - Lavenham's 1. solution - one must discard at least one of the above principles *P1-P5*. Lavenham's 2. solution is a denial of *P1*. In some cases $F(x)q$ is true while $P(y)F(y)F(x)q$ is false. It is, however, rather hard to find modern advocates of this possibility.

Lavenham's 3.solution discards *P5*, the determinateness of the future. According to this idea, nothing is true about the future unless it is necessary. This idea has many modern advocates. Though the denial of a determinate future and the consequent amalgamation of future with necessary future makes this position rather counter-intuitive from a common sense point of view, C.S. Peirce, A.N. Prior, and many of their followers have favoured this possibility. The 3. solution means that a statement like $F(z)p$ is true iff (if and only if) p is true after z time units for any future development. Hence $F(x)q$ is true at *N2*, while $F(x+y)q$ is not true (i.e. false, indeterminate, or truth-valueless) at *N1*:

The Peirce Model

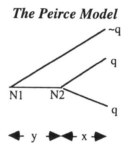

Accepted: F = NF - Rejected: F(x)A ∨ ~F(x)

The 4. solution, which Lavenham preferred, involves a denial of *P3*. I must admit that I for my part also find this position attractive. If *P3* is denied, then the inference from *(2)* to *(3)* may be rejected. According to Ockham and Lavenham, *P3* should only be accepted for statements which are genuinely about the past, i.e. which do not depend on the future. According to this view, *P3* can be denied since the truth of statements like $P(x)DF(x)F(y)q$ has not been determined as yet, since it depends crucially on the future. In this way one can make a distinction between soft and hard facts regarding the past. The truth of a statement like $P(x)q$ would be a hard fact, accordingly, whereas $P(x)F(x)F(y)q$ and $P(x)DF(x)F(y)q$ would represent soft facts.

The characteristic feature of Ockham's logic is his idea of *the true future*; this logic corresponds to a branching time model in which there is a privileged branch at any past, present or future branching point in the model. In consequence, $F(x)q$ is true at *N2* and $F(x+y)q$ is true at *N1*:

Peter Øhrstrøm

J.M. Fischer (1994) has recently questioned the Ockhamistic model. He has introduced a subdivision of the set of soft facts by distinguishing hard-type soft facts as well as hard-type soft facts and soft-type soft facts. W. Lane Craig (1989,p.236) finds that this analysis "has gone out of control", and I am apt to agree. Fischer's point can be stated in a much simpler way. His position is just that some soft facts are so hard that "they cannot be falsified without affecting some genuine feature of the past" (Fischer, p.127). According to Fisher, God's prior beliefs which represent his foreknowledge are such "hard-type soft facts" (p.118).

The key concept in Fischer's discussion, apparently, is the idea of "the state of God's mind" at a certain time. In my opinion there is no need to accept the relevance of this notion. Ockham himself clearly refused to say anything specific about the way in which God knows the contingent future. But Ockham was aware that communication was essential to his discussion especially, of course, the communication coming from God to human beings; and he claimed that God can communicate the truth about the future to us.

Ockham realised that a divine revelation of the future by means of unconditional statements communicated to a prophet is inconsistent with the contingency of the prophecy. If God reveals the future by means of unconditional statements, the future is inevitable because a divine revelation has to be true; in that case the soft fact corresponding to God's foreknowledge is turned into a hard fact. But as long as the divine foreknowledge remains unrevealed, it cannot qualify as more than a soft fact for which it is perfectly sensible to deny the application of the principle of the necessity of the past. Therefore, although there is no need for Fischer's distinction between hard-type soft facts and soft-type soft facts, the Ockhamistic analysis gives rise to a distinction between God's revealed foreknowledge and God's unrevealed foreknowledge.

In an interesting paper N. Belnap and M. Green have concentrated on another problem related to the Ockhamistic model. In fact, they have argued (1994) that the model should be rejected. Their reason is that the model not only has to specify a preferred course of history, past, present, and future. If one wants to insist on a concept of future which is different from possible as well as necessary future, it must further be assumed that there is a preferred branch at every counterfactual moment; but this leads to trouble.

Belnap and Green have based their argument on this example of a statement from ordinary language which any Ockhamistic logic in their opinion should be able to deal with (1994, p.379):

Peter Øhrstrøm

The coin will come up heads. It is possible, though, that it will come up tails and then later (*) it will come up tails again (though at that moment it could come up heads) and then, inevitably, still later it will come up tails yet again.

As Belnap and Green explains, the trouble is that, at (*), the example says that tails 'will' happen, not merely that it 'might'. The point is that (*) is future relative to a counterfactual instant (induced by the use of the concept of possibility). The above statement may be represented in terms of a tense logic, which corresponds to the branching time structure sketched below:

$$F_1 h \wedge MF_1(t \wedge MF_1 h \wedge F_1(t \wedge NF_1 t))$$
$$F_1 \equiv_{def} F(1) - \qquad \textit{for t read: tails -} \qquad \textit{for h read: heads}$$

4. Possibility: The Ockham Model

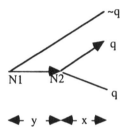

Problems: Which facts are soft? Belnap's & Green's problem

Belnap and Green hold that the Ockhamistic model cannot deal with such a situation because only one privileged branch is given in the model. They remedy this deficiency by introducing a function *TRL* (Thin Red Line) which to each instant assigns a preferred branch, the so-called "thin red line". The example shows that if the Ockhamistic model is taken seriously, then there must be a function TRL, which gives the true future corresponding to a given moment, *t*. Which conditions should the function *TRL* satisfy?

Belnap and Green have argued that the condition
$$TRL1 \quad t \in TRL(t)$$
should hold in general, and that in addition the following
$$TRL2 \quad t < t' \supset TRL(t) = TRL(t')$$
may be considered. However, they show that (*TRL2*) is inconsistent with branching time; in fact, it implies that the before-relation is forwards linear.

Peter Øhrstrøm

Therefore condition (*TRL2*) seems to be too strong a requirement. Rather than (*TRL2*), we propose the weaker condition

TRL2' $(t < t' \wedge t' \in TRL(t)) \supset TRL(t) = TRL(t')$

This seems to be natural in relation to the Ockhamistic concept of branching time and which is certainly consistent with it. Belnap has later accepted the relevance of (*TRL2'*) admitting that it "much improves the level of discussion" [E-mail discussion with Nuel Belnap, August 1996].

Belnap and Green have argued that any such *TRL*-function should give rise to a semantics in which the following formulas are valid:

(T1) $FFA \supset FA$
(T2) $PPA \supset PA$
(T3) $A \supset P_1 F_1 A$

No formal semantics is given by Belnap and Green; however, they seem to assume that tense operators are interpreted only relative to an instant. This amounts to interpreting tenses using a two-place valuation operator:

$T(t,Pp)$ *iff* $\exists t'$: $t' < t$ *and* $T(t',p)$
$T(t,Fp)$ *iff* $\exists t'$: $t' \in TRL(t)$: $t < t'$ *and* $T(t',p)$

Given such a semantics, it is straightforward to check that (*T1*) is valid without (*TRL2'*). On the other hand, (*T2*) is not valid without (*TRL2'*), but it is if this assumption is made. The formula (*T3*) is not valid even if (*TRL2'*) is assumed. To see why this is the case, consider a situation with an instant *t* such that $t \in TRL(t')$ is false for any $t' < t$. Assume that *t* is the only instant at which *A* is true. Then *PFA*, hence also $A \supset PFA$, will be false at *t*.

(If somebody would like to regard $A \supset PFA$ as invalid, one would have to say something like this: The counterfactual assumption of *A* does not invalidate the truth of the past prediction *PF~A*. Thus, if I am awake now, it certainly was true yesterday that I was going to be awake after one day. That prediction was true (but of course not necessary) even if I now - while being awake - imagine that I were asleep. For this reason one might say, that the truth of *A* and *PF~A*, where *A* stands for 'I am asleep', is conceiveable. But this piece of argumentation appears somewhat strained.)

Peter Øhrstrøm

It is not obvious how to extend the semantics described above to deal with necessity, however. The problem is that in an Ockhamistic branching time model, interpretation of the necessity operator involves interpretations relative to counterfactual branches. This amounts to interpreting necessity using a three-place valuation operator:

$$T(t,c,Np) \quad iff \quad T(t,c',p) \text{ for all } c' \in C \text{ with } t \in c'$$

There does not seem to be any reasonable way to combine this interpretation of necessity (which depends on interpretations relative to counterfactual branches) with the above mentioned interpretation of tenses (where branches are redundant).

I shall therefore propose another semantics of tenses and necessity.[2] As usual, we need a set, *TIME*, equipped with a transitive and backwards linear relation $<$, together with a function T which assigns a truth value to each pair consisting of an instant and a propositional letter. Furthermore, adopting Belnap and Green's idea, we assume the presence of a function *TRL* which to each instant assigns a branch such that the conditions (*TRL1*) and (*TRL2'*) are satisfied. A novel feature of the semantics we give here is the notion of a (counterfactual) branch with the property that at any future instant it coincides with the corresponding thin red line.

Given an instant t, the set $C(t)$ of such branches is defined as follows:

$$C(t) = \{ c \in C \mid t \in c \text{ and } TRL(t')=c \text{ for any } t' \in c \text{ with } t < t' \}$$

Note that the conditions (*TRL1*) and (*TRL2'*) together say exactly that $TRL(t) \in C(t)$. Also note that $C(t)$ may contain more branches than just $TRL(t)$. This allows for counterfactuality.

We shall now present a valuation operator T where truth is relative to an instant as well as to a branch with the above mentioned property. By induction, we define the valuation operator T as follows:

$T(t,c,p)$ *iff* $T(t,p)$ *where p is a propositional letter*
$T(t,c, p \wedge q)$ *iff* $T(t,c,p)$ *and* $T(t,c,q)$
$T(t,c,\sim p)$ *iff* *not* $T(t,c,p)$
$T(t,c,Fp)$ *iff* $T(t',c,p)$ *for some* $t' \in c$ *with* $t < t'$
$T(t,c,Pp)$ *iff* $T(t',c,p)$ *for some* $t' \in c$ *with* $t' < t$
$T(t,c,Np)$ *iff* $T(t,c',p)$ *for all* $c' \in C(t)$

Peter Øhrstrøm

A formula p is said to be valid if and only if p is true in any structure $(TIME,<,T,TRL)$, i.e. $T(t,c,p)$ for any instant t and branch c such that $c \in C(t)$. The tense operators P and F are interpreted as usual in Ockhamistic semantics. It is then straightforward to introduce metrical tense operators.

This makes all of the formulas $(T1)$, $(T2)$ and $(T3)$ valid. On the other hand, the necessity operator is interpreted differently in the sense that fewer (counterfactual) branches are taken into account. This invalidates the formula

$$F_1 M F_1 p \supset M F_1 F_1 p$$

which is valid in the usual Ockhamistic semantics.

The formula is not true in the following structure:

The model of Belnap & Green (p.379)

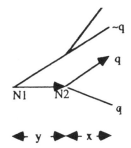

"The coin will come up heads. It is possible, though, that it will come up tails, and that later it will come up tails (though at that moment it could come up heads), and then, inevitably, still later it will come up tails yet again."

The Ockhamistic semantics given here should be further investigated. It can be said, however, that the idea of a semantical model in which truth is relative to a branch as well as to an instant is problematic from a philosophical point of view since the ontological status of branches is rather debatable. For this reason I prefer the so-called Leibnizian solution (cf. Øhrstrøm and Hasle, 1995). According to this system the branches in the branching time system have to be viewed as 'parallel lines' on the set of which there is defined a relation corresponding to identity up to a certain moment. In such a model made up of 'parallel lines' the TRL-function will be trivial.

On the Leibnizian view, $A \supset P_1 F_1 A$ is valid, whereas $A \supset P_1 N F_1 A$ (where N is the necessity-operator) does not hold:

Peter Øhrstrøm

5. Possibility: The Leibniz Model

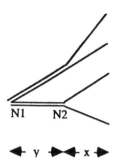

N1   N2

◄ y ►◄ x ►

Conclusion

I have discussed Lavenham's four solutions corresponding to a full acceptance of the argument, and to denials of *P1*, or *P5*, or *P3*, respectively. Of course, one might also consider denials of *P2* and *P4*. But it is very hard to see how such denials may be defended. The same can be said about rejections of other ingredients of the apparatus involved in Lavenham's argument.

I have demonstrated that the Ockhamistic model, including the idea of "the true future", can be defended in a modern context; but I have also argued that the Leibnizian model should be preferred.

References

1.   Belnap & Green, 1994: 'Indeterminism and the Thin Red Line', (Logic & Language), *Philos. Persp.* 8, 365-388.

2.   Craig, W.L., 1988: *The Problem of Divine Foreknowledge and Future Contingents from Aristotle to Suarez*, E.J. Brill.

3.   Craig, W.L., 1989: 'Nice Soft Facts: Fischer on Foreknowledge', *Relig. Stud. 25*, 235-246.

4.   Fischer, J.M., 1994: *The Metaphysics of Free Will*, Blackwell.

5.   Øhrstrøm, P., 1983: 'Richard Lavenham on Future Contingents', *Cahiers de l'Institut du Moyen-Âge Grec et Latin 44*, 180-186.

6.   Øhrstrøm, P., 1984: 'Anselm, Ockham & Leibniz on Divine Foreknowledge and Human Freedom', *Erkenntnis 21*, 209-222.

7.   Øhrstrøm & Hasle, 1995: *TEMPORAL LOGIC - from Ancient Ideas to Artifiical Intelligence*, Kluwer.

Notes

[1] See e.g. Craig (1998).

[2] This idea I owe to Torben Bräuner, Dept.Mathematics, Aarhus University.

Peter Øhrstrøm

LARS BO GUNDERSEN

FUTURE SPACE BATTLES
AND BRANCHING TIME

1. Introduction

Will there be a space battle tomorrow? Is there a fact of the matter as to whether there will be a space battle tomorrow? This question has often been tied up with *the realism/anti-realism dispute*: If the future is real there is a definite answer to the question. There is a fact of the matter, known or not, which settles the question. And if there happens to be a space battle going on tomorrow it is true today that there will be a space battle tomorrow. If, on the other hand, the future isn't real yet, but continuously comes into being, it might still be indeterminate whether there will be a space battle tomorrow. There is no fact of the matter as to whether there will be a space battle tomorrow. Not yet. Matters are not that simple, though.

The question of tomorrow's space battle might be unsettled despite the reality of the future. This being so if there is more than one real future, if, in other words, the future is branched. Only if there is exactly one real future will the question be settled. If there is less, as the anti-realist claims, or more, as a branching theorist claims, the question is unsettled. However, elucidating on exactly such a branching concept of the future, as is the intention of this paper, might shed some light on why it has proved so unmanageable to develop a satisfactory semantics for propositions expressing future contingencies and, hence, why it has proved so recalcitrant to provide a satisfactory answer to the question about tomorrow's space battle.

2. The Master Argument

Some philosophers have claimed that the semantics for propositions expressing future contingencies are straightforward: A contingent proposition is a future proposition, the claim is, so the semantics for future contingent propositions are the semantics for future propositions. A reduction of semantics for future contingent propositions to semantics for future propositions, although by no means simple, would certainly mark a significant progress. However, why should we believe contingency is synonymous with futurity? One line of argument, the *Master Argument* of the Megarean philosopher Diodoros Kronos, proceeds by demonstrating that the following is a trilemma:

D1   Every proposition true about the past is necessary
D2   An impossible proposition cannot follow from a possible one
D3   There is a possible proposition which neither is nor will be true

D3 is rejected in favour of the plausible *D1* and *D2*. Possibility is thus equated with Diodorian possibility as actuality or futurity, and necessity, accordingly, as actuality and forever futurity. Let us pause for a moment and examine the argument more closely. Are *D1* and *D2* really plausible, after all? And how can it be demonstrated they are inconsistent with *D3*?

3. Temporal de re and de dicto readings

The former question regarding the plausibility of *D1* leads us back to the discussion of *realism* versus *anti-realism*. If one, like the temporal realist, is disposed to think of the course of history from an abstract, non-temporal point of view, then there seems to be no good reason to think of propositions about any particular period of time, such as the past, as being more necessary than propositions about some other period such as the future. If, on the other hand, one, like the temporal anti-realist, is disposed to think of oneself as essentially immersed in time, then it seems plausible that anything prior to ones present temporal standpoint, i.e. the past, is unchangeable and in that sense necessary. We will call the former *a temporal de re understanding* and the latter *a temporal de dicto understanding*.

Just as *modal de re readings* invite us to conceive of other-worldly states of affairs as representable unmediated[1], while *modal de dicto readings* invite us to think of such states as representable only when mediated by a linguistic characterisation[2], in the same way temporal *de re* readings support the view that past and future states of affairs are representable unmediated and independently of the present moment whereas *de dicto* readings support the view that temporal states of affairs are representable only when mediated by a linguistic characterisation gaining its characterising force by picking out some temporal state of affairs relative to the present moment.

Hence, on a *de re* reading, the picture is that the whole world with its entire past and future, is spread out in front of us. We are observing the world from a timeless point of view independent of any particular temporal outlook. Every event in the world is temporally ordered as before or after some other event, but is not ordered relative to a standpoint within time, i.e., there is no privileged moment in the world we can pick out as the present and therefore no ordering in past and future. This might sound a bit queer, for how can a

Lars Bo Gundersen

proposition such as 'It is raining' ever be attributed any content if abstracted from the context of the present? Does it imply a strong claim that it always has been and always will continue to be raining, or does it mean that it is raining at some particular time, and in that case, which time?

But this is only a problem for propositions that are not time-indexed. Such non-indexed propositions seem to be ambiguous, referring either to a class of instances, viz. all rainy days, in the same way as a predicate such as 'red' refers to the class of all red objects, or to a truth value - viz. 'true', if it be rainy the day in question - just as 'this apple is red' refers to a truth value. Under the *de re* reading, proposition should be understood in this latter sense. But the difficulty, of course, is to sort out which day has to be rainy for the claim to be satisfied. How can such particular content be put into *de re* mode? And how is it possible to put different contents into the same mode?

This dilemma is very similar to the more familiar dilemma of giving content to modal propositions in their *de re* senses. How can we make sense of a sentence such as *Necessarily the number of planets is greater than seven* in its *de re* sense when abstracting from the real world in its uniqueness and asking whether *that* number is greater than seven in all other possible worlds? In its *de dicto* sense the question is fairly simple. The sentence can easily be evaluated in every possible world by checking in all these worlds whether "The number of planets is greater than seven" (or an adequate translation of that sentence into their language) is true. But taken in its *de re* sense it seems as if we were supposed to pick out a certain number, the number of planets, and investigate whether it is greater than seven in every particular world.

The question of course is, how do we initially pick out that number? And the answer is that we cheat. We do take a standpoint in one particular world, viz. the actual one, then we fix the reference of 'number of planets', and finally we abstract ourselves out into a worldless perspective. In the case of temporal *de re* propositions we do something similar. We take a standpoint at one particular time, the present time, fix the reference of 'it is now raining', and abstract ourselves out into eternity. So - when reading 'It is raining now' in its *de re* sense - we pretend to read it from outside any temporal context, but in doing so we still keep in mind one particular temporal context in which the reference of 'now' is fixed - hooked on to the temporal world, as it were - when we throw our minds out into this imaginary timeless reality.

The only difference from the modal case is that the reference-fixing modal runway is constant, i.e. the actual world, whereas the reference-fixing temporal runway moves (literally) as time goes by. The referent of a predicate

Lars Bo Gundersen

such as 'number of planets' in *de re* modal statements is fixed from the same possible world outlook on every occasion, viz. from the actual world, while the referent of 'now' in *de re* temporal statements initially has been fixed from a different temporal outlook from case to case. A *de re* statement in itself bears no witness of which temporal outlook initially has served as reference-fixing. Sometimes it can be traced from the broader context. But in formal representations of *de re* propositions no such context is available.

The alternative is to read 'proposition' in the temporal *de dicto* sense. In that case they are always interpreted within a temporal context; not some fixed context, but the arbitrary context provided by the time of utterance. Past, present and future tenses occurring in such *de dicto* propositions are thus absolute in the sense that something described in past tense statements is always prior to something described in future tense propositions. In contrast, something uttered in a *de re* past tense proposition might very well be posterior to something described in a *de re* future tense proposition.

It is now time to return to our two original questions: Are *D1* and *D2* so intuitively appealing as they appear? And how can it be demonstrated that they are inconsistent with *D3*? We shall see that the two answers depend on whether *D1-D3* are read temporally *de re* or *de dicto* and that there is a smooth dialectic between the two options: On a *de re* reading it is fairly obvious that *D1-D3* are inconsistent, but equally clear that *D1* must be wrong. *D1* is only plausible on a *de dicto* reading - on which, however, it seems impossible to demonstrate any inconsistencies between *D1-D3*.

F.S. Michael [1976] has offered the following argument that *D1-D3* are incoherent if taken *de re*. In that case *D1 & D2* is expressible as follows:

$D1'$ $(T(q, t') \,\&\, (t' < t)) \Rightarrow \Box T(q, t)$
If a proposition q is true at any time t' before t, then q is necessary at t
$D3'$ $\nabla T(q, n) \,\&\, (\forall t)(t \geq n \Rightarrow T(\neg q, t))$
There is a proposition q which is possible but false now and in all future

Now the argument proceeds by pointing out that q in $D3'$ must have been false also before n. For if $T(q, t')$ for some t' before n, we would have $T(q, t') \,\&\, t' < n$ and hence, according to D1', $\Box T(q, n)$, therefore, as against $D3'$, $T(q, n)$, thus $(\forall t)(t < n \Rightarrow T(\neg q, t))$. But according to $D1'$ this implies $\Box T(\neg q, n)$ which, by $\Box/\nabla$-interdefinability, is equivalent to $\neg \nabla T(q, n)$. But, again, this is against $D3'$. Hence $D1'$ and $D3'$ must be inconsistent.

Lars Bo Gundersen

It is striking that this conclusion, on Michael's account, can be reached without so much as introducing *D2*. Even more striking, perhaps, is that $(\forall t)(t \geq n \Rightarrow T(\neg q, t))$ from *D3'* likewise seems to be superfluous. However, as hinted at above, the reason is fairly simple: Michael understands propositions in their temporal *de re* reading which means that a proposition, if true once, always is so; especially, it will always have been true in the past. So, if something which was true is necessarily true now, as *D1'* claims, it follows without much ado that something once true is necessarily true now. And, by the same token, once false, always false, and thus impossible now. *D1*, read as *de re*, is thus equivalent to a collapse of the modal distinctions: $\Box T(q, n) \equiv T(q, n) \equiv \nabla T(q, n)$. Given *D1*, it is therefore no wonder that Michael can produce a paradox by assuming only $\nabla T(q, n) \, \& \, T(\neg q, n)$.

What is surprising is that Michael can opt for a *de re* reading of *D1*. Although his reasoning, thus understood, is indisputable, *D1* seems plainly false in its *de re* reading. The intuition underlying *D1* is that it is impossible to change the past and, hence, that truths about the past are now necessary. But truths can only be 'about the past' properly if considered from within some temporal context. The *de re* proposition q, if it is to have any content at all, must have been loaded with this content in a temporal context expressible by means of temporal indices. Thus q must refer to a fact which at time t was expressible as e.g. "It is raining today". This is the way q has been coded.

Hence, for q to be something past, it must be possible to decode it again in another temporal context later than t, where it has to be expressible by means of some other temporal indices, e.g., "It was raining x days ago". Only from this later perspective is q about the past. But to decode q from within a particular temporal context is precisely to conceive of q as a *de dicto* proposition whose prima facie value can be read off directly, relative to a certain temporal context. For *D1* to be plausible, it must therefore presuppose a temporal *de dicto* reading. Hence *D1'* is simply false.

The next reconstruction we will consider, which is due to A.N. Prior (1967 pp.32-33), does indeed take *D1* in its *de dicto* sense:

D1" $Pq \Rightarrow \Box Pq$
Every true proposition concerning the past is necessary

D2" $\Box(q \Rightarrow r) \Rightarrow (\nabla q \Rightarrow \nabla r)$
What is impossible does not follow from what is possible

D3" $\neg q \, \& \, \neg Fq \, \& \, \nabla q$
Something that neither is, nor will be, is yet possible

Lars Bo Gundersen

Prior, however, added two auxiliaries to the original premises:

P1 $\Box(q \Rightarrow HFq)$
      From something's being the case it follows necessarily
      that it has always been the case that it would be the case
P2 $(\neg q \ \& \ \neg Fq) \Rightarrow P\neg Fq$
      Of whatever is and always will be false,
      it has already been the case that it will always be false

Now the negation of *D3"* can be proved from *D1"*, *D2"*, *P1 & P2*:

1	$\neg q \ \& \ \neg Fq$	*assumption*
2	$P\neg Fq$	P2,1
3	$\Box P\neg Fq$	D1", 2
4	$\Box P\neg Fq \Rightarrow \neg \nabla q$	P1, D2"
5	$\neg \nabla q$	3,4
6	$\nabla q \Rightarrow (q \vee Fq)$	1,5

The negation of *D3"* was precisely what Diodoros set out to prove.

4. Diverging Semantics

As the argument here stands, two premises are worth examining in some more detail, viz. *D1"* & P1. According to one line of thought, which for (pseudo) historical reasons often has been called **Ockhamist**, *P1* is acceptable, but *D1"* ought to be rejected, or at least constrained such that it only applies to genuine past tense propositions, thus not to past tense statements such as "It was the case yesterday that I would tie my shoe laces two days hence" which really implies something future. According to another line of thought, the **Peircean**, *D1"* should be accepted, but *P1* denied.

The two responses agree on one important point: time is branched and not linear, as assumed by Prior and, in all probability, by Diodoros too. This metaphysical idea can be expressed as a structure consisting of a set K of moments a, b, c, and a temporal relation $<$, restricted by the two properties:

Connexivity: $(a < c \ \& \ b < c) \Rightarrow (a = b \ \vee \ a < b \ \vee \ b < a)$
Transitivity: $(a < b \ \& \ b < c) \Rightarrow (a < c)$

For this branching structure we also define paths, or histories, H:

Lars Bo Gundersen

A   *For all $a, b \in H : (a \neq b) \Rightarrow (a < b \vee b < a)$*

B   *If G is a subset of K satisfying (A), then $G \subseteq H \subseteq K$*

Now the main difference between an Ockhamist and a Peircean line of thought lies in the corresponding semantics for such a branching structure, in particular with respect to their treatment of propositions about the future.

One difference is that Ockhamists evaluate such propositions relative both to a moment, a, and a certain history, H, such that:

$$\mathcal{V}_{a,H}(Fq) = 1 \text{ iff } \mathcal{V}_{b,H}(Fq) = 1 \text{ for some } b \in H \text{ such that } a < b$$

As opposed to this, Peirceans operate with absolute truth in the sense that the evaluation of Fq is only relative to a moment :

$$\mathcal{V}_a(Fq) = 1 \text{ iff - for all } H \subseteq K - \mathcal{V}_b(q) = 1 \text{ for some } b \in H \text{ such that } a < b$$

So Fq is Peircean-true iff it is Ockham-true relative to each $H \subseteq K$. This is the reason why the Peircean, but not the Ockamist, can accept *D1''*, $Pq \Rightarrow \Box Pq$. The Ockhamist kind of counterexample to *D1''* would be: "If it was the case yesterday that I would tie my shoe laces two days hence, it was necessarily the case yesterday that I would tie my shoe laces two days hence". This is to say that something future, viz. my tying my shoe laces, is necessary. That counter example does not trouble the Peircean who conceives of future truth as absolute truth which, arguably, is equivalent to necessary truth.

Another semantic difference between Ockhamists and Peirceans is that the temporal point of evaluation changes as one moves through the layers in nested temporal expressions in a Peircean evaluation, while it is fixed and identical to that indicated by the outermost layer in an Ockhamist evaluation. In evaluating the 'inner' layer, $F_{\nu+\mu}q$, in the nested expression $P_\nu F_{\nu+\mu}q$, at a, the Ockhamist would do it from an a-perspective whereas the Peircean would do it from a b-perspective, b being ν days prior to a. This is the reason why an Ockhamist, but not a Peircean, can accept *P1*, $\Box(q \Rightarrow HFq)$. But despite these semantic divergencies, the reconstruction of Prior fails due to false premises on both the Ockhamist and the Peircean account.

We have seen how Ockhamist and Peircean semantics differ on two central issues: absolute versus relative future truth, and stable versus unstable evaluating perspective for nested temporal expressions; and we have seen how the differences impinge on the validity of *D1*, and on that of *P1*, respectively.

Lars Bo Gundersen

We have likewise observed that the Peircean stance on the former question verifies $D1''$ and that the Ockhamist stance on the latter question verifies $P1$. This suggests that a combination of the two semantics, which might be called G, and which agrees with the Peirceans in maintaining absolute future truth, but agrees with the Ockhamists in adhering to a stable temporal point of view for the evaluation of nested expressions, might be coherent with both $D1''$ and $P1$ and hence constitute a suitable semantic basis for Prior's reconstruction. But matters are not that simple, for with a semantics favouring a stable point of evaluation in nested temporal expression we are committed to accept:

$$G1 \quad F_\mu q \Rightarrow P_\nu F_{\nu+\mu} q$$
$$G2 \quad \Box(P_\nu F_{\nu+\mu} q \Rightarrow F_\mu q)$$

In fact, $G1$ & $G2$ are derivable from $P1$. But with $GG1\text{-}2$ added to $DD1\text{-}3''$ & $PP1\text{-}2$, a result much stronger than Diodorus' can be derived:

1	$P_\nu q \Rightarrow \Box P_\nu q$	$D1''$
2	$P_\nu F_{\nu+\mu} q \Rightarrow \Box P_\nu F_{\nu+\mu} q$	1, subst
3	$F_\mu q \Rightarrow P_\nu F_{\nu+\mu} q$	$G1$
4	$F_\mu q \Rightarrow \Box P_\nu F_{\nu+\mu} q$	2,3, trans
5	$\Box(q \Rightarrow r) \Rightarrow (\Box q \Rightarrow \Box r)$	$D2''$
6	$\Box(P_\nu F_{\nu+\mu} q \Rightarrow F_\mu q)$	$G2$
7	$\Box P_\nu F_{\nu+\mu} q \Rightarrow \Box F_\mu q$	5,6, subst, MP
8	$F_\mu q \Rightarrow \Box F_\mu q$	4,7, trans

If this principle is combined with the original result, the Diodorian concept of modality, $\nabla q \Rightarrow (q \vee Fq)$, we get, firstly, that possibility implies actuality or futurity, and, secondly, that futurity implies necessary futurity. In this way every possible, but presently false, statement becomes necessary! This result is even more radical than Michael's conclusion of modal collapse and it is, of course, an unacceptable consequence of Prior's reconstruction. These difficulties in reconstructing the Master Argument are rather surprising as possibility is usually understood to mean truth in at least one future branch. This definition seems to be in best accordance with the Diodorian conclusion, and it would thus be expected that it is a feasible project to vindicate the definition on the basis of some branch semantics. But, as we have seen, the project is not feasible: neither with Diodorean premises, nor with any other premises coherent with a branched concept of time.

Lars Bo Gundersen

This, I think, should be seen as evidence for the intricate difficulties that are always involved in implementing a combined tense-modal semantic. Any reconstruction of the Master Argument will have to make use of a combined language in order to derive futurity from modality. But there are reasons to think that it is impossible to develop a satisfactory semantics for such a combined language: On the basis of a linear model, it is possible to give a semantics for temporal expressions and hence to develop a tense logic. But it is impossible to give an exhaustive semantics for the modal expressions within such a linear model. Necessity and possibility cannot be exhaustively determined by merely a model of the actual world. It has to be determined relative to a model that is capable of representing otherworldly facts as well. But on a linear model only one world, the actual, can be represented.

By recurring to a branching model, on the other hand, it is at least to some extent possible to account for the meaning of modal expressions; this is usually made by likening possible worlds to future branches in the model. The past tense can likewise be given a satisfactory semantic on such a view. But problems emerge with respect to the meaning of future tense statements. In branching semantics we are offered two distinct proposals for this purpose: we can, as on an Ockhamist account, equate future truth with truth on at least one future branch; or we can, as on a Peircean account, equate future truth with truth on every future branch. But neither of them is especially successful: A claim that there is going to be a space battle tomorrow might very well come true although there is not a space battle on every future branch; likewise it might very well prove false although it is true on one future branch.

So neither the Ockhamist nor the Peircean semantics for future tense expressions appear intuitively appealing. That there is going to be a space battle tomorrow cannot possibly be read off a branched model. It can be derived from the fact that there is a space battle tomorrow on every future branch, but it is not synonymous with it. Rather than being evaluated relative to some manifested features of the model, it should be evaluated relative to the dynamic process of branch attrition. It is possible to picture that in a model, e.g. a model which represents the result of this branch attrition. But this would only lead us back to a linear theory in which we will have to refrain from giving a semantic account for the modal expressions.

Lars Bo Gundersen

References

1.   Michael, F.S., 1976, in: *American Philosophical Quarterly.*
2.   Prior, A.N., 1967: *Past, Present and Future*, Oxford.

Notes

---

[1] As when we talk about "possible events" or "a necessary being"
[2] As when we talk about "the possibility that something happens"

Lars Bo Gundersen

ANINDITA NIYOGI BALSLEV

TIME AND 'ANADI SAMSARA'
INDIAN VIEWS IN A CONTEXT OF CROSS-CULTURAL EXCHANGE

Seen in a cross-cultural and multi-disciplinary context, the body of ideas that is available to us concerning the themes of time and creation is remarkably rich. Hence this is a conspicuously fruitful area of investigation for initiating a conversation among philosophers and physicists, cosmologists and theologians. It is so not only because an enormous amount of material is readily accessible today from diverse sources but also because we are dealing here with a set of ideas where the concerns of scholars seem to glide away from their carefully drawn-out domains and intersect with other areas of human thinking. I suppose that we have all come across such writings where cosmological questions seem to unexpectedly take on a theological turn or that the physicist and the philosopher seem to draw closer to one another, struggling to fuse or to maintain the distinction between knowledge and belief.

To peruse the story of the philosophical wondering about the question "Wherefrom this creation?" [Kutah ayam visrsti?] - as the Vedic seer posed it - leads us to a wide range of answers. This intellectual journey is fascinating as it leads us, in a sense, to the network of ideas that form the crux of diverse thought-traditions. It discloses to us on the one hand, traditions that put forward the idea of a world-process having an absolute beginning, i.e., a beginning out of nothing, and on the other hand, to the startlingly different formulation of the notion of a beginningless world-process. Leaving aside for the moment the query about the significance and implication of such formulations, and resisting the urge to unmask such opposed expressions, let us note that, in both cases, what remains of central importance is their respective concern for the question of time. As a consequence, human reflections on the theme of time can be seen to have a very long history - perhaps longer than most other themes - introduced already in a period when there was no well-drawn demarcation between philosophy and science. Even when such disciplinary distinctions arose the question of time still remained at the centre of conceptualisation since "whether we are thinking of the nature of Nature or of the nature of the self, we cannot escape thinking of the nature of time" - as Charles Sherover (1975) has rightly observed.

In order to situate in a wider inter-cultural setting some of the basic ideas regarding these issues from the classical Indian sources, the strategy that I would like to adopt in the compass of this short paper is as follows:

First I will retrieve some of the exchanges between pre-Christian Greek and Judeo-Christian thinkers with regard to similar queries. This brief allusion to the immediate response of the pre-Christian Greeks to the idea of *creatio ex nihilo* is useful for discerning a few characteristics of classical Greek thought which resemble Indian modes of conceptualisations in many important ways.

Gradually, focus will be put on the technical theological significance of the idea of *creatio ex nihilo* from Judeo-Christian sources, in order to bring out the underlying concerns and their affinities and differences with some of the predominant modes of reflections on analogous issues in the Indian context.

Finally, I would like to make a few observations with the hope of indicating a conceptual space where the bridge-building task between these traditions may eventually be undertaken.

It is indeed amazing to note, as relevant literature amply exemplifies, how the discussions concerning the origin of the world-process lead, imperceptibly as it were, to the formulations of ideas about 'beginning', or 'beginninglessness'. In the process these ideas get impregnated with various related concerns revealing the multiple layers of complexities pertaining to the question of time and creation. I am aware that even the attempt to draw a bare outline of the network of ideas which reflect those concerns that we all seem to share, requires collaborative work. It seems to me that projects directed to an authentic comprehension of these ideas, which have been consequential to the unfolding of diverse cultural traditions, still remain largely neglected. Undoubtedly, such undertakings that seek to deal adquately with diverse cultural traditions will prove not only to be a difficult challenge but also to be an enormously enriching and beneficial collective experience.

Leaving aside all the subtle nuances of the doctrines of *creatio ex nihilo* in their early formulations, let me first enquire into how that expression came to be formulated. Erich Frank, in his book entitled *Philosophical Understanding and Religious Truth* (1945), writes this is "a rational expression evidently coined as counterpart of the philosophical formula *nihil ex nihilo fit*. It is foreign to Scripture where the idea of creation did not yet constitute a philosophical problem. It first occurs in the second century B.C. in the Greek version of Maccabeans (7.28). Subsequently, the formula is used by Christian thinkers, whenever they wish to express their idea of creation in terms of Greek philosophy."

Anindita Niyogi Balslev

What is to be noted is how the Christian theologians insisted on the idea, to quote St. Gregory of Nyssa, that "Non-existence (was) changed by the Divine Power into Being". But this idea did not find favor with the Greeks. "Nothing is ever produced by divine power out of nothing", said Lucretius. As Richard Sorabji writes (1985), the view that the universe has a beginning, "was denied by everybody in European Antiquity outside the Judeo-Christian tradition. That tradition's belief that God could have given a beginning to the material universe would have seemed to most Greeks to be an absurdity."

Whatever internal divergences there were in their own accounts about the material universe (recall all the speculations in the pre-Socratic period of Greek thought), there are two points in the controversy which are of special interest for the purpose of this paper: One pertains to the principle to which all rational thinking is supposed to conform, viz. that of the *ex nihilo nihil fit*, and the other is about what implications we may draw from this concerning the question of time.

The controversies among the pre-Christian Greek and the Christian thinkers have been preserved and these form a lengthy record. But instead of following up this story, I shall now draw your attention to the *Indian* scene. If a steadfast adherence to the principle of *ex nihilo nihil fit* - which Aristotle, in his Physics, claimed to be an idea about which all physicists agree - is a characteristic of pre-Christian Greek thought, it equally holds true of the Indian conceptual world.

Right from the earliest documents available to us, we see a record of an intensive speculation leading to a rejection of all those views about spontaneous, arbitrary origination which maintained that the occurence of an event has no necessary dependence on anything else. The fallacies of this mode of thinking were exposed in detail. Instead it was argued that the fact that an event occurs only at a particular time and neither always nor at any other time can be accounted for solely with reference to an antecedent, necessary and invariable cause.

However, the philosophical schools that appeared later in the history of Indian thought, within the Brahmanical, Buddhist and Jaina traditions, developed different views about time and causality (as would be expected in the case of any major philosophical tradition).

Nevertheless, they held in common the view that a contingent entity (which is sometimes there and sometimes not) must have a cause. Only that which is ever-present, viz. the eternal, or that which is never-present, viz. the fictitous, can be said to be uncaused.

Anindita Niyogi Balslev

To the question whether a 'cause' can be of the nature of non-being, a host of argumentation was forwarded to demonstrate the absurdities that would follow from such a position. The records of all these reasonings are carefully saved in the Indian literature, which testifies that there was unanimous agreement in favor of the idea that "being cannot come out of nothing".

It is indeed of great interest to read the philosophical arguments offered by both the Indian and the Greek traditional thinkers concerning why the idea of an absolute beginning of the world was not forwarded and notice the overlaps. First of all that would be a transgression of the priciple, 'being cannot come out of nothing' [cf. Bhagavadgita 2/16 : Nāsato' vidyate bhāvo]. It is possible to cite from various Brahmanical sources, but likewise from the Buddhist and Jaina literature, statements in support of the same idea.

Thus, despite many divergences, the Indian thought-traditions are in agreement that no absolute beginning can be attributed to the world-process. One important way to understand the idea of a beginningless world-process is to recognise that it implies there never was a time when the world was not. Note that apart from various logical arguments, which undoubtedly exerted considerable influence on all cosmological speculations in the Indian context, there are also important ethico-theological considerations supporting the notion of a 'beginningless world-process'.

But, before I proceed to explore some of these ideas, let me refer to the notion of cosmological cycles that played an important role in Indian culture as a whole. This is related to the widespread idea of repeated creation and dissolution of the world-process. One encounters a grand cosmological model where each world cycle is conceived in terms of billions of human years. It is important to comprehend how this idea is used in a soteriological framework. Indian mythology makes a lot out of this idea of world-cycle [Kalpa] by infusing the vast time, as measured in astronomical terms, with human significance. An interested reader can find any number of such narratives in the Puranas.

Unfortunately, this idea of cosmological cycle has sometimes been confused with the notion of cyclic time. Arnold Toynbee, to mention only one example, misconstrues the Puranic idea by taking it to be, as he writes (1972), "a philosophy of sheer recurrences, which intrigued without ever quite captivating the Hellenic mind, came to dominate the Indic mind". In fact, St. Augustine has repudiated a Greek (pre-Christian) view of 'circular time' claiming exact recurrence not only of cosmological processes, but also of individual destinies. Although the idea of generic recurrence is present, there is no idea of a mechanical recurrence of specific phenomena in Indian thought.

Anindita Niyogi Balslev

The idea of Karma implying efficacy of human action forbids that possibility. I have discussed this question elsewhere in great detail.[1]

However, as a word of caution, let me restate here that a perusal of the relevant literature shows that the attempts to situate the major thought-traditions in a global frame on the basis of the supposedly distinct cultural experience of time, have often resulted in setting these up against each other. Thus, it is commonplace to maintain that the Indo-Hellenic time is 'cyclic', as opposed to the Judeo-Christian understanding of time as 'linear'. This unwarranted use of time-metaphors has created serious obstacles for cross-cultural understanding and has blocked inter-religious exchanges.

What is even more disturbing, in the context of these improper metaphorical designations of cultural experience of time, is to note how the expressions 'linear' and 'cyclic' have gradually ceased to be simple time-metaphors and have come to be associated with such concepts as that of history, that of progress, and even that of salvation. A creative conversation, by consciously avoiding these age-old cliches, is needed to make room for fresh exchanges enabling the participants to appreciate the inner dynamism of alternative modes of thinking about this multi-faceted problem.

An outstanding characteristic of the conceptual world of India is to be seen in the weaving of a network of ideas that not only combines distinctly different views of time with various contending notions of creation and annihilation, being and becoming, space and causality, etc., but also in the manner in which it projects views concerning eternity and timelessness with a sharp sense of philosophical acuity.

Reference could be made to two Brahmanical schools, Sānkhya and Vaiśeṣika, to exemplify how, despite a common point of departure, they came up with different views about time and causality. For the Vaiśeṣika the effect is interpreted as a new 'beginning' [Ārambha] of that which was not there before the causal operation had brought it forth (hence, the theory is termed Asatkāryavāda). Note that the occurance of an effect [karya], the beginning of a contingent entity, is an event-in-time. Further analysis led the school to put forward the notion of an absolute time. The ontological features of this idea of a time *per se* were carefully noted. It is said to have no beginning or end, and to be all-pervasive, indivisible, and unitary. A distinction was made between this idea of absolute time [Mahākāla] and that of relative, conventional, time [Vyavahārika kala]. All conventional practices of time-divisions such as a minute, an hour, a day, a month, or a year, and so forth, are made possible by the use of a standard motion; the solar motion is the most rampant.

Anindita Niyogi Balslev

Those who shared this position all thought that without postulation of the objective reality of an absolute time, we will be confronted with a static universe. This event-in-time conception, however, is conspicuously absent in the literature of Sānkhya, held to be the oldest school of Indian philosophy. According to Sānkhya a philosophical account of change and becoming, or an explanation of the use of the three time-phases, past, present, and future, does not require the postulation of an empty time as an ontological category. These phenomena need to be understood, they insist, in the light of the Sānkhya theory of causality (Satkāryavāda). Unlike in Vaiśeṣika, the effect in this context is perceived not to be an entirely new beginning, but an actualization of that which was potentially existent prior to the causal operation.[2]

It is of great interest for our present purpose to note the manner in which the idea of beginning is interpreted in each case. For Vaiśeṣika, a beginning is always an event-in-time. They thought that without reference to an absolute, objective time no beginning is possible, or even conceivable, whereas - for Sānkhya - a beginning is only an emergence, an actualisation of that which was potentially present in its cause, there being absolutely no need for the postulation of a concept of empty time as a locus for temporal absence of an effect prior to the causal operation. Space, time and matter are aspects of 'Prakṛti' [Nature]. The Sānkhya understanding of nature precludes a pluralistic view of Prakṛti.[3] Both of these theoretical moves - divergent as these are - are made within a conceptual frame where no absolute beginning is attributed to the world-process, as both reject the idea of a beginning out of nothing.

If we now turn our gaze to the inter-cultural context and ask once more for further precision with regard to the conceptualisation of the idea of a 'beginning' of the universe, we find that it is common to conceive of a notion of beginning with reference to time. This common sense view also has its philosophical counterparts; among such formulations, note the first antinomy formulated by Kant in *Critique of Pure Reason*: "Since the beginning is an existence which is preceded by a time in which the thing is not, there must have been a previous time in which the world was not, i.e. an empty time."

This also explains why those who could not make any sense of the theological doctrine of *creatio ex nihilo*, asked, as quoted by Augustine: "What was God doing before he made the heaven and earth?". Augustine took the cited question seriously; commenting on Genesis, "In the beginning Thou madest the Heaven and earth", he boldly stated: "At no time then hadst Thou not made anything, because time itself Thou madest". This theological answer emphasizes the absolute dependence of the creation on the Creator.

Anindita Niyogi Balslev

Thus it seems that both in humanity's past and in present endeavours the search for the significance of human existence, or the failure to find it, is intertwined with the question of the Vedic seer: "Wherefrom this creation?" In fact, it is possible to sketch a narrative of the formation of diverse traditions of beliefs taking this theme as a point of departure.

Gazing at this wide canvas where a range of ideas about creation seem to be vying with each other to capture our attention, I would like to urge that the challenge that remains before us is to undertake in collaboration a cross-cultural intellectual adventure seeking to build bridges between these traditions. Startling as the contrasts of these formulations that confront us are, regarding whether this 'creation' has an absolute beginning or not, both views deserve conceptual exploration of religious consciouness in a soteriological context - a large topic into which I cannot delve in the compass of this short paper.

However, let me briefly take up the ethico-religious considerations that are operating in support of the idea of 'a beginningless world-process' [Anādi Samsāra]. Given the fact that the Brahmanical tradition holds this position in common with the Buddhist and the Jaina traditions, and granted further that the non-theistic schools of thought - whether it be Brahmanical, Buddhhist, or Jaina - had in no way the possibility of using a *creatio ex nihilo* paradigm in the absence of an Almighty God, the interesting question is, why couldn't any theistic Brahmanical school make use of that idea?

In fact, a conceptual possibility of this type was not unknown to them. Such a philosophical position called Īśvaravāda ("God-ism") has been referred to in the compendium of Madhavacarya, called Sarvadarsanasamgraha. However, the mainstream Brahmanical thinkers have unanimously rejected this position. A critical examination of the human situation where disparities and differences of various sorts are there right from the very moment of birth, induced them to argue that a God who creates *ex nihilo* must be the one who alone is responsible for such a creation. Consequently, such an Almighty God can be charged with being cruel and biased, conferring favors to some and depriving others of the same.

In other words, the idea of God for the Indian theistic thinkers, is not one of simple arbitrary power, it also entails mercy, compassion, and justice. Thus a deepening of an ethical query about God as well as about the human situation made it impossible to have any room for the idea of a first creation with an absolute beginning in Indian thought. Note in this connection that the idea of Karma, in theistic as well as in non-theistic soteriology, is a pan-Indian concept built into the idea of a beginningless world-process.

Anindita Niyogi Balslev

At this point let me repeat that the question of 'beginning' and 'beginninglessness', whether it is to be attributed to the world-process or not, are ideas that are prompted by as much ethico-religious as by cosmological considerations. A philosophical encounter of world-religions will be required to deal with these issues. A very interesting sequel of ideas pertaining to the diverse interpretations of the notion of creation is that of time and causality.

In the theological context of different traditions across cultures, one often runs into the idea that the temporal is totally dependent on the timeless and that the latter is the cause of the former. The resolution of these apparently contradictory formulations that we have been dealing with is to be sought at this juncture. What is interesting to notice here is the theological reading of the Idea of Cause - *not* as that which is 'temporally' prior but in the sense of being the indispensable ground for the occurrence of the effect.

Let me finally observe that time is not only a multi-dimensional issue, but of great significance for the self-understanding of cultures as a whole. This is precisely why it is not only St. Augustine who comes up with a triumphant declaration that he has found the answer to the "Why not sooner?" question through the comprehension that God does not create in time, but is Himself its source, its creator - but even Leibniz seems to think that, by for-warding a relational concept of time, he was not only providing an alternative to the absolute time of Newton but was also answering the "Why not sooner?" -question. If one asks such a question, "We should reply", Leibniz wrote, "that his inference would be true if time were something apart from temporal things, for it would be impossible that there should be reasons why things should have been applied to certain instants than to others, when their succession remained the same. But this itself proves that instants apart from things are nothing, and that they only consist in the successive order of things."

Even today, when certain physicists and cosmologists speak of the commencement of time, or even suggest of an absolute beginning of the universe, it does smack of the same urge that a given cultural soil provokes.

Conclusion

The theme of 'time and creation' indeed seems to be particularly well-suited for initiating a conversation among diverse philosophical and religious traditions. Instead of continuing with the stereotypes that any given tradition cherishes about the 'otherness' of other traditions, what we need is a re-examination of these construals of otherness and the opportunity for deeper acquaintance with the historic consciousness of specific thought-traditions.

Anindita Niyogi Balslev

A glance at the contemporary global scene can convince any critical onlooker that the early formulations of philosophers and theologians are not merely of antiquarian interest, these are still forces to reckon with and are to be perceived as contributing to the various sorts of group-identities. Perhaps a cautious review of the stock of philosophical and religious views, myths and symbols concerning these key-issues in a global framework could lay bare before us the distinct conceptual contents that constitute the multifarious paradigms, enabling us to recognise the inevitability of this multiplicity of views for unmasking time-experience. It is obvious that such an enterprise calls for a co-operation of scholars trained in multiple traditions as well as disciplines, allowing the possibility of fresh responses to perennial questions.

An increasing academic involvement with fundamental themes such as time and creation is likely to have significant impact on the meeting of world-religions, perhaps far beyond the confines of the academic scene. It might very well create new avenues of thinking that could benefit all those who find themselves at the cross-road of cultures.

References

1.   Charles Sherover, ed., 1975: *The Human Experience of Time*, NY.
2.   Erich Frank, 1945: *Philosophical Understanding & Religious Truth*, Oxford, pp. 74-75.
3.   Richard Sorabji, 1985: *Time, Creation & the Continuum*, London, pp. 193.
4.   Arnold Toynbee, 1972: *A Study of History* (rev. and abr. by the author and J. Caplan), N.Y.
5.   St. Augustine, 1966: *De Civitate Dei* (P. Levine, transl.), Cambridge.
6.   For Sankhya, Prakrti is one [Eka], although of composite nature cf. my 1983: *A Study of Time in Indian Philosophy*, Wiesbaden.
7.   Immanuel Kant, 1970: *Critique of Pure Reason*, Kemp-Smith transl.

Notes

---

[1] See my paper "Time and the Hindu Experience", printed in *Religion and Time*, Balslev & Mohanty eds., E.J.Brill 1993.
[2] Note that precisely this idea of 'prior absence' [Prāgabhāva] as a temporal idea was advocated by the Nyāya-Vaiśeṣika schools.

Anindita Niyogi Balslev

CHRISTIAN LINK

GOD AND TIME
THEOLOGICAL APPROACHES TO THE PROBLEM OF TIME

Are your days like the days of mortals, your years like human years?
asks Job (10.5). We know the answer: No, God's time is different, for God's
years 'endure through all generations', his days 'have no end' (Ps 102.24-7).
Human life moves and develops in time which divides us into future and past.
This is limited time. Our lives are 'only a breath' (Job 7.7); human days are
'like a passing shadow' (Ps 144.4).

Time, the fundamental structure of the world, bestows upon the world
its finitude and frailty, its triviality, and its need of salvation. Time 'tends
towards not-being',[1] and is dominated by the past. That is why the experience
of time is foremost an experience of suffering. From this springs the certainty,
held from Plato to Hegel, that "true" being - the "meaning" of being - can be
recognised only in contrast to time, not in terms of time.

In the same way, the aim of human religious and philosophical
endeavour has been deliverance from the power of time - a paradoxical aim, if
deliverance means actual liberation from a context whose very universality
makes escape impossible. For the dominion of past over future is universal in
the world as we know it and defines the 'compulsory character' (Adorno) of
existing reality. That is why the hope of human beings, labouring under their
past, has always been founded upon the coming of a "new" time, and on the
idea of "eternity" as absolutely different to time.

The extent to which this hope shapes the kernel of the biblical
message can be seen from the opening of Mark's gospel which summarises the
core of Jesus' preaching and thus the highest expectations of God's salvific
intervention in the words: *The time is fulfilled, and the kingdom of God has
come near; repent and believe in the good news* (Mk 1.15). Nowhere else
does the gospel focus so clearly on the taking place (or, to coin a phrase, the
taking time) not of new phenomena in time, but of time itself. These words are
related to those of Paul: *When the fullness of time had come, God sent his son*
(Gal 4.4). The salvific significance of God's incarnation in the man Jesus is to
be recognised in time, as time's 'fulfilment' (*kairos*). The unique importance
of the work of salvation is interpreted in terms of statements about time.[2]
But how? None of the keywords - neither 'nearness', nor 'fulfilment' - can be
interpreted in terms of a traditional understanding of time.

The message of the fulfilment of time clearly cannot be understood as a statement about the course of time, but must be seen as a statement about time's content. The question which will be considered is the following: What is time, if birth and development, maturing and decay, shape its nature? What happens to time, when in it not this event or that, but God himself, comes into the world? How does God fill time? Can God fulfil time in the same way as things or events which belong to our daily experience? And further: How can God enter into our time at all? How can he be prophesied and proclaimed as the one who comes, when, according to biblical tradition (Ex 20.4), he cannot be incorporated into any image of our world?

1.   World's time and God's time

To accept the biblical message about the coming God is to enter into the complexity of this theme. This becomes clear if one compares the biblical understanding with an interpretation which answers these questions by focussing on our own experience of time. In Sophocles' *Aias* we read:

> *Time in its slow illimitable course*
> *Brings all to light and buries it again.*[3]

Here time is encountered as *nomen actionis*, as an active element which brings growth and later concealment. Time is the power which gives birth to everything: in Greek it is *physis*, in Latin *natura*. For that reason the two fundamental modes of time are not, in fact, past and future, but rather 'bringing to birth' and 'giving over to decay' - in Plato: *genesis* and *phthora* - i.e. processes running through different phases named 'earlier' or 'later'.

The Greeks did not see time as an abstract series of temporal points, but as a dimension of the appearance, development, and disappearance of that which truly is. So understood, time is a phenomenon of context: everything that exists, exists "in" time. To ask about the essence of time is to ask about the origin and the composition of this context. The philosophical definition, accordingly, sees time as 'an eternal moving image of that Eternity (*Aion*) which remains forever the same'.[4] Aion is lifetime, the time which makes up a life, although here it is the life, not of a human being, but of God, which lasts forever. Put concisely, Aion is the eternal present, *nunc stans aeternum*, time before it became temporal. The 'long and illimitable course' of time (*chronos*), which allows appearances to grow in the world, is only an image. In it, the Aion is represented, and it is this representation of the Aion which defines the essence and course of passing time. Here it makes sense to ask the questions What *is* time? And *what* is it?

Christian Link

In his oft-quoted meditation on time, Augustine expressly addresses this question while at the same time giving the problem an angle that affects all attempts - especially theological ones - to find a solution.[5] For he phrases his question about the essence of time in such a way that time is isolated as an object of thinking, which means that it has to be understood as a substance. But because the substance is precisely that which remains identical through the changing of accidents with time, a problem arises: 'Paradoxically, the metaphysical axiom of the timelessness of truth is already present in this question of the essence of time'.[6] The true being of time must, therefore, be that aspect of time which is not affected by time. Kant paraphrased this idea with the words: 'time itself remains and does not change.' For this reason he defined time as a pure form of intuition existing before all experience.[7]

Time is thus precisely described in terms of those things which are experienced in it, and so the chosen route is that which describes time as a sort of empty formula into which series of events, 'data', must first be entered. Apart from the fact that a qualitative differentiation of the modes of time, as we doubtless experience them, is no longer possible, the question of how God, once made a part of this scheme, can be distinguished from other objects of experience (whether through a larger, or even infinite, quantum of empty duration) simply cannot be answered. On the basis of these theories it is impossible even to pose the question of time in the same terms as those used by theology to address the problem set by God's 'coming'.

God "is" not "there" in the same way that the world or human beings are there. He comes with his name to the world. When the Bible speaks of the one *who is, and was, and is to come* (Rev 1.4) the progression has an internal order, but not one in which the first element can be recognised as meaning the *eternal* Son of God (which is how Augustine interpreted this verse). The point here is about God's "being" in time, in yesterday and today. Otherwise our thoughts would have to push their way into a reality which lies behind this name, and seek there the explanation of what 'appears' in time. God's 'transcendence' would be another world, a world behind our world.

This idea is clearly contradicted throughout the biblical tradition. God disempowers the order of being, which in Greek terms has no other status than the revealed and the concealed. *God as God is essentially revealed in his coming,*[8] and this coming precedes every present.

God's time is time before every present. How - and here our problems begin - can the relationship between God and world then be described?

Christian Link

How is God's coming experienced, and is "experience" in fact an appropriate approach, one that can bring us close to and make us aware of God's time? For the popular concept of experience (however imprecisely it is usually defined) cannot be separated from the power of the present to bring unity, or from the idea of making present and unity.

From its first to its last pages, the Bible reports the ways in which God "breaks into our time", and there is no doubt that these are experienced. One need only think of the calls of the prophets or of the New Testament parables. The things which are experienced here take place on the level of the world's time, and for that reason they remain ambiguous. Our experience does not tell us whether we are really dealing here with God rather than with a product of our own imagination. What we experience is in the medium of the world's time, and thus familiar to us, but at the same time it is a pointer to a different sort of time: the totally unfamiliar time of God. If we are to experience the arrival of this time, its breaking into our time, we have to look beyond all our ordinary experiences and the everyday contexts of time.

In theology, a simple recourse to experience very quickly becomes a betrayal, leading to the confusion of appearance and content. The God who refuses every image cannot enter the temporal context of consciousness and become present in the same way as a historical phenomenon.

2.   Time beyond consciousness

The most precise identification of these difficulties has been offered by Lévinas. His philosophy focuses on the imageless God, to whose transcendence our consciousness must first "awake". Traditional attempts to think about God have failed, God is not an idea subordinate to our understanding. He is, as Lévinas formulated it in the radicality of early dialectic theology, the *absolute other*,[9] from which I am separated, which stands, incomprehensible, in opposition to me; this outside cannot be integrated into my consciousness. He is the God whose face Moses was not allowed to see (Ex 33.20); the God who in an absolute sense has "passed by". The idea of God is no object of philosophical, let alone historical, "memory". How can one speak of the time of this God without confusing it with that which is temporal?

Lévinas speaks of a past 'before time', one that was 'never present',[10] and thereby draws the consequence from that theophany (Ex 33) which gives to the senses nothing that experience can measure. For this past is not a mode of our calendar time. It is a form of time which touches us when, "in search of the infinite" (without making it an aim), we come into relationship with God.

Christian Link

Then we have an experience, in 'the only radical meaning of that word',[11] namely an experience which takes us out of ourselves by questioning our familiar categories and putting them on the line.

Lévinas' is the most coherent modern attempt to solve the theological problem of time. It evades the time context of consciousness which loses itself in a river of events, for it stands in a tradition of thought which sees, not time as closed in upon itself, but moments which are open to eternity. Time is bound to eternity, as the life of the individual is bound to society, and from eternity shines a light which breaks into time, keeping time open. Messianism places human beings in this absolute instant, this time break, in which 'deeds (human action) and time (divine action) encounter each other'.[12] This break affects human consciousness. Here philosophical reflection begins: How does eternity - "older" than any thinkable present - break into time? How does the incomprehensible transcendent God come to be thought?

Transcendence - and this is the significant change to take place here - is understood by Lévinas as an 'event' possessing its own time structure. 'Transcendence takes place (*se passe*)'.[13] In the wounds and traumas of a consciousness marked, like Jacob at Jabbok (Gen 32.25), by God's "passing", transcendence can be recognised as an ineradicable trace. The metaphysical tradition sees transcendence as the breaking through of an eternity which is beyond time. God's time is the *nunc stans aeternum*, and here transcendence is understood to be radically temporal. The questioning of consciousness is at the same time the touching of the consciousness by the "un-fore-thinkable" past of God, which has no origin in the time of thought. This past cannot be "remembered"; it cannot be brought into the present; and therefore it cannot enter any present of our world. The meaning of the God-idea discloses itself only "an-archically", without any origin in the consciousness and therefore "always already older" as every manifestation which reaches our memory. Its time lies beyond the border of *chronos*.

But if God's time - eternity - is the 'source and refuge of the past',[14] how can it affect us, as is clearly assumed in the ethical turning to the other? How is God's coming to the world, which fills the Bible from beginning to end, thinkable? The theological concept of time which would be most appropriate to this event could be described with the paradox of 'the closeness or arrival of one who is absent'.[15] But how can such closeness come about? Just as in the imagery of prophecy it is suggested that, when the eternal one leaves his own place, under his feet *the mountains will melt under him and the valleys will burst open as wax near the fire melts* (Mi 1.3-4).

Christian Link

Without the images: in the moment in which consciousness splinters and its conviction of freedom is broken, its context ceases to impose its needs and worries, and the order of our present world loses all its weight. In this disintegration - that is the point most deserving of thought - occurs the transition to the 'reign of an invisible king', namely the reign of the 'non-contemporary, i.e., non-present God'.[16] His kingdom, as is said in the Gospel of John (18.36), is 'not of this world'. With this transition comes the transition to a time which overtakes the context of the world because it is - always already - ahead of the time of my own consciousness and my own actions. In this time those things which, today, under the pressure of the world's reality which we all know, take refuge in sickness, pain, and suffering, are preserved and finally attain their rights. The philosophical name for this time is 'the time of the other'.[17] Its biblical name, also according to Lévinas, is the time of 'God's reign'.[18] Unforethinkable past becomes unimaginable future.

3.   The fulfilment of time

God's time is seen by Lévinas as coming from beyond the horizon of our history. According to biblical witness, God's time is eternity, which until now has ruled as 'other to itself', not as an eternity of infinite, empty duration, but as time that preserves and saves, a function which even in ancient thought was seen to annihilate 'the uncountable row of years and the flight of times' (Horace). This is the time of history which has been freed for itself; time which makes whole that which was only fragmentary. This is time which in no way allows itself to be separated from the content of the lives that are lived in it, and so it is described in the New Testament as the 'fulfilment' of time.

This fulfilment is certainly not a state; nor is it a duration which is somehow available, or with which we can reckon - even if only in the way that the mystics reckoned with the 'eternal moment'. It remains an event, a present, which evades our grasp. Therefore the Bible - rightly - does not speak of God's reign in terms of a manifest presence. The gospels proclaim the nearness of this reign, and by doing so confront thinkers with almost insurmountable problems,[19] for in this nearness 'now' and 'then' are related in a way which contradicts normal conceptions of the relationship of different modes of time. The kingdom of God is 'near' and yet it has 'arrived'; it is future and present at the same time. This relationship must be understood in such a way that the present nature of the kingdom in no way relativises its future nature. We cannot anticipate its future, and yet it shapes the present. Nevertheless, this present *is* the nearness of the kingdom.

Christian Link

Theunissen has spoken of the 'proleptic' structure of the present, in that what occurs is shaped by 'the occurrence of time in itself'.[20] The presence of 'coming' time - a present which is no longer a representation - defines the true time-structure of the kingdom of God. For that reason, its coming or approaching does not have the character of an appearance and cannot be made comprehensible from the perspective of the idea of epiphany, as can the present of the platonic *Aion*.[21] If one wishes to find a comparison, it might be said that it takes place much more as a kind of touching, like the sounding of a tuning fork, which affects all three modes of the time which is known to us, so that the hope of the living includes also the dead in the most distant past and the promise made to them of a certain future (Is 26.19).

One may have a particular problem with the idea that the kingdom of God has a temporality which does not make itself comprehensible historically. This temporality has no common measure with the time of our history, and that, precisely, is the theological point. For it is in this incommensurability that the temporality of God's kingdom matches the biblical God who does not allow himself to be categorised through any image of history. Therefore, it is at the point where the time of his kingdom touches our historical present that a new description of the world, such as that which is offered to us by the parables of the New Testament, is born.

Parables are theological discoveries. They portray the world as it looks when God's future imposes its conditions, the world as it looks when it has been touched by the fulfilment of time. Everyday happenings then become 'what they were not before, and what they cannot be in, and of, themselves. ... the material [of these events] is everywhere transformed, and there is an equation of the kingdom with them, and of them with the kingdom'.[22] The world breaks through the dimensions of its reality into a possibility which does not belong in any thinkable way to the sphere of what we already know, but which imposes itself upon us from outside - from a future beyond our future - and in doing so destroys any conceptually constructed image.

In the parables, God's incomprehensible future creates a model of that which is to come. As long as we attempt to bring about the future through our own plans and predictions, it remains shackled to the consequences of our decisions and is threatened with suffocation by the past. When the future touches the time of God's reign, it is liberated from these shackles, and in its light the world is seen to be what it was 'in the beginning' - that is: *creation*.

Christian Link

4.   **The time of creation**

Creation is the theological name for the aspect of the world which, as nature, is the object of scientific research. But this is not simply a different, religious, name for the same phenomenon. The name also stands for a different perspective on experience, and this perspective, I have suggested above, is opened up by a different shape of time.

According to Kant's classical definition, nature is: 'the existence of things, in so far as it is defined by general laws'.[23] This description sets nature under the leadership of a certain mode of time, the present, and upon the same level as the representation of logical concepts (although this cannot be shown in detail here). In this perspective, it is precisely those aspects of nature's past and its future which show themselves in the present - namely the actual and the possible - that are experienced. In their conventional form, natural sciences and technology thus describe the world as the embodiment of all 'objectifiable' phenomena, for they know only one form of time, a linear duration from the past into every possible present.

The biblical description of the world as creation moves on a different level of representation showing us things against a different temporal horizon. It is the expectation of a contingent, inaccessible future - a horizon of possibility, which opens itself up before us - which lays open the world as it transcends its obvious nature in its hidden character as God's creation. This is what gives the world, as created, both its meaning and its rights.

My thoughts here draw upon the suggestion, made by Thomas F. Torrance, that it is necessary 'to operate with a ... distinction between created time and uncreated "time", that is, between the created time defined by its contingent nature, and the uncreated "time" of the eternal life of God defined by his divine nature'.[24] I also follow Torrance in that I assume that God's "time" 'penetrates and embraces' the contingent time of the created world. What effects does this distinction have for our understanding of time?

a.   Firstly, it has a formal parallel in the theory of open systems ('non-equilibrium thermodynamics') which offers the widest horizon against which the question of creation can currently be discussed. These systems are characterised by the irreversibility of the processes which they describe. The future state of the system is always different from its present state. In contrast to closed systems, open systems show the direction of time - from the past, towards the future - which means that the structure of time is defined in terms of a qualitative difference between future and past which can be 'experienced' in such systems.

Christian Link

The openness of the system is determined by temporality, in the original sense which shows itself in the move from one epoch to another (with the end of childhood we enter a new age). However, this temporality can no longer be represented in the linear parameters of classical physics. The most important discovery to be brought about by this insight into the structures of open systems has been the discontinuity between the classical concept of time (i.e. the empty time co-ordinate, which can "run" in both positive and negative directions) and evolution's concept of time. 'Tomorrow is no longer contained in today'.[25] As it appears in open systems, time points to a world which is open to the future. The theory intends to integrate 'the concept of history' with 'the concept of nature'. It only makes sense to speak of time and its future as being in principle open if there are reasons for assuming that the world, understood as becoming, is an anticipatory system, which cannot remain in any one state, but which goes on from any stage once attained to develop new, richer possibilities.

b.   Evolution gives us sufficient grounds for making this assumption. Today's knowledge indicates that time in physics is indeed more than a duration of certain courses of events which can be represented in terms of a continuous series of numbers (linear parameters). Instead, time is understood as the horizon which surrounds all that is. For everything that *is*, is *in* time. This simple statement loses its triviality if the three modes of time are understood in terms of the modalities of logic: the past is the region of the factual; the future is the realm of the possible; the present is the real, the ways in which phenomena appear. For now it can be seen that time not only *has* a structure, but *is* itself a structure. Time lies in the horizon of physics and must be describable with its media of representation.

The 'laws of nature', the context in which we encounter the structure and logic of time, would be impossible without the particular structure and logic of physical time. When we speak of the 'structure' of time, we are re-cognising something essential about time, without which the particular form of objectifiable experience would not exist - but we have not described time in its fullness. If we admit the existence of a "richer" time, for instance, that of everyday experience, then we extend our possibility of experience. We step beyond the world as it is conditioned by the laws of nature of physics into the world of art or religion.

Hence time is the horizon against which we experience all that we experience and think all that we think. How we experience and know and what we experience and know is dependent upon the time in which we move.

Christian Link

The forms in which what we sense appear - whether in the 'concepts' of physics or the 'revelation' of theology - can be understood as shapes of time. But then the methodological difference in the ways in which theology and natural science access one and the same world (and explain it as 'creation', or as 'nature') must be explicable in terms of the different ways in which time shows itself in theology and in natural science.

c.   The future is the most important of the three modes of time for the experience of the world as creation. In contrast to the traditional understanding of time, here the perspective does not allow the future to be understood as the consequence of the past; therefore, the future cannot strictly be seen as an analogus mode to our calendar time. Rather, as the condition of the possibility of all new things in an apparently closed relation of regularity and law, the future is at the same time the reason why 'now' the present becomes the past. It is the permanent presupposition for all facticity.

Here the familiar ideas are reversed: if the source of time itself manifests itself in the temporality of time, and in the becoming of the world, this future must be seen as the source from which time and the world spring and renew themselves (adventus).[26] As creation, the world lives from the giving of time. It takes place in the flowing of time, in the setting free of forms of time, which in turn reflect forms of the world. Here the future takes over the foundational function which classical metaphysics assigned to a necessary, timeless ground of the world. Theologically speaking, God's place in the world is the future - a future which remains irrevocable, even when it continually appears in the form of the present. It allows God's relationship to the world to be thought of in terms of time. All this implies that, following biblical tradition, God is understood not as one who somehow is, and who is thus necessary, but as one who is coming, and who is therefore free.

God cannot be introduced as a hypothesis for which we bear the burden of proof. Rather, God remains the foundation, who is not accessible to us, but who is the foundation of and basis for everything and who makes our explanations possible. To understand God as the source of a time unrolling itself means to expect that God comes close to this world in every moment of its temporal existence, in that he gives his time to our time to be the foundation of its future in the world. This is the point at which we make the link with the theory of open systems. Our world is dependent upon a source of its future. It realises itself in the duration of forms of time, both those which are already present and those which are contingently new, which we experience as evolution in the limited selection of what could be possible.

Christian Link

Seen like this, time can be said to be the common horizon against which theology and natural science move.

What consequences does this have for our understanding of time? The difference to the general understanding becomes particularly clear when one opens oneself to an experience which describes our status as creatures. In Ps 104.18ff it is said: *These all look to you ... When you hide your face, they are dismayed; when you take away their breath, they die and return to their dust. When you send forth your Spirit, they are created, and you renew the face of the ground.* If this experience is interpreted in the language, and against the background, of the European tradition, the deep difference to the familar 'Greek' understanding of the structures of time are clear at once.

Past and present are not part of a unity, or at least not of a unity which can be understood in terms of a self-evident presupposition about what is, from the perspective of what is now. Here the unity of time is clearly constructed differently from the way one would expect it to be understood by a neutral observer of the course of the world. From the viewpoint of the Psalms, both dimensions of time break apart over the experience that the future in no way comes about as a consequence of the past.

It seems here to be impossible to see the past as no-longer-being and the future as not-yet-being from the perspective of the being of now in the way that Greek thought does. The idea that a regular flow of time has its only being in the now of the present, and therefore knows no qualitative difference between past and future, is unthinkable to the Hebrew thinker. What is experienced as time here disintegrates into the past, for which human beings are grateful, and that which is to come, which they expect from God. Understood in this way, creation is *ex nihilo* in a basic sense, by eliminating the possibility that the world, having no future, could again become dust.

The time that makes possible the future for which all that has been created "waits" is clearly not itself one of the modes of our experiential time, but one of the conditions of that time. It is the time of beginning of creation, and is thus at a distance from the time concept of our everyday life. It can be strictly distinguished from the time parameter of modern physics by the fact that this time cannot be used to observe, or to measure, intervals of time. Unlike physical time, this time is not available to us in the persistent present, and it is not ours to command. For this reason it must, as Heidegger has argued, also be held clearly apart from the idea of an original temporality according to which human existence calls forth the future as an *exstasis* out of the strain of care and trouble according to its own plan.[27]

Christian Link

The idea of the creation also presupposes that the world is dependent upon God in every moment of its temporal existence. This is only possible when one seeks the 'heart of time', its unity, in the future which is given the biblical name: eternity. This future stands for a dimension of time which we theologians call 'eschaton', and as such it is also the time of the history of God 'before the foundation of the world' (Eph 1.4). Here we stand, so to speak, at the source of our historical time. In order to understand the mystery of the creative beginning, we would have to understand how this time is related to - and restricted by - the time of our experience and our thought.

But here we are at the limits of what we can know, unable as we are to move beyond metaphorical language. God can bestow existence to the world by calling it into being. His time comes into the world as a renewing force, like the Sabbath, which allows time to enter now in its fullness and therefore completes creation (Gen 2.2). God can do away with the time of the world, or with human time, by calling his creation to him and by rebuilding it in a new form which has shed all earthly conditions (Rev 21.1). Understood as creation, the world exists in the difference between two forms of time which are not reducible to one another. With its claim to God's eternity, it is placed in time and protects its created status in that it finds itself on its way to fulfilment as new creation. Therein lies its difference to itself as mere nature, adequately described by the chronological understanding of time.

In this discussion, the direction of the question of time has taken a new turn. Wherever the attempt to think of time in its different modes as a unity has been successful, whether in Plato's theory of time or in Husserl's phenomenological consciousness of time, it has been an attempt to understand time from the present. The fundamental biblical experience with which we began, namely the experience that precisely this present is not self-evident, did not fit with this basis of European thought. It has been methodologically suppressed, and with it any question of a future which evades every form of portrayal in which it is made present as representation.

If this future has imposed itself upon us as the "heart" of time, it has not done so arbitrarily, but out of a recognition that we can only realise our temporality as creatures when we are able to move beyond the chronological structure of our existence and the universal reign of time which it manifests. The traditional question of the unity of time is thereby left behind us; the step that is required here does not depend upon the appearance of an "eternal present" in time, as it does in philosophical thought, but upon the expectation that history's continuum could be interrupted, its assault halted.

Christian Link

The biblical tradition lives from the conviction that this expectation has been fulfilled in the event of Israel's Messiah. Therefore the time of God's reign must be understood in terms of the content of this expectation - that is, in New Testament terms: Christ's past, present and future - and not as if it could be related to a specific date of our history. It remains an event which "from the beginning" takes place "in" or, better, "on" our time and in that way defines its sense, its "whereupon", anew.

5.   God's openness to time

This way of approaching the theological problem of time by means of a differentiation and classification of two forms of time is also an attempt to overcome the traditional opposition of time and eternity. Therefore, this difference is not associated with ideas of limited, or unlimited, duration but with the different content which fills these forms of time, and our experience. Hence its opposition to a chronological concept of time.

God's eternity opens itself to time in the life of Jesus of Nazareth and impresses this time with its seal - this is a well-established Christological conclusion.[28] But is the reverse not also true: that this opening also leaves its trace in God's eternity, just as the imagelessness of God does not prevent his binding to that image of himself which he gives us by creating the world? When he allows the man Jesus to enter into the mystery of his name, and lets himself be represented by him (John 14.13), he not only makes him a part of his own life, but also takes part in the earthly fate of his witness, allowing himself to be deeply touched and affected by his sending and death.

God's promises are so bound up with the temporal trace of his name that this trace not only shapes the expectations and hopes which are based upon his historical actions - but it also shapes the rhythm of his eternal life. It is not merely God's eternal relationship to himself, as suggested by classical doctrine of the Trinity, with its imagery of "processes" within the Godhead, which constitutes his inner life but also his relationship to the created world: 'He lets his acts in the world's time affect him, he receives it into himself'.[29]

The purpose of his coming is to make possible the achievement by the whole of creation in its temporal course of what it should have been 'in the beginning' - this is the point of all biblical narratives. In order to realise this aim, God makes himself dependent upon the ways and changes of his people, and upon the hopes and the fulfilments of Jesus. What we see illuminated parabolically as eternity is in time only fragmentary, not yet completed. God has not yet realised his aim, his time has not yet come to itself in ours.

Christian Link

Jewish theology has drawn a most important consequence from God's openness to time in the doctrine of the *Schechina*, impressively developed by Franz Rosenzweig.[30] It is impossible to think of God as giving himself up to destiny by selling Israel, while sharing his fate, without understanding God as one who differentiates himself. God separates himself from himself. After the destruction of the temple, the holy city and the king, his glory goes with his people to misery in foreign lands. This picture makes it possible to speak of something that to us seems deeply strange and alien, but of which the difference between God's time and our time, the diachrony between his truth and ours, forces us to think that God shares our temporal destiny and - by so doing - is himself "in need of salvation"!

Christians of all eras have hoped to be liberated from time and its sufferings (Rom 8.18). The promise of Revelation (21.3) which was inherited from Jewish prophecy (Ex 37.27) reminds them that this hope should also be a hope for God. For 'the home of God among mortals', the divine appearance of God as God, goes beyond the possibilities of the world and is therefore only thinkable when time, now coming in its true fullness, breaks the spell of the world's time, i.e. when eternity makes time whole by bringing it to itself.

So understood, the end of time liberates even God himself from the burden of the unredeemed world. No apocalytic scenario is necessary for this. If God has bound himself to his creation, he will not fulfil his aim without it. Almost like a foreign body, the unknown author of 2nd Peter includes in his drama the exhortation for 'precipitating the coming of the day of God', and thus keeps alive the Jewish consciousness that there is an active human participation in redemption. This is made possible because - with the first sign of the time to come, the resurrection of Christ - the power of what was previously known has come to an end.

Christian Link

References

1   Augustine: *Conf. XI*, 14, 17: *... tendit ad non esse.*

2   F.-W. Marquardt has drawn attention to this aspect of the problem of time in his work: *Das christliche Bekenntnis zu Jesus, dem Juden. Eine Christologie 2*, Munich 1991, p. 238ff, especially p. 245.

3   Sophocles: *Ajax*, 646/47, cited after G. Picht: *Wahrheit*, p. 301.

4   Plato: *Timaeus* 37 D

5   W. Schoberth: 'Leere Zeit - erfüllte Zeit', in Roloff & Ulrich eds., 1994: *Einfach von Gott reden,* Stuttgart, pp. 124-41, esp. 126ff, referring to Augustine, *Conf. XI*, 14, p. 17ff.

6   W. Schoberth: 'Leere Zeit', p. 127.

7   I. Kant: *Critique of Pure Reason*, edition B, 37a.

8   K.H. Miskotte: *Wenn die Götter schweigen. Vom Sinn des Alten Testaments*, Munich 1963, p. 212.

9   E. Lévinas: 'Die Philosophie und die Idee des Unendlichen', in: *Die Spur des Anderen. Untersuchungen zur Phänomenologie und Sozialphilosophie*, Freiburg/Munich 1992-3, p. 197.

10   E. Lévinas: 'Fragen und Antworten', in idem, *Wenn Gott ins Denken einfällt*, Freiburg/Munich 1985, pp. 96-131, p. 128.

11   E. Lévinas: *Die Spur des Anderen*, 197.

12   E. Goodman-Thau: *Zeitbruch. Zur messianishen Grunderfahrung in der jüdischen Tradition*, Berlin 1995, p. 12.

13   E. Lévinas: 'Gott & die Philosophie', in: B. Caspar, ed., *Gott nennen. Phänomologische Zugänge*, Freiburg/Munich 1981, pp. 81-123, p. 105, p. 118.

14   E. Lévinas: *Die Spur des Anderen*, p. 229.

15   E. Lévinas: 'Wenn Gott ins Denken einfällt', p. 124, turns this around, and thus excludes any intentional sense. Time is 'patience waiting for God, an excessive patience, but waiting ... for that which can be neither objective nor end'.

16   E. Lévinas: 'Jenseits des Seins', p. 126

17   E. Lévinas: *Die Spur des Anderen*, p. 217

18   E. Lévinas: 'Jenseits des Seins', p. 126

19   Compare M. Theunissen: *Der Gebetsglaube*, p. 326f.

20   Ibid., p. 327.

Christian Link

21   For the understanding of time as the epiphany of the Aion, see
G. Picht, 1991: *Glauben und Wissenschaft*, Stuttgart, p. 159ff.

22   According to one of the most speaking descriptions of New
Testament parables, K. Barth: *Church Dogmatics* IV/3, p. 113.

23   I. Kant: *Prologomena to Any Future Metaphysics*, §14.

24   T. F. Torrance: 'Creation, Contingent World-Order & Time', MS, p. 18.

25   I. Prigogine / I. Stengers, 1980: *Dialog mit der Natur*, München, p. 25.

26   See, for instance, A. Mercier: *God, World and Time*, MS, espec. p. 1f., p. 27

27   Heidegger, 1962: *Being and Time*, London, §65, especially p. 370ff:
'Temporality as the ontological meaning of care.'

28   Compare K. Barth: *Church Dogmatics* I/2,§14.1 and III/2,§47.1.

29   F.-W. Marquardt: *Das christliche Bekenntnis*, p. 433.

30   F. Rosenzweig: *Stern der Erlösung*, p. 455ff. Cf. also J. Moltmann:
The Coming of God: Christian Eschatology, Ld.1996, p. 302ff.

Acknowledgment

The final translation of this paper is due to Dr. Charlotte Methuen, Bochum.

Christian Link

THOMAS F. TORRANCE

CREATION,
CONTINGENT WORLD-ORDER, AND TIME
A THEOLOGICO-SCIENTIFIC APPROACH

1.   The concept of the creation of the universe out of nothing, *creatio ex nihilo*, originally derived from the Hebraic tradition, and became part of the Christian tradition from the beginning, but it was radicalised through the doctrine of the self-revelation of God in the incarnation and resurrection of his Son in Jesus Christ. He is the divine Word or *Logos* by whom all things are made and without whom no created thing has come into being, and through whom they are given temporal being in utter difference from God"s eternal Being, and endowed with a distinctive rationality dependent, or contingent, upon his transcendent rationality. The specific notion of *contingence* was developed by early Greek patristic theology in order to express the nature of the universe as freely created in *matter and form* by God out of nothing, endowed by him with an orderly reality of its own, utterly different from God yet dependent on him. By creation out of nothing was meant not created out of something called nothing, but not created out of anything. It was this Christian doctrine of the created universe and its contingent order that made up the ultimate basis upon which all modern empirical science rests.

In line with this understanding of creation of the universe in form and being out of nothing, Christian thought rejected the prevailing dualist outlook of Greek science and philosophy, expressed in the sharp disjunction between *cosmos noetos* and *cosmos aisthetos*, or *mundus intelligibilis* and *mundus sensibilis*, as St Augustine spoke of it. That represented a far reaching epistemological revolution, for it meant that the whole universe of invisible and visible or celestial and terrestrial realities was regarded, while creaturely and not divine, as permeated with a unitary rational order of a contingent kind, which could be investigated and understood only in accordance with its inherent nature, and not in accordance with any prior assumptions or logical reasoning from them. This gave rise to a strict understanding of knowledge, ἐπιστήμη, as the controlled understanding of things strictly in accordance with their divinely given or contingent nature, κατὰ φύσιν. (4) In this way Christian thinkers broke new ground and put forward a new scientific method in showing how a conjunctive and synthetic mode of inquiry could penetrate into the nature of things and interpret them in accordance with their inner relations and intelligible structures. It will be sufficient for our purpose to refer only to thought of three leading Christian thinkers, Athanasius, Basil, and John of Alexandria called Philoponos.

St Athanasius was convinced that when our minds act in obedience to the nature of created being, they are in tune with the rational order immanent in the created universe, and are already on the way of truth that leads to the really existent God. This does not mean that human beings can reach God by logical reasoning, but rather that through communing with the providential and regulating activity of God in the symmetry (συμμετρία), and order (τάξις), concord (ὁμόνοια), symphony (συμφωνία) and system (σύνταξις) of the cosmos, which point to the Creator, the human soul is directed to look away from creaturely rationalities to the uncreated and creative Logos of God. This is not some immanent reason in the universe, but the personal Autologos of the living and acting God who is other than created realities and all creation, the good Word of the good Father, who has established the order of all things, reconciling opposites into a single harmony. Thus Athanasius laid immense emphasis upon the one common order of the created cosmos, the intrinsic rationality of things, and so he held that there is everywhere not finally chaos and disorder but one world order or harmonious system of the cosmos (κόσμος παναρμόνιος συντάξις) which is enlightened and regulated by the one creative Logos, in a sustained rejection of the dualism, pluralism and polymorphism of Hellenic philosophy, religion and science. The entire universe of visible and invisible, celestial and terrestrial, realities is a cosmic unity due to the all-embracing and integrating activity of the divine Logos, so that a single rational order pervades all created existence contingent upon the transcendent rationality of God. The universe created in this way he characterised as flowing or fleeting (ῥευστός) in its temporality and as contingent (ἐνδεχόμενος) in its order.

It was in line with this changed outlook upon the universe that St Basil wrote his influential work, *Hexaëmeron*, on the six "days" of creation, by which he did not mean calendar days but periods of unspecified duration, reflecting the biblical or Hebrew notion of *òlam*, the longest duration that can be conceived. Like the earlier Greek Fathers he spoke of time as created out of nothing along with the matter and form of the universe. He held that creation out of nothing means that there is an absolute origin to the universe, a transcendent beginning beyond all material and temporal beginning, which in the nature of the case we can know only by divine revelation.

Thomas F. Torrance

Basil argued that the created universe is intrinsically incomplete; in no way physically or logically necessary, self-sufficient or self-explanatory, it is ultimately to be understood from its contingence upon God beyond itself. He pointed to the Genesis account of creation by the majestic fiat of God: "Let there be". This means that, although acts of divine creation took place timelessly, the creative commands of God gave rise to orderly arrangements and sequences and enduring structures in the world of time and space. It was the voice of God in creation that called forth the laws of nature. So all laws of nature, all its intelligible order, are to be regarded as dependent on the Word of God as their ultimate source and ground. Even physical law points beyond itself to a transcendent ground of intelligibility in the Mind or Word of God the Creator, and it is upon that ground that its constancy and order reposes.

According to Basil man himself belongs in body and mind to the realm of contingent being, but as created in the image of God he is the one being made to "look up" to God, and so to be the rational constituent within the created order through whom the secret of its purpose in the wise providence of God may be known. It is through the peculiar place of man on the boundary between heaven and earth, the invisible and the visible, that the rational order in the physical and moral laws of the universe deriving from God may be discerned. This concept of order presupposes an ultimate ground of order transcending what we can comprehend but of which we are dimly aware in our minds under the constraint of which human beings generate order in all rational activity, such as the formulation of laws.

Now let us turn to John Philoponos of Alexandria in the 6th century, the first great Christian physicist whose theological understanding of creation out of nothing led him to question the concept of the eternity of the world put forward by Platonic and Aristotelian thinkers and to apply a powerful conception of contingence to a scientific understanding of the cosmos, evident for example in his *De opificio mundi*, indebted to Basil's *Hexaëmeron*, his *De aeternitate mundi contra Proclum*, and his *De aeternitate mundi contra Aristotelem*. By contingence he meant that as freely created by God out of nothing the cosmos has no self-existence and no inherent stability of its own, but is nevertheless endowed by the Creator with an authentic reality and an intelligible order which points beyond itself, and is as such the ground of (empirical) scientific inquiry. By contingent order is meant, then, that the orderly universe is not self-sufficient or ultimately self-explaining but is given a rationality and reliability in its orderliness dependent on and reflecting God's own eternal rationality and reliability.

Thomas F. Torrance

My concern now is particularly with the way in which, within that general perspective, Philoponos sought to apply the theological distinction between uncreated light and created light to his understanding of the created order.[1] In doing so, he came up with the discovery that light has weight, and that light moves at what he called a timeless or practically infinite speed! John Philoponos then offered an account of time and space in terms of the movement of light, which was an astonishing anticipation of relativity theory. His importance for our consideration here, however, is with his suggestion on the analogy of the relation between created and uncreated light that the visible things came forth from the invisible. Hence we do not explain the invisible in terms of the visible, but the visible in terms of the invisible. This applies to law, physical and moral law alike, for the rational order which they involve derives from and points back to an ultimate ground of invisible order in God.

What does this say about World Order? The cosmos with its "world order" is in no sense an emanation from God or necessary for his being God. God was not compelled to create the universe, and the universe has no reason in itself why it has to be and continue to be what it actually is and becomes. Therefore the universe is described as contingent, for it depends entirely on God for its origin and for what it continues to be in its existence and order. The baffling thing about the created universe is that since it came into being it contains no reason in itself why it should be what it is and why it should continue to exist: it is not self-contained, self-sufficient or self-explaining, though it would be impossible to prove this from within the contingent nature and order of universe itself. It is ultimately to be understood from beyond itself in its relation to the Creator. Far from being closed in upon itself, the universe is intrinsically open and elusive in its existence and structure, and constantly surprising in its manifestation of new features and patterns.

It was, then, in the light of what became disclosed in this way about the nature and rationality of the creation, that Christian theologians developed the basis for a new understanding of the nature and order of the universe. This they found to be neither accidental nor necessary, but as characterised by an inherent intelligibility which could not be construed in terms of either necessity or chance. As already indicated the term they employed here was ἐνδεχόμενος, suggested by Athanasius, to express the contingent character of created nature and its intelligible order. This was a profound movement of thought which had the epoch-making effect of altering the very foundations of knowledge and science in the ancient world, and of laying the epistemological basis of what we now call empirical science, for it meant that cosmic realities

Thomas F. Torrance

and events may be understood only in accordance with their actual nature, $\kappa\alpha\tau\grave{\alpha}\ \phi\acute{v}\sigma\iota\nu$, through heuristic science, $\epsilon\grave{v}\rho\epsilon\tau\iota\kappa\grave{\eta}\ \dot{\epsilon}\pi\iota\sigma\tau\acute{\eta}\mu\eta$.

The concept of contingence was taken up by Boethius in the West who rendered the Greek verb $\dot{\epsilon}\nu\delta\acute{\epsilon}\chi\epsilon\tau\alpha\iota$ by the Latin *contingit* and gave us the term 'contingent'. However, under the guidance of Aristotelian philosophy and logic it was understood in relation to the concept of $\sigma\nu\mu\beta\epsilon\beta\eta\kappa\acute{o}\varsigma$ or the 'accidental' on the one hand and to the concept of $\dot{\alpha}\nu\alpha\gamma\kappa\acute{\eta}$ or 'necessity' on the other hand, and as such was not regarded as subject to true scientific knowledge. Contingent events thus came to be regarded by the Latins as irrational chance events. It was in that Boethian way that contingence was understood and used by St Thomas in developing the relations between Christian theology and Aristotelian science. He operated with the classical model of science, *more geometrico*, according to which the object of scientific investigation must be necessary and universal, together with the Aristotelian way of relating matter, form and causality - everything particular, incidental or accidental being excluded from genuine knowledge. It was by John Duns Scotus that the contingent nature and order of the created order was given its best expression, but it was unfortunately not Scotist but Thomist thought that came to prevail for centuries in western science.

2.   Modern science devoted to the investigation of empirical phenomena could not have arisen in the classical form given to it by Galileo and Newton if it had been restricted to a purely *a priori* approach. It arose out of the way of understanding of the universe as created by God and endowed by him with a created or contingent rationality of its own dependent upon his transcendent rationality. This means that while the contingence of the universe cannot be demonstrated from the world itself, nevertheless scientific understanding of it is reached only through giving attention to the universe itself, apart from God. And yet - this is the baffling feature about contingence - the independence of the universe from God is itself dependent on God and is sustained by him. That coupling and decoupling of the contingent universe with God lies deep in the foundations of our western science, but the decoupling loses its significance when its relation to the coupling of God and science is neglected or severed, as happened in the Enlightenment. That is the problem, as I see it, of the history of empirical science since the 17th century.

Empirical science rests upon the concept of the contingent nature and order of the universe which does not contain a sufficient explanation within itself, yet it was pursued through the development of self-explanatory modes

Thomas F. Torrance

and systems of thought in the development of non-contingent necessitarian conceptions of the universe, which threatened the very base upon which it rested and had to go on resting as empirico-theoretic science. But that is not the whole story, for the all-important empirical ingredient in our science, knowledge of things strictly in accordance with their nature, kept prompting the renewal of scientific inquiry into the intrinsic intelligibility of things, demanding new modes of rational formalisation appropriate to them. Epistemological and scientific reconstruction of that kind has actually been going on since the middle of the 19th century, with the result that the concept of contingence and contingent rationality has kept forcing its way back through the hard crust of necessitarian and determinist thought covering it.

I now wish to point to some areas in the development of science where contingence has increasingly become evident, and where contingent order is found by science to belong to the essential nature of the universe.

It is to James Clerk Maxwell that we must turn first.[2] In his account of the behaviour of light and electro-magnetism he developed the concept of the continuous dynamic field as an independent reality in which he broke away from the mechanistic interpretation of nature elaborated in Newton's system of the world. Instead of thinking in terms of particles acting externally on one another he thought of them as continuously and dynamically inter-locked with one another spreading with a velocity equal to the velocity of light. This called for a way of thinking not analytically from parts to a whole but rather from a primitive whole to constituent parts which led to new experimental facts and required a new mathematical *mathesis*.[3] This he set out in mathematical equations representing the dynamic structure of the field. According to Einstein, the discovery of the mathematical properties of light and the formulation of these differential equations constituted the most important event in the history of physics since Newton's time, not least because they formed the pattern for a new type of law. In this way Clerk Maxwell probed into a deeper level of intelligibility, disclosing a new reality, a concept for which there was no place in a mechanistic description of nature. And thus he began to uncover something of the contingent nature of the intelligibility that permeates the created universe.

Contingent events cannot be treated like random or chance events, for they have a distinctive intelligible order of their own but one nevertheless accessible to appropriate mathematical formulation. How, then, can they be coordinated with the chains of physical causes formulated in classical physics, and with the concept of a final cause? Causal connections, Clerk Maxwell argued, have to be looked at on two different levels, a lower level where subordinate centres of causation operate, and a higher level where we have to do with the operation of a central cause, the first being treated as a limiting case of the second. In his investigations the scientist, he said, has to focus "the glass of theory and screw it up sometimes to one pitch of definition and sometimes to another, so as to see down into the different depths", otherwise everything merges dimly together.[4] Thus, through a proper adjustment of "the telescope of theory", he is enabled to see beyond the subordinate fact of physical acts and their immediate consequences, to the central focus or cause where he is concerned with the original act behind all subordinate causal connections. However, far from thinking of this final cause as the Unmoved Mover in the medieval concept of *Prima Causa* or the absolute inertial framework of the Newtonian system, Clerk Maxwell thought of it after the analogy of a moral or personal centre of activity, that is to God the Creator. As a Christian he understood this central cause or focus of reference in the light of the dynamic nature of the living God as revealed in the incarnation of his Son in Jesus Christ. Thus for Clerk Maxwell the contingent nature of the universe brought to light in his dynamical theory of the electromagnetic field called for a new and deeper way of coupling our thoughts of God and science. We must not overlook here the fact that the finite speed of the propagation of light and electromagnetic waves carried with it a deeper understanding of the universe as finite in nature and extent and thus as not self-sufficient or self-explanatory but as pointing beyond itself altogether. Thus with Clerk Maxwell the notion of contingence, smothered in classical science, broke out once more into the open in a decisive way demanding scientific recognition.

We turn next to Albert Einstein, and the epistemological revolution brought about by general relativity theory in the integration of empirical and theoretical factors in scientific inquiry. With his sharp distinction between absolute and relative, true and apparent, Newton had operated with a radical dualism in which empirical and theoretical factors were related externally to one another; thus he explained physical features of the world within the rigid framework of Euclidean geometry, a theoretical system of necessary relations independent of time and space. This led to a closed system of a deterministic structure built up out of static concepts; but Einstein realised that it had been undermined by Clerk Maxwell's concept of the continuous dynamic field. Moreover, with the rise of four-dimensional geometries of space and time, Einstein pointed to the damaging effect of Euclidean geometry as an idealised abstraction from empirical reality. It had been erected into a self-contained conceptual system, pursued as a purely theoretic science antecedent to physics in which we develop our actual knowledge of the world. Rather, geometry must be lodged in the heart of physics, where it is pursued as a non-Euclidean geometry in indissoluble unity with physics as the sub-science of its inner rational or epistemological structure and as an essential part of its empirico-theoretical description of reality. While integrated with space-time reality in this way as a "natural science" geometry is not a conceptual system complete in itself, and is consistent as geometry only as it is completed beyond itself in integration with the material content of physics. It is the real geometry of a finite but unbounded universe. All this implied a rather different view of mathematics which led Einstein to argue that as far as the propositions of mathematics refer to reality they are not certain; and as far as they are certain, they do not refer to reality. Maybe the most important inference to be drawn here is negative: logic closely related to Euclidean geometry is suitable for flat spaces but not for curved ones. This calls for a more realist logic along with a more realist mathematics appropriate to the nature of our space-time universe. It was realisation of this profound concord between mathematical thinking and the intrinsic intelligibilities of nature that enabled Einstein to resist the pressure to apriorism in his development of relativity theory.

Here let me refer to an issue that seems to be particularly significant for our discussion. It concerns the way in which Einstein, as interpreted by Hermann Weyl, generalised the rôle ascribed to light by Clerk Maxwell, attributing to it a unique metaphysical and physical status in the universe. In the case of bodily motion, motion is defined relationally in terms of space and time, while space and time are defined relationally in terms of light. Light itself, however, is not defined in relation to anything else for its status is unique: here our science comes to a meaningless stop! Or does it? In a very interesting lecture in 1929, *On the Present State of Field-Theory*, he argued that in pressing toward the goal of an ultimate logical uniformity we do not just want to know how nature is, but want to know why nature is what it is and not otherwise. No doubt, he granted, there is a Promethean element lodged in the very concept of logical uniformity for it implies understanding empirical lawfulness as logical necessity even for God! This is an area in scientific reflection, the inner core of nature's secrets, which he always found fascinating; it is, he said, "the religious basis of the scientific enterprise".

In raising the question "why?" Einstein was asking a question, set aside during the Enlightenment, about the ultimate reason or justification for the laws of nature. He realised that far from being self-explanatory, the laws

Thomas F. Torrance

of nature are open-structured and contingent upon an ultimate rational ground of order beyond themselves. In theological terms Einstein's "why?" indicates that natural laws as laws of the contingent universe have a limited validity, and are what they ultimately are as laws by reference to the commanding and unifying rationality of God the Creator and Sustainer of the universe.

Unlike Clerk Maxwell, Einstein did not think of this in a personal way, but his frequent speaking of "God" shows something of his appreciation of the open contingent character of the universe and the limitless, indeed transcendent, nature of its incomprehensible *Verständlichkeit* (rational order). That was reinforced by his acceptance of the incompleteness theorem of Kurt Gödel which showed, as Bertrand Russell expressed it, that we must think in terms of a series of rational levels that are open to one another upward but are not reducible downward. It was with quantum theory that the biggest break with the strict causality of classical physics took place, so that the way was opened for a deeper appreciation of contingence through recognition of the elusive non-determinist, and apparently discontinuous, behaviour of wave-particles in the sub-atomic structure of nature.

As I see it the main issue was pin-pointed by Einstein in his reaction against the idea that nature acts discontinuously so that in abandoning the strict causality of classical physics resort had to be made to a way of accounting for the behaviour of sub-quantum particles only through the calculation of statistical probabilities, which has in fact proved remarkably successful empirically. Empirico-theoretical science, as Einstein understood it, has to do with the apprehension and description of realities themselves at a deeper level of intelligibility, and not merely with the probability of their occurrence, far less just with our observations of their occurrence. In his belief that "God does not play dice", Einstein was accused of lapsing back into determinism, but that, I believe, was an unfortunate misunderstanding, for as Wolfgang Pauli showed in an important letter to Max Born, Einstein was a "realist", "not a determinist", as has been confirmed with Bell's theorem.

In quantum theory Einstein called for a form of continuous, dynamic relatedness inherent in reality, such as had forced itself upon him in relativity theory, but that meant operating with a rather different and deeper conception of rational order for which both classical causality and a chance-necessity, or indeterminism-determinism dialectic, were irrelevant. Einstein did not deny causal connections as such, without which we cannot get on at all, but he wanted a deeper more refined dynamic concept of causality, which he called Übercausalität, a principle of super-causality calling for "new mathematical

Thomas F. Torrance

thinking" and appropriate to the subtle nature of things and their intelligible interrelations. Hence, as he regarded it, the development of quantum theory required a really deep change in the basic structure of scientific thought. For Einstein it was a realist coordination of mathematics in an appropriate way with the rational structures of the empirical world that probes into the contingent character and nature of its order, and thereby discloses the deep levels of intelligible relations embedded in empirical realities. This calls for a closer consideration of what Eugene Wigner once called "the Unreasonable Effectiveness of Mathematics in the Natural Sciences."

Mathematicians are, it is often claimed, either formalists or realists. In that distinction the formalists regard mathematics as reducible to a strictly logical system of propositions without ontological reference beyond themselves, and the so-called "realists" are not really realists, but idealists, for the real entities to which they hold mathematics to refer are of a Platonic kind. That is to say they do not operate with the Judaeo-Christian view that *creatio ex nihilo* applies not only to matter but to rational, including mathematical, form, as well as matter. It was that insight which originally gave rise to the conception of the contingent nature of the universe and its rational order upon which all our empirical science ultimately rests. In mathematics, of course, we elaborate symbolic systems as refined instruments by which we may extend the range of our thought beyond what we are capable of without them. The significance of mathematical symbolisms, however, is to be found not in the equations themselves but in their bearing upon non-mathematical reality. As far as I can see, mathematics is effective in physics because it belongs to the actual contingent world, and reflects or mirrors its immanent intelligible patterns, even though these cannot be captured in abstract mathematical form. That is why Clerk Maxwell has called for a mathematics of "embodied" kind concerned with "physical relation" and "physical truth". I link this with the point of Einstein cited above that if mathematical propositions are certain they are not real, and if they are real they are not certain. In their coordination with the dynamic structure of physical reality, mathematical propositions share with the universe its open structure which belongs to their truth.

Mathematics rigorously used does not lead to a closed necessitarian or self-explaining system of the world which lends itself to aprioristic thinking, but to an open contingent universe. Whenever mathematics is regarded as intimately correlated with the structures of the empirical universe it operates with open-textured or incomplete symbols, for in rigorous operation it is found to have a reference outside its own system which limits the validity of

Thomas F. Torrance

its formalisation. That insight ranges across modern science from Blaise Pascal through Georg Cantor to Kurt Gödel and Alan Turing, but it eluded some of the greatest mathematicians of modern times, viz. Karl Gauss and David Hilbert. With reference to mathematical proof Pascal pointed out that it is impossible to operate only with explicit definitions, for in defining anything in one set of terms we must tacitly assume other terms that remain undefined, and to define them we have to presuppose still other terms, and so on in an endless process. Thus even in the strictest mathematical operations we rely upon informal thought-structures, but these informal structures become known only as we rely upon them in developing formal structures. This applies, for example, to the all-important concept of order with which we operate at the back of our minds in all rational and scientific activity but cannot prove, because we have to assume order in all proof and disproof. Let me refer here to the development of an arithmetic of the infinite, and of set-theory by Georg Cantor, a Jewish Christian mathematician in Halle, born of Danish parents. He regarded a completed set as an infinite magnitude, but he distinguished it as transfinite in contrast to the absolute infinity of God. He held that mathematics has to do with a form of rationality which God has imposed upon both the human mind and the universe. It is created harmony between them that gives the universe its rational unity. Hence mathematical deductions from rational structures in the created universe open the way to new discoveries, yet so that finally they point transfinitely beyond themselves. Cantor produced a classical example of contingent rationality when he drew his distinction between transfinite numbers, which exist in the human mind, and the absolute uncreated infinity, which is beyond all human determination and exists only in the mind of God. Since the universe freely created by God might have been other than it is, no scientific deduction from nature must necessarily be so, for it depends upon a transfinite explanation beyond itself.

This brings us to the thought of Kurt Gödel in his famous 1931 essay *On formally undecidable propositions of Principia Mathematica and related systems*. In their *Principia Mathematica*, Whitehead and Russell had tried to transcribe pure mathematics into a completely formalised consistent system of logical notions and relations. Gödel showed that this was not the case, by demonstrating that in any formalised system of sufficient richness there are, and must be, certain propositions which are not capable of proof or disproof within the given system and hence that it cannot be decided within the system whether the axioms of the system are consistent or mutually contradictory. Thus he demonstrated the inherent limitation of the axiomatic method in

Thomas F. Torrance

which all arithmetical truths are logically derived from a given set of axioms. The consistency of such a formal system, if it is consistent, cannot be demonstrated by a proof from within it. If it is consistent it is incomplete. Moreover, in line with Cantor, Gödel showed that the source of the incompleteness attaching to formal systems of mathematics is to be found in the fact that the formation of ever higher types can be continued into the transfinite. Thus undecidable propositions presented in formal systems become decidable through coordination with higher types. A similar result holds for the axiom system of set theory. This demonstrates that in the last analysis we operate in formal systems with basic concepts and axioms which cannot be completely defined, so that we cannot know what the axioms ultimately mean - their truth and meaning lie ultimately beyond themselves. Thus Gödel brought the insights of Pascal and Cantor about the ultimate openness of mathematical propositions and relations to definite proof.

We must connect with Gödel's incompletability theorem the brilliant work of Alan M. Turing who through an idealised computing machine tested the provability of certain mathematical theorems and ended up by discovering incomputable numbers and statements.[5] Such statements are incomputable not simply because like mathematical statements in Cantor's transfinite set-theory they require an infinite time to compute, but because, although they may be true, they are inherently non-computable. With Cantor we have to do with contingent intelligibilities which finally outstrip the grasp of our minds for they impinge upon them from beyond the created order, from the absolute infinity of God the Creator. Gödel was influenced by Cantor's concept of transfinite relations in set theory; his incompletability theorem both vindicated Cantor and reinforced his recognition of the transcendent ground of order on which mathematics ultimately relies for its effectiveness in natural science. These developments certainly dealt a mortal blow to purely logicist views of mathematics; however, far from undermining mathematics they eventually strengthened it and contributed to our understanding of its effectiveness. Let me quote from John Barrow's 1988 article on *The Mathematical Universe*. "If the universe is mathematical in some deep sense, then the mysterious undecidabilities demonstrated by Gödel and Turing are part of the fabric of the universe rather than merely products of our minds. They show that even a mathematical universe is more than axioms, more than computation, more than logic - and more than mathematicians can know."[6]

All this has given considerable impetus to the return of mathematico-scientific thought to an understanding of the nature and rationality of the

Thomas F. Torrance

universe as open-structured and contingent, thereby restoring to their integrity the very foundations upon which classical and modern science are built. The consistence and completeness theorems of Gödel and the non-computable functions of Turing, apply not only to mathematical science, but to the whole universe of mathematics, understood as open-ended and incomplete, yet as completed beyond itself transfinitely in absolute Infinity.

By its open-structured contingent nature the orderly universe points to God as the transcendent ground of all order. We have to do here with a semantic not a logical reference, however. In the nature of the case there can be no logical argument from a contingent universe to its Creator, for as contingent the universe is not self-existent and does not contain a sufficient reason for itself - otherwise it would not be contingent, but would be self-existent and necessary.

3. Let us consider again the coordination of mathematics and physics, and let us think of this from the theological perspective not only of creation but of the incarnation of the creative Word of God within time and space. Through the incarnation, time and space are correlated closely with the ultimate rational ground and the endless possibilities of the Divine Creator. This explains why nature is endowed with the contingent kind of rational order that steadily surprises us in its manifestation of unexpected features and structures which could not be deduced from what is already known, but which always turn out to be consistent with other known features and structures. All this clearly manifests the contingent intelligibility of the created order. We have to do here with the astonishing flexibility and multivariability of the universe arising out of the correlation of the contingent freedom of the created order with the transcendent freedom of the Creator. That has the effect of reversing the classical approach to physical law, for it means that physical laws are to be formulated under conditions of contingence, where contingence is held to be not just an essential presupposition but a constitutive factor in the mathematical structure of physical law. What we need, therefore, is a new kind of realist mathematical thinking.

Further consideration may now be given to two questions, viz.:

A) *the bearing of mathematics upon contingent order*, and

B) *the nature of time in the contingent universe*.

A) We have noted above that in its coordination with physical reality rigorous mathematics proves to have an open-ended character reflecting the contingent nature of the created world order and its reference beyond itself.

Thomas F. Torrance

A two-way relation is involved here between mathematics and contingence, for it is conformity of mathematics in an appropriate way to the contingent nature of physical reality that gives it its heuristic thrust in scientific inquiry. This means that more attention should be given to the distinctive kind or mode of intelligibility that permeates the created order. The need for this becomes apparent when scientists again and again fall back upon the notion of chance even when they seek to counteract its irrationality through repairing to statistical law. As we have already noted, resort to chance is really a way not to think even when it is coupled with necessity, for it cuts short rational probing into deeper levels of intelligibility. Perhaps at best appeal to chance may be a way of pointing to independent modes of elusive intelligibility beyond the scope of hitherto formalised law, and so indicate that physical laws are what they finally are through a reference beyond themselves to what cannot be defined in terms of these laws. That would bring us back to the incompletability and incomputability disclosed through rigorous mathematical operations. However, it is not enough to bring our thinking to a halt there. We must give more attention to contingence, not simply as a factor at the boundary conditions of world order where our abstract mathematical thinking breaks off, but as a primary and profound kind of intelligibility immanent in world order for which we must develop new forms of thought appropriate to its subtle nature. A primary feature of the intelligible nature of contingent order is that it is not timeless but temporal, and cannot therefore be properly grasped and explained in conceptual or mathematical forms of thought which do not take that into account. But does time have a distinctive rational order of its own? Is there an order of time, a $\tau \acute{\alpha} \xi \iota \varsigma \; \kappa \rho \acute{o} \nu o \upsilon$?

B)   This brings me to the problem of trying to understand an essentially dynamic, continuously expanding, universe through the deployment of static timeless concepts in mathematics and logic, which seems to me to lie, in part, behind some of the bizarre difficulties arising in so-called "chaos theory". This was a problem bequeathed to science through the Newtonian System of the universe conceived in terms of the static absolutes of time and space. That problem was only partially overcome by the relativistic understanding of space-time, where time still remains an external operator, for the dualism between particle and field has not been entirely eliminated, as Einstein hoped. Attempts have recently been made, however, to bring what Bergson called "real time" and Prigogine calls "internal time", not the abstract metric time of classical physics, into the central focus and thrust of scientific inquiry.

Thomas F. Torrance

Real on-going time which, in metaphorical parlance, *flows* or *passes* is intrinsic to all contingent reality and must be interpreted as such, with an open structure like all contingent forms of order. Time thus understood is elusive and cannot, of course, be objectified but requires appropriate modes of apprehension and articulation, and as such needs to be brought into scientific inquiry, not as a linear instrument for measuring velocities, but as an internal dynamic functioning of contingent order. In the real on-going time of the expanding universe continuity and novelty bear upon one another under a sort of "invisible hand" or in a kind of spontaneous feed-back way. I think here, in particular, of the work of Ilya Prigogine and his collaborators in their account of non-equilibrium thermodynamics, which has led them to develop dynamic notions of being as becoming, and to speak of "the redemption of time" in the emergence of ever richer patterns of order arising spontaneously upon the random or disorderly fluctuations that occur far from a state of equilibrium. To express this they have put forward mathematical equations for the passage of thought between dynamic and thermodynamic states of matter, but even here, as far as I am able to judge, while time is brought as an internal operator into physics, real time relations are still not built into the warp and woof of mathematical induction and explanation. That is certainly understandable in respect of traditional mathematics. But what we need is a radically new way of dynamical reasoning in mathematics in which real time relations belong to and operate within the basic equations and structures of mathematics.

Similarly what we need is an adaptation of traditional logic formed in connection with classical ideas of substance and causality in order to cope with the kind of intelligible relations that obtain in dynamic fields of reality. We now require something like a logic of verbs adapted to becoming rather than static being, logic in which time is built as an essential factor into the process of reasoning. As far as I am aware, the nearest that has been produced in this respect is the work on tense logic initiated by the late A.N. Prior.[7] The problem had already been raised by Kierkegaard in relation to the idea of "becoming", referring to the Johannine statement "the Word became flesh". This requires a kinetic mode of thought appropriate to the movement (*kinesis*) of the Word in becoming flesh in time and space, and that calls for movement or change to be given a central place in the categories governing all thinking in time and space. The effect of this would be to give the categorial structure of the understanding a dynamic rather than a static character, and to obviate the transposition of temporal into logical relations.

Thomas F. Torrance

In working this out Kierkegaard found he had to abandon a way of thinking from a point of absolute rest, which was a way of "thinking movement or becoming by abrogating it", and to develop a new dynamic yet realist way of thinking in which he could be true to objective movement, whether in God's interaction with us in time and space or in any authentic historical event, without the *metabasis eis allo genos* of converting becoming into necessity. That was an astonishing anticipation of the way that modern physics was to take, but unfortunately Kierkegaard was misunderstood in the rise of existentialist philosophy according to which there was no inherence of *logos* in *phusis* or any notion of the intrinsic intelligibility of empirical events. There had to take place a rejection of the Kantian synthetic *a priori* as a way of coordinating theoretical and empirical factors in knowledge while maintaining the disjunction between them, and at the same time the realisation that contingent events have an inherent objective intelligibility in the light of which they are to be understood and explained.

That is precisely what took place with general relativity theory which demolished Newton's dualism between two kinds of time: absolute, true, or mathematical time, and relative, apparent, or physical time. Epistemologically the effect of general relativity was to heal the breach between geometry and experience, and to show that theoretical and empirical factors inhere in one another in nature itself and in every level of our scientific knowledge of it, and thus to lay the basis for a unitary understanding of the world as finite and unbounded. This implies, not only that empirical events are essentially contingent, but that they are endowed with a contingent intelligibility of their own, and that therefore historical events are properly to be interpreted not in terms of alien patterns of thought clamped down upon them *ab extra*, but in terms of the distinctive rational order they possess in their own right. The unique importance of this Einsteinian revolution for our understanding of history was the deliverance of real motion and real time from a mathematical analysis into still small points strung together in linear connection in accordance with rigid logico-mathematical law. Everything changes when the empirical and the mathematical are intrinsically coordinated with the continuous objective structure of the on-going universe, for then we may seek to understand motion and time only through abandoning a point of absolute rest, and removing the possibility of reducing what we understand to closed conceptual explanations of abstract mathematical formalisations.

When the equations of general relativity predicting their own limits were matched by empirical evidence of the microwave background radiation,

Thomas F. Torrance

it became evident that the universe had been expanding for some fifteen billion years, more or less, from an originally incredible dense first state. This beginning of the world, Einstein held, "really constitutes a beginning". This led Henry Margenau of Yale to show that the equations of general relativity theory have the effect of negating objections to the biblical concept of *creatio ex nihilo*, with which Einstein himself agreed. It became clear that the universe was in fact an immense, and of course unique, historical event with a real beginning. This has helped to force real ongoing time back into the essential subject-matter of scientific inquiry and knowledge. It is now evident that all scientific inquiry within the on-going expansion of the universe has to do with time-dependent dynamic order. This reinforces the conviction that world order is fundamentally contingent not only in its nature but in its inherent rationality and temporality. All scientific truths and all physical laws are as contingent as the universe itself. This means that rather baffling problems have to be faced: how to meet the compelling claims of contingent structures in nature and its history through the invention of appropriate formulations of scientific truth, and in particular how to write time into the fundamental equations of physical law. As we have already noted this calls for a new kind of "embodied" mathematics. Mathematical formulations of rational structures embedded in the time-space continuum of the universe must take the form of incomplete symbols, which to be consistent have to have a reference outside their own system in limitation of their formal validity but not of their truth. That is to say, time is what it is by relation beyond itself to what is not temporal but eternal, so that the order of time ($\tau\acute{\alpha}\xi\iota\varsigma$ $\kappa\rho\acute{o}\nu o\upsilon$) must be of a teleological kind, with a beginning and an end.

What then is time? We all know what it is, for we all experience time as a form of life and existence, but we do not know what we are saying when we utter the word "time"[8] As time belongs to the contingent nature and order of the created universe, we must try to grasp and interpret it in accordance with what it is in itself, and yet since it was created by God out of nothing along with the universe, we must allow our relation with God to play a role in our understanding of time. As we have seen, that applies to the very notion of contingence which by its nature is neither self-sufficient nor self-explanatory - its origination, ground and sufficient reason lie outside the universe, in God. But we need not reject an empirico-scientific approach to the understanding of time, for as with everything created out of nothing, we must look away from God in order to know it in accordance with its contingent otherness. So far, however, scientific inquiry has not been able to carry us much beyond

Thomas F. Torrance

reference to time as a standard for the measurement of velocity, which gives rise to an abstract metric concept of time. It is the contingent nature of time, created with the world out of nothing, that makes it so elusive for us to grasp. This is especially difficult for science. While time is intrinsically real, as real as anything else in the created universe, and must be understood properly in accordance with its own intelligible reality, by its very nature time cannot be objectified and described by us, any more than we can capture the present moment, a progressive "now-point" in the stream of experience, which is no sooner present than it is gone. Yet time keeps on flowing, coming or going.

We recall that it was when working with the distinction between the uncreated light of God and the created light of the world that John Philoponos was able to overthrow the Platonic and Aristotelian conceptions of the eternity of the world, and to make such astonishing progress in the physics of light. It also led him to reject Aristotle's idea of measuring motion by time and time by motion,[9] though he held that time and motion are devised for one another like relative concepts. John Philoponos brought to full development the early Christian doctrine of the creation of the world *ex nihilo*, with a beginning and an end, and of the intelligible nature and unitary order of all things visible and invisible under God, including the contingent nature and reality of time, unceasingly upheld through and in the Word of God incarnate in Jesus Christ. May it not be helpful, then, to operate with a parallel distinction between created time and uncreated "time", that is, between the created time of the world defined by its contingent nature, and the uncreated "time" of the eternal life of God defined by his divine nature, in the hope that this may enable us to grasp something of the reality, nature, and order of contingent time?

As a Christian theologian I am convinced that we must reflect more realistically about the implications of the Incarnation, of God the Creator personally incarnate in time and space, and his redemptive purpose in the history of the world. God's coming among us and as one of us was an utterly astonishing event, something quite new, not only for the created world order, but even for the ever living God![10] The fact that though God was always Father he was not always Creator, and the fact that though he was not always incarnate he became incarnate in Jesus Christ, means that there is a "before" and "after" in the eternal life of God, and thus a kind of divine "time", identical with the ever living and acting God. What are the implications of this, especially of the Incarnation of God the Creator become creature in time and space, of the eternal become temporal, for our understanding of time?

Thomas F. Torrance

The incarnation of God himself, the Creator of heaven and earth, in Jesus Christ, in the time and space of created world order, means that a deeper ontological bond has been forged between uncreated time and created time, which undergirds its contingency and establishes its ongoing nature, reality, and order in a new way. Here we think of the eternal time of God incarnate as penetrating and embracing the contingent time of our creaturely world thereby giving it features which it does not have merely in virtue of its creaturely nature. What are these features?

In the first place, the ongoing time of our passing world has been given a fortified reality - it is not just something merely contingent that is subjected to random chance and futility. While time has been created along with the world as having a contingent reality, it is not left to its contingence away from God, but is rather undergirded and reinforced in its contingent dependence upon the Creator, so that in all its fleeting character it is held together and made to consist in the upholding presence and affirming activity of the Logos or Word of God incarnate in time and space.

In the second place, the ongoing time of our world has been given a real end or goal, a teleological thrust in its direction and order. That was a primary effect of the once and for all nature of the Incarnation, something absolutely decisive for all time to come. Such an absolute within the empirical relativities of temporal existence and history, with an unrepeatable before and after, changes ongoing time quite fundamentally, decisively, and irreversibly. This is marked for Christians by the dating of historical events before and after Christ, which left such profound impact upon understanding of historical thinking, thus liberating Greek thought of time from the tyranny of the ever-recurring processes in nature, such as the endless cycle of cosmological events or the continual succession of day and night and the seasons of the year. The fact that in the Incarnation something happened which is decisive for all time and all people had a revolutionary effect on the concept of history, for history was thereby given an end or a goal, and in this way history becomes real history, emancipated from chance and illusion.

In the third place, we must take into account what St Paul spoke of as the redeeming of time. In Jesus Christ, God became man in our alienated disorderly world without ceasing to be God, and the eternal became time within the temporal structures of our decaying creaturely existence without ceasing to be eternal, thus anchoring the world in the redemptive love of God. Our human life is characterised by decay and mortality, for from our birth we are involved in an ineluctable process of decay and sooner or later tumble

Thomas F. Torrance

down into the grave. In some inexplicable way there is evil at work in the universe, giving disorder a crooked twist so that it is not just an entropic feature of nature on its way toward order, but is fraught with destruction. In this event the redemption of the universe from disorder requires more than a rearrangement of form like the resolving of dissonance in music, namely, the radical defeat and undoing of evil. In Christian theology that is precisely the bearing of the Cross upon the way things actually are in our universe of time and space. It represents the refusal of God to remain aloof from the disintegration of order in what he has made. It is his decisive personal intervention in the world through the Incarnation of his Word and Love in Jesus Christ. In his life and passion he who is the ultimate source and power of all created order has penetrated into the untouchable core of our contingent existence in such a way as to deal with the twisted force of evil entrenched in it, and bring about a redemptive reordering of temporal existence.

Thus in Christian theology we think of the advent of Christ into our temporal and mortal existence within the structures of time and space as having a redemptive purpose with ontological as well as moral implications. This is held to apply not only to the human race but to the whole created world, in vanquishing its latent disorder, in overcoming its estrangement, and in reconciling all things, visible or invisible, to one another in cosmic harmony with the Creator. In the Incarnation of God the embracing of created time by the uncreated time of his eternal life has been established in such a final way that created time can no more vanish back into nothing than God himself can cease to be. But the finalising of that ontological relation between created time and uncreated time has an intrinsic teleological thrust toward overcoming the irrationality of evil and disorder that have inexplicably invaded the creation. In this way, far from negating created time, uncreated time fulfils it and enriches its reality. Christian theology thus thinks of the Incarnation of the Creator Logos of God as penetrating back through created time to the very beginning unravelling the twisted skein of evil, recapitulating all things in himself, as St Paul expressed it, in order to liberate us from the tyranny of the guilt-conditioned irreversibility in which our life has become trapped and so to heal our nature of disorder and direct it forward to the renewal and consummation of all things in God. This has the effect of giving to the future a slant of a teleological as well as an eschatological kind, which is reflected in the way the New Testament speaks of Christ as the First and the Last, A and Ω, whose Advent or Parousia ($\pi\alpha\rho o\nu\sigma\iota\alpha$) is a coming that is a presence and a presence that is a coming. Hence, in the redemptive purpose of

Thomas F. Torrance

God, created time is set on a new basis in which it is given a built-in end yet to be fulfilled. New things happen - new time flows from the end to come giving a perspective to time and new meaning to the past and to the present. That is the redemption of time, for instead of running down, time is directed onward and forward toward an ever higher and richer pattern of order in the promise of a future that will increasingly take us by surprise.

It may be helpful to consider this redemptive effect of the Incarnation upon time in connection with recent development in thermodynamical theory through Katsir, Landsberg, Prigogine and others.

According to the second law of thermodynamics, which applies only to closed systems, all physical and chemical processes tend toward an increase of disorder or entropy ($\grave{\epsilon}\nu\tau\rho o\pi\iota\acute{\eta}$). In its classical form this "law" is relevant only to macroscopic processes, and does not apply either to micro-systems or to the universe as a whole, which limits its usefulness in our understanding of the expansion of the universe, or to the development of living organisms. While the classical formulation of the second law for closed isolated systems is not challenged, startling new developments in the thermodynamics of open systems such as living organisms have necessitated a restatement of the law on a different level necessary, if we are to cope with the ways in which order is found to emerge in the universe. According to classical thermodynamics, increase in order is always at the expense of increase of disorder, which implies that fundamental change takes place irreversibly only in that one direction, even though there are pockets in nature that deviate from this rule. How is it, then, that the whole expansion of the universe shows a steady upward gradient in the emergence of ever richer patterns of order from the "primeval soup" of its earliest minutes to the wonderful complex order of the human brain and indeed, scientific knowledge of the universe?

Prigogine and others, who have been mainly responsible for the development of non-equilibrium thermodynamics, have shown that order is found to arise spontaneously upon the random or disorderly fluctuations that occur far from a state of equilibrium, that is, in the behaviour of open systems in which an exchange of matter and energy takes place between them and their environment. In a closed determinist world which is governed by logico-mathematical connections and the statistical laws of thermodynamics, the arrow of time moves with ineluctable increase in entropy or disorder. In the open-structured world of relativistic quantum theory and non-equilibrium thermodynamics, on the other hand, the arrow of time moves in the opposite direction with a spontaneous increase in order and new structures emerging.

Thomas F. Torrance

In the former world, time is an external parameter governing nature in a geometrically absolute way without being affected by what happens in the empirical world, and as such it closes the door to the future - thus, the future is determined by the present and the past. In the latter world, however, time inheres as an essential dynamic property of nature and operates as an internal parameter in its on-going processes, and as such it opens the door to the future, and thus the future is indeterminate. In the former the irreversibility of time means that time is unredeemable, but in the latter the irreversibility of time means that, as Prigogine expresses it, time is redeemable. Thus strangely the law of entropy operates in a closed deterministic way near the state of equilibrium in terms of the disintegration of structure, but in open systems, such as living organisms, it allows for a creative functioning far from the state of equilibrium in terms of the transformation of structure through fluctuation. The paradox is that order should emerge spontaneously, and inexplicably, out of disorder, that is, not in spite of entropy but because of entropy. This happens, for example, with living organisms which are open systems in which matter and energy are exchanged with the environment.

In our theological account of the effect of the incarnation of the Creator Word within the finite time and space of our world, and its decaying disorderly nature, we spoke of it in terms of the way in which the uncreated time of God's eternal life embraces created time, and of its redemptive effect upon created time in bringing order out of disorder. It may help us now in our theologico-scientific approach to creation, contingent order and time, to think of it after the analogy of the way the environment bears creatively upon open systems in such a way as to bring about the spontaneous emergence of new structures of order, thereby redeeming time from being subjected to a deterministic world of ineluctable decay. In Christian theology we hold that in Jesus Christ the order of redemption has intersected the order of our world, judging, forgiving and healing it of malevolent disorder, and making it share in the wholly benign order of the divine life and love. Since in Jesus Christ there became embodied within time the very Word of God by whom all things are made and in whom they cohere, the redemption of time is to be regarded as applying not just to the human race but to the whole created universe of things visible and invisible. If we think of world order as an open system in this kind of way within the redemptive embrace of the uncreated time of the divine life, we cannot but have a different understanding of world order and time. Scientific accounts of creation, world order and time, will inevitably disappoint us if we think of them within the theoretical framework of a closed

Thomas F. Torrance

system, that is, of a system closed off from God, but it will be quite otherwise if we learn to think of it within the creative and redemptive embrace of the life and love of God. It is to him that the open structures of our contingent world, mathematical and physical, point transfinitely beyond themselves.

4.   The role of moral order in world order

Moral order has an essential role in world order, if only because it is a form of the rational order with which our minds are attuned in an ultimate belief that, whatever appears to the contrary in so-called random or chance events, the universe to which we belong is intrinsically orderly, and reflects as such an ultimate ground of order as its all-important sufficient reason. That ultimate ground of order is and must be hidden, for in the nature of the case it cannot be conceptualised, far less explained, in terms of the orderly arrangements within the universe itself that are indebted to it. In a strange way it is known in not being known, or known only in a tacit or subsidiary way as the comprehensive presupposition for the understanding of all order; without it everything would be meaningless and pointless. The belief in order, together with a refusal to accept the possibility of an ultimate fortuitousness, lies deeply embedded in our moral as well as our religious consciousness.

Two points about this moral order may be made. In the first place, it has arisen together with science, art, and religion, as part of that expansion of the universe towards richer and higher patterns of order which we seek to understand in rational and scientific inquiry. Hence moral order cannot be set aside in rational and scientific inquiry, for it belongs to the universe, and as such calls for a reconsideration of "the nature of nature". The embedding of the human being in nature means that the moral order is not extraneous but essential to the nature of nature and its rational order. In other words, it tells us that moral obligation is ontologically integrated with the commanding intelligibility inherent in the being and becoming of world order.

In the second place, the realisation that moral order has a place within the expanding order of the universe is reinforced by the rethinking of classical thermodynamics in application to open systems, in which, as noted above, order is found emerging spontaneously far from states of equilibrium where instead of random fluctuations or chaos we find more organised or higher levels of order. The kind of order that arises here may be regarded as "entropy-consuming": that is an orderly movement against a tendency toward an increase in entropy or disorder. But that is after all, what science itself is, an entropy-consuming activity, geared into the entropy-consuming activity of

Thomas F. Torrance

nature, and dedicated to the understanding and maintaining of order in the face of the "natural" inclination of nature to degenerate into states of disorder. Hence it may be said that the inner compulsion which prompts and drives our science is an extension of the rational compulsion under which we human beings live our daily lives. This inner compulsion, which R.B. Lindsay has aptly called "the thermodynamic imperative", is reflected in the way we feel bound to live and act in producing as much order in our environment as possible, that is, to maximise the consumption of entropy.

That is very evident in the relation between pure science and the developing of technology in order to transmute available energy into higher and more complex patterns, through which the inherent forces of nature are encouraged to function in accordance with their own latent possibilities for increase in order. I believe that we must discern behind this imperative to increase the degree of order, whether in nature or in human life, something much more compelling, like a requirement or obligation emanating from the ultimate ground of order and echoed by the claims of created reality upon us. This is the imperative of which we are acutely aware as we tune our minds as faithfully as possible to the intrinsic structures of the universe, for it generates within us what we call the scientific conscience. It is an imperative which the scientist as scientist cannot in rational conscience disregard or disobey, but to which he is wholly committed. It is this imperious order, the ontic truth of things to which we are rationally committed and over which we have no control, which stands guard over all our scientific inquiries and theories from discovery to verification. How are we to think of the relation between this thermodynamic imperative with which we have to do in natural science and the categorical imperative with which we have to do in moral science or ethics, under the commanding authority of the ultimate ground of order? They cannot but belong together and affect one another in world order.

The nub of the problem facing us here is that inherited from the Enlightenment, the deep rift torn in human knowledge between the 'how' and the 'why', between the 'is' and the 'ought'. It is to that rift that the unhappy splits in our modern culture go back, and not least the damaging separation between the physical and the human sciences, or the natural and the moral sciences, and between natural science and theological science. Can we ever reach a unified field theory, even one of an open-structured kind, unless we heal that rift? In order to do that we need to operate within a dimensional perspective which transcends that separation, that is, theologically speaking, from within the relation of God to the universe and its order. As Max Planck

Thomas F. Torrance

once claimed, the unified view of the world demanded by science requires in some way a coordination between the power of God and the power that gives force to the laws of nature, which would have the effect of giving those laws a definitely teleological character.

As we have seen, important developments in basic inquiry are now taking place in which rigorous questioning refuses to be halted at artificial barriers laid down in the past by a myopic view of scientific knowledge, and reaches out across the 'how' to the 'why' and beyond the 'is' to the 'ought'.

Let us recall again the point made by Einstein that science cannot remain satisfied merely with describing the laws of nature, but must press beyond knowing how nature is what it is, to knowing why nature is what it is and not something else. That means that rigorous science must be concerned with the inner justification of nature's laws in order to disclose the reasons for them, and so is bound to be concerned with how things ought to be as well as with how they actually are. There Einstein was in fact questioning the artificial dichotomy between the 'how' and the 'why', and indeed between the 'is' and the 'ought' which was built into western science by the Enlightenment. This implies that the laws of nature are to be understood not just in the way they relate logically to one another but in the light of their relation to an ultimate ground of rational order. As I see it this means that scientific inquiry, whether a scientist is aware of it or not, must conform to the contingent nature of the universe and respect the openness of its immanent rationality to the transcendent Rationality of God the Creator.

Einstein's claim that science must be concerned with the inner reason or ultimate justification of natural law also has powerful implications for the moral and social sciences. This was already evident from the massive recovery of ontology in the foundations of knowledge brought about through the integration of theoretical and empirical factors in general relativity theory. Recognition of the coinherence of truth and being in nature and in our knowledge of it, to which this gives rise, radically changes the attitude to reality and deepens the sense of obligation generated in the scientific mind under its compelling claims. The effect of this is to call in question the positivist notion of *Wertfreiheit* or value-free science that has become entrenched in the social sciences, together with the separation of the 'ought' from the 'is' in moral and legal science, and to call for the recovery of ontology in their fields also. This integration of the 'ought' with the 'is', must not be confused with "Hume's principle" or the "naturalistic fallacy", i.e. the identification of what may be regarded as natural, factual, or conventional

Thomas F. Torrance

with what is positively obligatory. Instead, it opens the way for an ethic grounded upon an imperative latent in reality in which we not only think and speak of things in accordance with their nature, that is, truly, but act toward them in accordance with their nature, that is, truly. At the same time the way becomes open for realist moral and social science in which questions of truth and falsity are no longer artificially bracketed off from serious investigation. It would thus seem incumbent upon all science for the moral imperative to function as an internal operator, and not just in an external utilitarian way. Once the artificial separation between the 'is' and the 'ought' is set aside, a profound element of moral obligation demands to be built into the essential process of scientific inquiry, so that the 'ought' becomes essential to the rational structure of scientific inquiry as a significant factor of control. It will be granted that the scientist finds himself operating under a compelling claim of nature, to which he ought in scientific conscience to yield, but how far is this claim grounded in nature to be understood as a moral imperative?

How are we to think of the relation between natural and moral law? We need not be concerned at this particular moment with the divine ground of law, but with its open character. This has become very clear today in realist science in which scientific concepts and theories point beyond themselves to the nature of the objective realities into which we inquire and by which they are governed and in the light of which they continue to be revisable. By their nature realist laws are incomplete and open-structured, for they have their truth in the realities which they indicate beyond themselves, but which they are unable to capture completely within the net of their theoretical concepts and formalisations. The realist objectivity of natural law and its openness belong essentially together. All scientific theories and formulations of natural law, while objective and true, are open-structured and provisional, for the universe, together with its natural laws, cannot be understood completely out of itself, but requires an explanatory reference beyond itself. Thus even the most rigorous mathematical equations are intrinsically incomplete and call for completion beyond themselves. I believe that this applies not only to physical laws, but to moral laws, however axiomatically and logically formalised, for they also derive from and point back to an ultimate rational ground beyond themselves. If moral laws are logically certain they are not necessarily true, but if they are true they are open-structured and may not be subjected without falsification to complete and logically certain formalisation. I believe that this is a matter that legal science needs to take into account

Thomas F. Torrance

today, for legal science has too long been infected with positivism, and needs to recover a realist open-structured conception of moral and juridical law.

We must now consider how natural law and moral law are related to one another. This has become very important today for medical science, particularly in the field of genetics where difficult problems arise and crucial decisions have to be made. The basic question that arises here, for example in embryology, is whether research or experimentation with embryos is in the interest of the embryo or in the interest of the scientist in his desire to advance knowledge and his own reputation. This is a clear instance where scientific and moral integrity are inviolably one - any refusal by a scientist to meet the obligation imposed upon him by the nature of what he is investigating is a rejection of the compelling claims of reality upon him. In both science and ethics we are obliged to know things and behave towards them strictly in accordance with their natures, and may not confuse the ends with the means. The scientific conscience will not allow the scientist to do otherwise. To say the least, he is aware of an obligation to be faithful to the actual facts, and may not "cook the results" of his experiments. However, this has also to do with the relation of scientific inquiry to the inner compulsion of the universe in its expansion toward maximum order, the imperative immanent in the natural order to which we with all nature belong. In his commitment to order the scientist is committed to its entelechy toward the maximisation of order. That is to say, in his obligation to behave in accordance with the nature of things, the scientist comes under the compelling claim of nature to further its immanent thrust toward fuller and richer patterns of order, which he seeks to fulfil through appropriate inquiry and in technological development harnessed appropriately together. But how far may the scientist impose upon nature a pattern of order of his own devising alien to it, if only to satisfy his curiosity? This is the area where pure science and applied science often conflict in confusing ends with means, where strict behaviour in accordance with the nature of nature may clash with technological manipulation governed by some professionally or socially desired end. Surely any refusal by a scientist to meet the obligations imposed upon him by the nature of what he is investigating is a rejection of the compelling moral claims of reality upon him.

How then are we to think of the relation between natural law and moral law? Let me recall here the basic principle on which the Royal Society in London was founded, succinctly formulated in its motto, *Nullius in Verba*, in which expression is given to the nature of science when it is pursued strictly on its own ground and under the compelling claims of the realities

Thomas F. Torrance

being investigated, and not on the ground or "say so" of an external authority. Scientific inquiry and discovery are pursued in rigorous attention to the intrinsic intelligibility of nature throughout the universe without imposing extrinsic patterns of thought on our understanding of it. This implies that natural law may not and cannot rightly be related to moral law in any external way, but only on a rational ground and under a compelling authority common to both scientific and moral inquiry, the intrinsic intelligibility of the created universe which points to an ultimate ground of rationality and constancy beyond itself. We have to think and act here under the imperative of an ultimate ground that is both rational and moral. It is only on that common ground that natural and moral law may be related rationally and properly to one another in such a way that each may be true to itself without conflict with the other. That is surely what should happen in the field of medical ethics, where difficult decisions have to be taken but where it is often very difficult today to determine what is morally right, yet merciful and beneficial. This is of crucial importance in genetic engineering which can be of such enormous benefit in treating and even obviating disease. Unfortunately this is not how current science always operates when, for example, appeal is made to some form of utilitarian ethics to justify some "helpful" act of genetic manipulation, which may be backed up by a local statute law, but not by realist common law. Utilitarian ethics is of course the kind of ethics to which all fascist and communist governments appeal in their self-justification. In so doing natural science sins gravely against its own nature and the rule, *Nullius in Verba*.

The more strictly scientific inquiry concerns itself with the intrinsic intelligibility of the created order, the more it finds it has to operate with open structures or incomplete formalisations which through the nature of their inherent rationality point beyond themselves to an ultimate ground of order. Far from that open or incomplete character being an indication of deficiency or falsity it is found to be essential to their truth. The more profoundly realist scientific theories or formulations of natural law are, the more they indicate much more than they can express, and have their truth beyond themselves, in the light of which they continue to be revisable. I believe it is in much the same way that rigorous moral and legal science operate, under the compulsion of a transcendent ground of rational order to which they point and in the light of which their formulations continue to be revisable.

What are we to make of the fact that both natural law and moral law are what they are in their contingent relation to the ultimate ground of order and function under its commanding imperative? Here let us recall again the

Thomas F. Torrance

fact that all rational and scientific thought tacitly presupposes that the world is inherently orderly, otherwise it would not be understandable or open anywhere to rational investigation and description. This fundamental belief in order is not something that we can prove, for it has to be assumed in all proof and disproof, and arises irresistibly as a decisive operator in our consciousness under the impact of reality from beyond ourselves. As such it is, so to say, built into the inner walls of our minds where it exercises a regulative function in scientific inquiry, explanation and verification. Within scientific operations we cannot but submit our minds to the compelling claims of reality and its intrinsic rational order, so that we have to reckon not only with an ontological basis for knowledge but with a normative basis with which our scientific intuition resonates. Thus we think rationally and scientifically only as we think under the compelling claims of reality and its intrinsic intelligibility. We find ourselves up against an immanent imperative in nature in response to which we frame our understanding of its objective, dynamic arrangements in terms of physical law, and we are aware of an obligation thrust upon us from the ultimate ground of order which gives rise to the scientific conscience.

In holding that both physical and moral law are what they are in their contingent relation to the ultimate ground of order and function under its commanding imperative, we cannot but affirm that there are not, and cannot be, two ultimate grounds of order - we do not live and cannot think rationally within a schizoid universe! No more than we can think of there being two Gods can we think of two ultimate grounds of order, one rational and the other moral, and therefore of two different imperatives laid upon us. However, if physical and moral law, for all their difference, have a unitary ontological ground beyond themselves, to which they are open and in the light of which they are to be justified, they must also be locked together in the compelling claims they make upon us. This is apparent in the fact that in all inquiry in natural and moral science we are obliged to respect, know and act toward, realities of whatever kind strictly in accordance with their natures in a true and faithful way and not otherwise. All true and right behaviour respond to the imperious constraint of a single transcendent reality which we cannot rationally or morally resist. This is surely an essential part of what we mean by conscience, whether scientific or moral, the functioning of a moral imperative as an internal operator in the determination of natural and moral law which are both ontologically grounded in the nature of ultimate reality. In other words, the unconditional obligation of which we are aware in our conscience is an ontic as well as a moral obligation. If natural science and

Thomas F. Torrance

ethics overlap in their epistemological and ontological structure at this crucial point, it seems clear that the sharp cleavage between science and ethics commonly accepted since the Enlightenment must be rejected in order to do justice to the double fact that there is an inescapable moral ingredient in scientific activity and an inescapable rational ingredient in ethical behaviour. The recognition of their common relation to a unitary intelligible ground in ultimate reality will help to reinforce the moral imperative latent in physical law, and the rational imperative latent in moral law.

I believe that a rethinking and restructuring of fundamental scientific inquiry and method in setting aside the rationalistic dichotomy between the 'is' and the 'ought', and an inclusion of the moral imperative as an essential factor of control in an appropriate way within the formulation of natural law is being forced on us at every hand. This is nowhere more evident than in the field of ecological research concerned with the conservation of the planet on which we live. But above all it is becoming more evident day by day in medical science where bioethical issues of the greatest importance for the survival of the human race have been raised. The ground for this change has already been prepared in the recovery of ontology and the role of belief in the foundations of knowledge, but that requires to be nourished through the heuristic vision of an ultimate unitary basis in the rational and moral order of the created universe, to which Christian theology is committed.

Thomas F. Torrance

1   See the excerpts made by Walter Böhm from the works of Philoponos about light, Johannes Philoponos, Grammatikos von Alexandrien, München, 1967, pp. 56f, 103, 195, 307ff, 315f, 419f.

2 Cf. my edition of his work:
A Dynamical Theory of the Electromagnetic Field, Edinburgh, 1982.

3 See especially *A Treatise on Electricity and Magnetism*, Dover Edition, London, 1954, vol. 1, p. IXf, and vol. 2, pp. 174-77.

4 See L. Campbell & W. Garnett, *The Life of James Clerk Maxwell*, with a selection from his correspondence and occasional writings and a sketch of his contribution to science, London, 1882, pp. 226, 237ff.

5 See A.M. Turing, *The Mind's I* (Hofstadter & Dennet, eds.), Basic Books, 1981.

6 *Natural Science*, May 1989, p. 311.

7 See M. Wegener & P. Øhrstrøm, *A New Tempo-Modal Logic for Emerging Truth*, in: J. Faye et al. (eds), *Perspectives on Time*, Kluwer 1997, pp. 417-41.

8 Cf. St Augustine, *Confessions*, XI, 14 : "What then is time? If no one asks me, I know; if I want to explain it to a questioner, I do not know."

9 Cf. the paper of Prof. Park, this volume (*editors' remark*)

10 For the following refer to the thinking of Athanasius about this which I explain in *The Trinitarian Faith, The Evangelical Theology of the Ancient Catholic Church*, Edinburgh, 1995 reprint, pp. 84ff.

Thomas F. Torrance

MOGENS WEGENER

TOWARDS A NEW
METAPHYSICS OF TIME & CREATION

Contents:

What is Metaphysics?
Philosophy, and the Logics of Time
Cosmology, and the Worlds of Physics
Mythology, and the Ethics of Creation
Time = Creation = Grace

Summary:[1]

A *metaphysics* of time and change, in order to be possible, will necessitate a redefinition of the original idea of metaphysics which can no longer be understood as ontology, but will have to be based on tempo-modal logics with clear implications for cosmology, so it will have to be interpreted as *chrono-logics*, or *cosmo-logics*.

According to traditional metaphysics truth is either timeless or eternal. This stance is here challenged by proving it both possible and consistent to view contingent truth as ephemeric, bound to emerge and perish with the reality it depicts, past contingents being determined for all future, and future contingents being as yet undetermined, hence unknowable. In this way *time* is assimilated to *creation* in a very radical sense.

Contingency implies a world-wide simultaneity - in spite of relativity, but in clear agreement with the standard principle of cosmic isotropy which can be regarded as a principle of the equivalence of observers, a principle of obvious importance to ethics, if decoded by analogy. An ethics of creation allowing for evolution may be based on the principle of trial and error which is pointless without resurgence ultimately based on forbearance.

A.   Introduction: What is Metaphysics?

Since a librarian of ancient Alexandria associated the phrase *tà metá tà fysiká* to the *próte filosofía* of Aristotle, metaphysics has been interpreted as *ontology*, or the doctrine of being as being, for centuries hailed as the most fundamental of sciences. According to Aristotle, *reality is thing-like*, all real beings being of the nature of things. The whole universe consists of nothing but things, and the highest thing is called God. God is just a being, or thing, and in this sense "he" is on a par with other beings, or things. The final step of Aristotle, viz. to identify God with the very being of all particular beings, hence with universal being, or the universe, is then very small, indeed.

A different kind of metaphysics is found in Plato, Aristotle's teacher. In contrast to Aristotle, Plato did not write treatises: he wrote dialogues, and the very gist of his thinking is dialectical which is the opposite of dogmatical. According to Plato, knowledge is related to being just as opinion is related to becoming - but higher than being is goodness, the ultimate cause of being. Thus he invented a philosophical monotheism in order to be able to explain the origin of the *pantheon* of gods together with the creation of time and change and thereby the entire universe of becoming and deceasing. Goodness, which inhered in the Divine Craftsman, was the lofty Paradigm needed to create a Kósmos out of Cháos. Chrónos, first of motions, arose together with Kósmos and became indirectly measurable by means of the heavenly circuits of sameness and otherness. Kósmos thereby emerged as a perfect synthesis of structure and process - i.e., of Parmenides and Heracleitos.

A modern philosopher, Heidegger, spoke much about metaphysics. The ambitious goal of his thought was to defeat traditional metaphysics by reverting to Parmenides and rethink his vision which aimed at uncovering the very truth of being. According to Heidegger, *logic has blinded metaphysics and made it forget true being* by concentrating on the various forms of being, instead of focussing on being itself, so his subtle plan was to break the rule of logic in science by confronting it to - nothing! Face to face with great nothing, true being reveals itself as a presence which embraces past and future, and the task of philosophy, according to Heidegger, is to rethink being as a temporal unity, avoiding the vulgar image of time as a linear succession of instants.

To a logically minded person all this sounds like sheer obscurantism, except for its rejection of vulgar time and of the current reification of being. As I do not share the enthusiasm for fundamental ontology displayed by most disciples of yon master of linguistic opacity, I shall prefer to clear the table by

Mogens Wegener

forsaking the central issue of his discipline in favour of a concern for our basic experience of events. So I shall devote my efforts to developing a logic of time and change, indeed of creation, which may serve as the *organon* for a new metaphysics very different from ontology. This philosophy will borrow its inspiration partly from Plato and partly from Kierkegaard; both were able dialecticians, eager to unveil nonsense disguised as wisdom.

Metaphysics: Dialectics ≠ Ontology

Plato → Dialectics 1 // Kierkegaard → Dialectics 2
Aristotle → Ontology 1 // Heidegger → Ontology 2

1.   Philosophy, and the Logics of Time

Philosophy is the incessant search for *wisdom*, whereas science is the relentless quest for *truth*. Is philosophy a science, then, the queen of science, or perhaps the roots of "the tree of sciences" whereof physics is the trunk?[2] Truth is total,[3] Hegel said; and philosophy is the universal science of truth. But *is it true to say that truth is the sole aim of wisdom*?

According to Aquinas, being is the same as being one, being true, being good, and being beautiful; all these predicates unfold various senses of what it is to be. This philosophy may appear to be beautiful, good, and true. But if we do not want to accept ontology, or the doctrine of being, as our first philosophy, we shall disagree; and there are plenty of reasons for doing so.

Ontology, whether revealing *ultimate reality* or *the truth of being*, must be expressible in propositions, sentences unifying subject with predicate by means of the copula "is": only propositions can exhibit the value of truth. But *language is infinitely richer than the realm of propositions*, true or false. It is therefore unwise to base our notion of language upon that of descriptive sentences unified by a copula, defining meaning in terms of truth-conditions. Likewise is it rash to define philosophy as the universal science of truth unless one is willing to accept that there are different senses of truth.

The point is that *the truth of statements*, universal or particular, differs from *the truth of a totality* of statements, as well as from that of a metaphysical system, and truth *in* a logical system is obviously different from the truth *of* a logical system. The notion of truth is basic to logic which is the universal instrument of human reason. Logic can be defined provisionally as a philosophical *discipline stating the rules for a valid transport of truth-value (true, or false) from given premises to their conclusion.*

Mogens Wegener

Now, if a unique logic could claim to be the only valid system, problems might be less. But as a matter of fact, even on the basic level there is more than one system, such as the intuitionist logic ascribed to Brouwer, and the three-valued system of Lukasiewicz; and when it comes to tempo-modal logics which are not directly translatable into truth-value semantics, these *intensional systems turn out to form a tree-like hierarchy.*

All logics have two aspects: a syntactical one and a semantical one. From the point of view of *syntactics*, a logical system consists of rules for well-formed formulae, definitions, assumptions, and principles of inference. Assumptions are also called *axioms*. Some formulae are valid because of their form, irrespective of how they are interpreted; such formulae which are provable in the system are called *theorems*. Jointly, axioms and theorems are called *theses* of the system. The question of the truth of formulae which are not valid solely in virtue of form is not decidable independently of their interpretation. In general, the question of truth is not syntactic, but semantic. From the point of view of *semantics*, the logical system is described in a language which, by its internal structure, models certain very general features of the real world; due to their generality, these features are compatible with a variety of different facts, each maximal set constituting a "possible world".

Now *possible worlds*, which I take to be nothing but models, free *constructions* of our intellect, can differ not only as regards *contents*, but also with respect to *structure*; and this will be the case when the models concerned relate to different logical systems. As long as we stick to some basic system, its models will differ merely with respect to their contents, and the validity of its theses will be expressible solely in terms of truth-tables; when we pass on to other systems, notably intensional ones, truth-tables do not suffice, and that brings us to a secondary sense in which to speak of different possible worlds. Before proceeding further in this direction it deserves mention that there is always *a close connexion* between the syntactical and the semantical aspects of a logical system. The crucial condition for claiming a particular system to be sound and complete is that a one-to-one correspondence can be shown to hold between its syntax and semantics: the system is *sound* iff[4] all its valid formulae, or theses, are provably true no matter what their interpretation, and it is *complete* iff[4] all provably true formulae are theses in the system.

In a sound and complete *system of logic* the theses are just empty tautologies. It is customary to distinguish tautological propositions from those which are empirical. The traditional view is that *tautological* propositions are true solely in virtue of *form* whereas *empirical* propositions, when true, are

Mogens Wegener

true in virtue of their material *contents*. In what follows I shall identity a fact with a true proposition which is not provably true in virtue of form alone; such a proposition presumably tells us something about *reality*. However, I shall here claim that the tautological propositions of a logical system in fact may tell us more about the *structure* of reality than empirical propositions can ever do. The reason is that *the semantical model* serves as an intermediate, thus providing us with *a tertium comparationis* which enables us to compare a system of *logics* with a theory of *physics*. We shall later find occasion to compare different interpretations of quantum mechanics to various systems of tense logic which are translatable into models of a branching future.

It is commonplace to distinguish *the humanities* which are mainly *historical* and *idiographic*, aspiring to *describe* and *interpret* the individual traces of a factual past, from *the social and natural sciences* which are mainly *theoretical* and *nomothetic*, attempting to *explain* and *predict* the general trends of an unknown or fictitious future. Without discussing the adequacy of these characterisations it seems safe to say that *history investigates the past* while *theory prepares us for the future*. Thus it is natural to conclude that the *distinction of past from future* constitutes *a transcendental condition* which is fundamental to all branches of human knowledge. Indeed, the very possibility of experimental science depends crucially on this transcendental condition: without the distinction we cannot distinguish experience from prediction.

Let us now take a closer look at the possible worlds semantics of formal logic. It is pretty clear that *experience* involves a factual knowledge of the past whereas *prediction* implies that notions of possibility and necessity be applied to the future; the cognisance hereof invites us to consider the formal systems of tempo-modal logic. In tense logic it is usual to distinguish between *dated* propositions which are determinate and *undated* propositions which are indeterminate; still the latter are genuine propositions. According to *Leibniz*, who did not realise the importance of temporal distinctions, *a possible world* is a maximal consistent set of propositions which together describe a linear succession of events, hence a world is *a total succession of individual states*. Contrary to most later views, Leibniz took possible worlds to be virtually real, and - such worlds being *B-series*, not *A-series* - their time does not flow.[5]

According to Leibniz, a proposition is possible iff it is true in some possible world and necessary iff it is true in all possible worlds; but this will need further elaboration. The point is that, in order to account for the seeming flow of time and the appearance of possibilities pointing towards the future, Leibniz not only depicts worlds as linear orderings of successive world-states.

Mogens Wegener

He also imagines the totality of possible worlds, which he takes to constitute the eternal contents of the Divine Reason, in the picture of an infinite bundle of world-lines that converge towards the past, but diverge towards the future. The final picture is that of a parallel "bundle" of world-courses diverging at every instant in the direction of the future, the present being identified as their actual point of diverging into different "branches". This is the classical vision: Its indication of *the present*, however, remains illusory.

The very same objection can be raised against the system of *Ockham* which may be viewed as a forerunner to that of Leibniz. The main difference between these two systems of logic is that the past according to the Leibniz-system can be depicted as a bundle of fibres, whereas the past according to the Ockham-system may be likened to a massive trunk. This means that the set of possible world-courses (relative to some given now) in *the Ockham-system* is a set of different futures coupled to the same past, whereas a similar set of different futures in *the Leibniz-system* only seem connected to the same past: an Ockham-world splits up every second, a Leibniz-world never bifurcates.[6]

The systems are nevertheless on a par as regards the status of truth-value which is given of eternity to any proposition if it refers to some given instant of a given world; this holds even if instants are interpreted as *instant-propositions* in the manner of Prior.[7] So a proposition which is dated relative to a given world fulfils the basic principles of *identity*, of the *excluded middle*, and of non-contradiction, or *consistency*, without exception. Another way of expressing this fact is to say that the operator representing dated future is transparent to negation, so that an outside and an inside negation together produce an affirmation. The two systems are also on a par in the sense that both allow us to distinguish the *simple future* from a merely *possible future* and a strictly *inevitable future*; this fact is itself interesting and makes them accomodate closely to ordinary linguistic usage.

Two other systems of tempo-modal logic are interesting because they do not allow us to identify the simple future as distinct from a possible and a necessary future. These systems, named after *C.S. Peirce* and *S. Kripke*, resp., differ from the two just mentioned by making a difference between outside and inside negation of the operator for dated future, thereby leaving it opaque to double negation. In the Kripke-system the future is not determined, hence it softens the principle of consistency by accepting all future contingents including their inner negations.[8] In the Peirce-system the future is determined, hence it slackens the principle of the excluded middle by rejecting all future contingents including their outer negations.[9] Both systems are similar to that

Mogens Wegener

of Ockham as regards the past which is backwards linear; but in the Kripke system time is branching into different futures which are all real, while in the Peirce system only future possibles branch, and such possibles are imaginary.

We shall briefly touch on the interesting, but not very clear, logic of *Kierkegaard*. In his *Philosophical Fragments*, and in *The Concept of Dread*, we find elements which can be combined in a way that at least resembles a plausible system of tempo-modal logic. In one place he identifies the future with the possible and the possible with the future, in another he claims that time is perfectly linear: these combined lead to determinism.[10] Kierkegaard, however, was no determinist, but a resolute defender of human freedom; nor was he a chump, so we should rather interpret his views in a reasonable way. Let us assume that, when assimilating the possible to the future, he was speaking of the indeterminate, or undated, future. Let us also suppose that, when claiming time to be linear, he was referring to determinate time - time as a succession of instants, or dates. The calendar, as an abstract ordering of dates, is linear. Future possibles are branching. Kierkegaard also insisted that *possibility is temporal* whereas *necessity is atemporal*. This debars the usual definition of necessarily as not-possibly-not or of possibly as not-necessarily-not; but that may after all be regarded as a question of language.

I will now sketch a logic akin to Kierkegaard's in certain respects.[11] We start by taking over the *branching structure* of the systems of Peirce and Kripke with their linearity of the real past being correlated to the branching of future possibles. What we shall call necessary, then, is what was always inevitable (always impossibly false). We next introduce instants by means of *clock-propositions*, i.e., propositions which are true only once, neither earlier, nor later, covering all branches indifferently. By this means we construct a calendar as *a completely ordered set of world-instants*: such an ordering is abstract, devoid of contents, but a world-instant can be intuited as significant by assuming it to be *indexed by its relation to some particular possible world*, "a possible world" being defined as: a maximal consistent set of propositions. It seems natural to restrict the name of future to what is considered to be determinate; consequently *indeterminate future is mere possibility*, hence true future must be dated, and a dated future must, properly understood, be linear because our dating is universal. That imputes a kind of inevitability to the future without making it timelessly necessary. What is necessary was always inevitable, but *the future is what is inevitable just now, and our future now may have been merely possible, or even unstatable, a moment ago*. This logic, I contend, is a promising base on which to found a new metaphysics.

Mogens Wegener

PHILOSOPHY
The Science of Truth?

LOGIC
Instrument of Reason
Syntactics ≃ Semantics
Soundness & Completeness

Tautological Statements ≠ Empirical Statements
Truths of Reason: Necessary ≠ Truths of Fact: Contingent
(True in All Imaginable Worlds) (True in The Only Real World)

Logics differ by the Systems of their Tautologies
A Hierarchy of Intensional, or Tempo-Modal, Logics
Truth in a System ≠ Truth of a System

If Anything is a Factual Truth
it will forever inevitably have been true but
may not always have been going to be true
Eternal Necessity & Future Possibility

Conditions of Knowledge
History focusses on the Past
Practice focusses on the Present
Theory focusses on the Future

2. Cosmology, and the Worlds of Physics

Passing on to cosmology we must ask: What entity is this world? Meaning the one and only real world, not one of the imaginary constructions called possible worlds, it is certainly unique. Plato, in his famous dialogue *Timaios*, declared:[12] *So, in order that this cosmos might be eminently like (its paradigm which is) the most perfect of living beings, the Divine Craftsman produced neither two worlds, nor an infinite number, but our world is the only one to have been created, and will ever be.* If he had been asked how he could be so sure of that, he might have answered: this is simply what we mean by the term 'universe', it is just a matter of correct definition. In its essence, *the universe is the totality of everything which can be said to exist.*

Mogens Wegener

This totality is outside the scope of anyone's experience except God's. We conclude that the term 'universe' denotes a limiting concept in the sense of Kant: it is intelligible and, like an angel in scholastic theology, it is the only one of its kind. The idea of the universe as the total sum of existing reality - a totality which, transcending all experience and intelligence, is unobservable and unknowable - is clearly paradoxical, but also indispensable if we are to understand the perceptual contents of our experience. What we perceive is a confused multitude of sensory impressions: they impinge upon us and, by perceiving them, we are aware of events: past, present, future. Time, as discerned by its *modes of past, present, and future*, I shall hence insist, is the timelessly *necessary concomitant of any possible world*, including the actual one.

The contents of all possible worlds are *temporal happenings* - events. A universe in which nothing happens simply makes no sense, such a world cannot be real; therefore a pure Parmenidean universe, devoid of Heraclitean streams, is against reason. Indeed, we might take a further step identifying a world with a temporal world-course: *the real world, then, is nothing but the actual world-course of events observable to us*, together with all those events which we must presuppose as their necessary conditions. This, in fact, brings us close to the view of Prof. André Mercier who has proposed to identify the universe with a relativistic so-called *super-time* of at least four dimensions.[13] I sympathise with Prof. Mercier's metaphysics which states that *temporal flux* is real in the sense of being *the bearer of reality* or existence, his idea being very original: *reality is what is given to us as time flows from future to past*. But I am convinced that, to vindicate this idea, a final step must be taken.

This step will no doubt seem radical to all who, like Prof. Mercier, have been engaged with Einsteinian relativity theory: It implies a revival of absolute simultaneity! Furthermore, *the idea of time-flow* is closely connected to modern tense logic, and this logic does not make sense unless the temporal modes can be considered absolute: the cut between facts, past or present, and our fictions of the future must be sharp. Likewise, our concept of existence, signifying the endurance in time of something that did once arise and may once expire, is bound up with the concept of interval. But Special Relativity, by discarding absolute simultaneity, also relativises the concept of interval: granted that the existence of something (a lump of radioactive matter, say) be limited to a definite temporal interval, it may be the case for three observers in fast relative motion that, by meeting in mutual coincidence, the first reports that the lump perished long ago, the second that it is still there, and the third that he has not yet observed anything of the kind in that place.

Mogens Wegener

This paradox may be viewed as *a universal conumdrum of existence.* According to the theory of relativity, the concept of existence is individual and relative to the reference frame of a particular observer. In logic this idea simply does not work.[14] *The relativisation of simultaneity is the most fatal blow ever given to scientific realism. The only question is: when will reality hit back in order to eliminate this image of the world?*[15] To the observer, an existent always emerges as a series of causally connected events; this is a cue that our concept of a thing may be composed from our notion of an event, but whether such a definition will do in logic or in physics is not my point here. My point is that, howsoever we conceive of *existence* - whether we define it, or use it as a primitive: a concept of existence which is *not transitive* simply makes no sense at all because, if the concept is intransitive it is particular or private, which is *next to illusion.* It is of no use to postulate the existence of a four, five, ten, or three hundred and sixty, dimensional space-time because existence, then, must mean something quite different. If existence means appearance in space-time, then space-time itself does not exist; and if space-time exists, then everything in it has timeless 'being' - whatever that is.

Some philosophers have gone so far astray as to defend physics by proposing a metaphysics which reduces events to be nothing but timeless properties of coordinates. According to this view, absolute *super-space* is the sole reality, all details being merely the modes of a super-being which would have gratified Parmenides as well as Spinoza. Both Strawson [16] and Quine [17] appear to be potential proponents of such a world-picture which constitutes the final implementation of *the scientific program of Einstein*, the purpose of which it is *to reduce everything in natural science to space-like concepts.* Now, what is empirical in physical geometry is of topological, not of metrical, nature; on this issue I prefer to side with Poincaré rather than with Einstein: *Coordinates are conventions, like the metrics incorporating them, and should not be hypostatised to abstract properties characterising an absolute nature.* Neither is it well founded to concoct a temporal metaphysics based on those absolute entities called instants, or dates, whether they be of universal or of merely local validity: dates, when arranged in linear series, form calendars, but calendars do not inhere in the universe. That, of course, does not prevent us from constructing calendars based on scientific considerations.[18]

But philosophy should not be reduced to the interpretation of science. *Philosophy is not a maiden of theology, but neither is it a maiden of physics.* So it should not disgrace itself by accepting a restriction to mopping-up work, its real obligation being to combine profound analysis and visionary synthesis.

Mogens Wegener

However, philosophising is not the prerogative of academic philosophers. Scientists are also free to think, and Eddington, astronomer and cosmologist, in a philosophical vein once pointed out that *the physical world* is, in fact, very different from the world of the physicist - or, as we should say, for indeed there are many: *the worlds of the physicists*. What he meant was that the real world, our actual physical universe, is one of a kind, is unique; and, as the only kind of similarity our intellect can grasp is similarity of *structure*, the only way for us to come to know anything about the real world is to construct *models*, the structure of which can then be compared to that of the real world. *The world as a 'thing in itself', independent of observation, is unfathomable; what is left to know is the world as a 'thing for us', but this world is plural. How do we come to know the real world? By devising structural models of the world and by testing these models by means of observation and experiment.*[19]

Cosmology has not yet succeeded in producing a viable grand unified theory, although some attempts in that direction have been made. As yet we possess only partial theories, fragments of world-models. Even a unification of relativity theory and quantum mechanics is still in jeopardy due to the vexatious emergence of infinities, and the standard renormalisation procedure used for their removal is ad hoc. As pointed out already by Heisenberg,[20] the great stumbling block is the relativistic dissolution of classical absolute simultaneity. More recently John Bell has admitted that the cheapest solution to the problems presented to physics by the experiment of Aspect might be: *to go back to relativity as it was before Einstein, when people like Lorentz and Poincaré thought that there is a preferred frame of reference, an aether.*[21]

Personally I would prefer a solution which would make a new and more radical kind of relativity compatible with a refined form of absolute, or invariant, simultaneity, and it is indeed interesting to see that such a strange combination is possible mathematically.[22] However, the prevailing tendency at the biennial conferences on relativity which I have attended in later years shows a preference for some kind of substratum theory. Indeed, such a theory would solve the problem by invoking a preferred reference frame as defined by the 3K cosmic background radiation, in accordance with Weyl's principle. This reference frame, of course, would no longer be stationary, but expanding, and it is therefore natural to assume that it would possess dynamic properties that would make it possible to search for an explanation of the phenomenon of gravitation in terms of spontaneous accelerations explainable by local deviations from universal symmetry and homogeneity.

Mogens Wegener

Such explanations have been proposed by some Greeks, by Descartes, and later by others, among whom the most recent are Milne and Landsberg. The latter two developed their cosmologies in conformity with the so-called Hubble-law of universal expansion, so these are characterised by their consent to a cosmological principle implying certain minimal requirements as regards isotropy and homogeneity. Indeed, Milne was the first to make that principle an effective instrument of cosmology.[23] Now it has been proven by Robertson and, independently, by Walker that any world-model in which the average distribution of matter-in-motion conforms to the cosmological principle can be described in terms of an expansion-factor where a statistically defined time parameter serves as the argument, a parameter which is universally invariant. Therefore we are entitled to conclude that an absolute and universal time is definable, at least statistically, for any standard Robertson-Walker model.

This fact, as I see it, is exceedingly important. If it is possible to estimate the size of the fluctuations in the average density and distribution of matter in the universe, we must be able to specify: Deviations from what? From the universal mean, of course! Now atomic clock rates are retarded by dynamic forces, so we must be able to specify: Retardations relative to what? To the universal time, of course! Hence I shall follow Whitrow by claiming that the internal oscillations of atoms must ultimately be determined by a cosmic rhythm which remains invariant within an ideal class of equivalent fundamental observers conforming to the principle of perfect cosmic isotropy. I shall also insist, against Whitrow, that the rhythm cannot be intrepreted as merely statistical, but that it reveals the participation of phenomena in a basic idea of pure reason. This metaphysical conjecture further opens the possibility of revolutionising our understanding of gravitation: instead of explaining the retardation of clocks by the influence of gravitation we might as well attempt to explain gravitation in terms of the retardation of atomic clock-rates.[24]

So there is no reason to discard the notion of absolute simultaneity. On the contrary, there is every reason to retain it in order to vindicate a tempo-modal logic lending formal support to the idea of a permanent flow of time - from the future, towards the past. Before drawing any further consequences of this new metaphysics of time and change, I shall briefly hint at the structural similarities between the various semantical models of tempo-modal logic and certain interpretations of classical and quantum mechanics. First, it appears that the Leibnizian idea of a possible world as a linear series of instantaneous world-states, the past being pregnant with the future and the future preserving every trace of the past, corresponds closely to the determinism of Laplace.

Mogens Wegener

Given a complete description of a single world-state, all other world-states, whether past or future, are then exactly computable to the tiniest detail. Secondly, it seems that the Ockhamist idea of possible worlds as a tree, linear towards the past and branching towards the future, but with one privileged world pictured as a line discerned by marks hidden to any finite observer, clearly resembles the image given by Bohm of the classical world as causally imbedded in the sub-quantum world. Thirdly, the many-worlds interpretation of quantum mechanics given by Everett and de Witt appears very similar in its structure to a possible world of the Kripke-system, there being no privileged sequence of its world-states, but only a brushwood of branches budding from bifurcations and framing a diffused infinity of virtually real futures.[25]

To these three systems of logic which are more or less deterministic in their manner of construction I shall oppose a system that, in my opinion, is the only one to embody in a satisfactory way a development which is radically indeterministic in the sense that all causal determination is seen to depend on *creation* defined as *time-flow*. This does not imply that causality is absent, or impotent, but it means that *causality is contingent*: that it depends on a continued flow of time from the future to the past which is itself correlated to the fact that all our experience originates from becoming. The logic alluded to is that of Peirce, refined by Prior and akin to that of Kierkegaard.

The system, outlined by myself in joint work with Peter Øhrstrøm,[26] conveys the impression of a structure-under-construction, a picture similar to that produced by the covering theory of classical and quantum mechanics devised by Tom Phipps.[27] His is the only one among current physical theories to offer a formal justification of the arrow of time, in contrast to the factual justification given by thermodynamics; it further frees us from fiddling with quantum logics and non-Boolean algebras. It is a source of persistent surprise to me that the theory of Phipps has got much less attention from scientists than the rather dubious time operator devised by Prigogine.[28]

This type of logic, which is a logic for a "time-bound" truth emerging together with the reality it depicts, is uniquely well suited to reveal the feature of contingency, so crucial to our understanding of the idea of creation.[29]

LOGICS $\simeq$ PHYSICS
The Syntactics of 'world-states'
The Semantics of 'possible worlds'
The Cosmology of 'world-models'
'Super-Time' $\neq$ 'Super-Space'

Mogens Wegener

Cosmic Isotropy
UNIVERSAL TIME
Absolute Simultaneity
Gravitation *is* Time

THE FLOW OF TIME
Past ← Present ← Future
Inevitability ≠ Factuality ≠ Possibility
Experience ← Observation ← Prediction
A Steady Change of Temporal Modalities
Time's Flow ⇒ Time's Arrow

3. Mythology, and the Ethics of Creation

Antique philosophy is marked by a transition from *mythos* to *lógos*, and it has since been a matter of major concern to many thinkers, ancient and modern (except maybe the greater names), to free philosophy of "the gods". By contrast, the unity of *lógos* and *mythos* is central to Christian doctrine. The majestic *prologue* of the Gospel according to St. John (*KATA IΩANNHN*) begins precisely by proclaiming the marvellous myth of the Divine Logos:

'Εν ἀρχῇ ἦν ὁ λόγος ... *In the beginning was the Word, and the Word was with God, and God was the Word. The same was in the beginning with God. All things were made by him, and without him [became not one (thing) which has become]. In him was life; and the life was the light of men. And the light shineth in darkness; and the darkness comprehended it not ... And the Word was made flesh, and dwelt among us (and we beheld his glory, the glory as of an only-begotten of a Father), full of grace and truth.*[30]

According to the *Concise Oxford English Dictionary*, 1934, a myth is: *A purely fictitious narrative usually involving supernatural persons, etc., and embodying popular ideas on natural phenomena.* The tenor is positivistic: *fictitious* contrasts with *factual*, just as *popular* and *supernatural* contrast with *scientific* and *natural*. But *COED* is a reliable indicator of educated opinion. As our point of departure, we thus have to face the fact that the central idea of Christianity which is the Incarnation of Christ (God's Anointed) in the man Jesus of Nazareth, and his baptism as the "only-begotten" Son of the Father - according to a general academic consensus peculiar to the era of modernism, is nothing but (oh, that "nothing-but'tery" of our enlightened age) the fantastic core of a fairy tale traded down to us by generations of illiterate people.

Mogens Wegener

If we turn to the most famous Christian thinker of the modern age, Søren Kierkegaard, there is no help to be found, and we shall be no better off. According to Kierkegaard, the Incarnation - interpreted as the unification of God and man, a temporal manifestation of Eternity - is the *Absolute Paradox*, a sheer absurdity to non-believers, unfathomable to anything but revelation.[31] In the same vein, *proofs of the existence of God are simply ridiculous*, for if He exists, they are superfluous, and if He does not, they must be inconsistent. However, as I have argued elsewhere, this way of reasoning is superficial.[32] God having created the Universe, which is the totality of everything that can be said to exist, it makes no sense to ask whether the Creator himself exists, as *the only significant question is whether God did once exist* - viz. as a man. Secondly, as conceded by Kierkegaard, proofs of God might be reasonable, and even useful, if they were expressly designed to elucidate the Idea of God; but this was precisely the motive behind the dialectical proof of St. Anselm. As I have shown elsewhere, his proof is valid when reconstructed in terms of modern symbolic logic, its premises being implicitly granted by the atheist.[33] So the claim of the atheist, that there is no God, is silenced by formal logic: either he does not realise what he is talking about when denouncing it as an illusion (viz. the *quod-nihil-maius-cogitari-potest*), or he contradicts himself. Both horns of this dilemma severely threaten his intellectual integrity.

If, by *mythology*, we do not imply merely *a narrative body of myths*, but also *the formal study of myths*, it is of the utmost importance that their sensitive interpretation is not hampered by the erection of artificial barriers between illusion and reality, fiction and fact. To the fulfilment of this purpose St. Anselm's proof, by succesfully defending the Christian Idea of God against the attack of so-called "enlightened" atheism, represents a major step forward. The next step in paving the way for a deeper understanding of the Christian *Lógos-Myth* would be to refute the insinuation that the Christian Idea of God, when interpreted as a *unitary idea*, is beset with contradiction, or incoherent.[34] This claim which is based on the seeming conflict between *Divine Providence* and *Human Freedom*, however, was already countered in the Middle Ages.[35] Nevertheless, the difference between consistency and plausibility is important and, in order to overcome the doubt lingering, other solutions may be needed. Moreover, I have long felt a growing suspicion that the idea of timeless truth is an import of Greek origin which is foreign to Christian tradition, and that the associated idea of Divine Providence as encompassing "eternal knowledge of future contingents" is an unfortunate construct that needs re-interpretation. Maybe "providence" just means: *God's active care to fulfil his promise.*

Mogens Wegener

With this proposal to re-interpret traditional Christian ideas in light of the (Jewish-Christian) Bible, I have taken my inspiration from J.L. Lucas.[36] In the same vein is a passage which stems from our national bard, Grundtvig: *The creation is a divine experiment.* A natural implication of this sentence is that even God does not know the outcome of his own experiment in advance because, if he did, it wouldn't be an experiment! What the Gospel says is that he is on our side in fighting against evil and has promised us the final victory. One may ask: What if creation is planned, and all truth is known of eternity? This, of course, is the engrained view of tradition: Why should that be wrong? Because, if God knew everything in advance, all creation would be pointless! What reason could convince God that it was good to redouble his own vision? More important than any reasoning, however, is the indisputable fact that the idea of a God who is living and acting in time, caring for his beloved creature, is much closer to the Bible than the traditional idea of an eternal, immutable, and dispassionate deity transcending the times and sufferings of man.

If the creation of the universe, with the life it contains, is in fact a divine experiment, then not only its outcome, but also the laws determining that outcome - or at least some of them - may be supposed to be unknown. Perhaps the laws of nature are just its "habits", as suggested by C.S. Peirce? Maybe laws of nature are not given of eternity but are the results of evolution? If that were the case - *if laws were customs* - then *lex* would be akin to *mos* and *nómos* to *éthos*; and then the difference between laws of nature and laws of society, or morals, would be a matter of degree rather than a matter of kind. Nevertheless *it can be argued that creation must be performed in accordance with certain trancendental conditions if a universe is to be produced* at all.[37] Models of the universe are invented by scientists who have a double rôle in the great play of life, being at the same time both participants and observers. A first condition of *objective knowledge* is that they be able to communicate and thus ensure that they use the same definitions for their exchange of data; to this purpose they will have to agree on the use of *transformation formulae* which are *invariant* to the transformation of laws between different observers. We are therefore entitled to conclude that a primary condition for a rational universe is that it allows the definition of a universal class of fundamental observers which are equivalent in the sense of possessing congruent clocks. The *cosmological principle*, which generalises the principle of relativity by claiming the existence of *a universal class of mutually equivalent observers*, is *indispensable* if our universe be supposed accessible to rational science. This fact is of great significance not only to science, but also to morals.

Mogens Wegener

The point is that the cosmological principle can be interpreted as normative rather than descriptive: *In the absence of evidence to the contrary: treat all observers as if they were equivalent!* Although the fundamentality of observers may thus be regarded as a matter of approximation or degree, it is utterly important that the principle provides us with *a cosmic norm or ideal.* For this reason it assumes a status which makes it comparable to that of the *principle of universality* in morals; but we shall return to this principle later. Perhaps also other elements of cosmological or physical theory are derivable from purely epistemological considerations, as suggested e.g. by Eddington.[38] However, when it comes to the laws of higher order in nature, such as those of biology, it seems evident that these are the results of incessant trial-and-error in energetic systems which are subject to the principles of thermodynamics. Many attempts have been made to deduce the "laws" of thermodynamics from those of classical physics, but in vain; one of the latest is due to Prigogine.[39] In fact, his main conclusion is right: considerations of entropy do not suffice to distinguish between the positive and the negative directions of time, hence physics needs a principle of selection in order to know which is the right one. However, he didn't clearly realise that physics of itself is unable to provide us with such a principle; to do that we urgently need an instance outside physics. Fortunately it is pretty clear that a proper logic of time can do the job.

One of the greatest attempts in history to frame a moral philosophy is that of Kant. His metaphysics of moral conduct is appealing and appalling at the same time, at once a natural object of admiration as well as abomination. The main problem with the ethics of Kant is that it is impotent: it blocks our motivation in advance by presenting duty as foreign to all human emotions. Kant's fault was to invent a chasm separating law and duty from life and love; for this reason his concept of morality appears in the disguise of inhumanity. How would it have to be changed, in order to be baptised in the river of time? First of all we would have to alter his priorities relating causality to freedom: instead of seeking a loophole for freedom in the context of natural causality we would have to seek a place for natural causality in the context of freedom. So we should begin by constructing an indeterminist logic of time; and then we should continue by investigating the implications of that logic to physics and biology, pointing out that the existence of our universe is conditioned by a principle of equivalence while life evolves by creating higher laws of its own. That is: we should, in fact, have taken precisely the course we have followed; and the way is now open for us to further inquiry into the relations between time and creation, order and purpose, science and morality.

Mogens Wegener

We follow Kant by conceding that nothing but the will can be good. But the spontaneity of divine love, motivated wholly by itself, transcends duty which is a need for action motivated by reverence for life and human dignity. A good will, which is the completion of duty, is a condition of human dignity; when good, it is good by itself, not by its end or purpose - its value is intrinsic. The dignity of man as a frail "image" of God derives from the fact that man is a rational animal, subject to morality and empowered to act according to duty. Among the moral imperatives, some are hypothetical and others categorical; whereas compliance to *a hypothetical imperative* is motivated by *desire* for what appears under the aspect of good, obedience to *a categorical imperative*, by contrast, is motivated by *respect* for what appears under the aspect of duty. The only principle giving rise to a categorical imperative is *the principle of universality* which says: "Thou shalt act so that the rule of thy action could be a universal law of human conduct without impairing life or human dignity!" that this tacitly implies the *universal equivalence* of human agents is obvious; its meaning is: "Do unto thy neighbour as you would he should do unto you!" Acting according to this principle, the human will assumes a legislating role; by choosing its rule of action it determines a law of social behaviour.

Autonomy, the power of a will enlightened by reason to produce and obey its own laws of esteem for life and human dignity, is the core of freedom. Natural causality imposes heteronomy. Spiritual exigency furthers autonomy. The idea of *freedom* is a latent logical possibility in each human individual; as heir to that idea, each human individual is a *person* entitled to membership of a spiritual realm of moral purposes referring directly to its divine creator. In order to be truly free it does not suffice to act under the aspect of freedom, the real difficulty being to vindicate freedom in the practice of moral action; freedom of will is not a human property, but the ultimate goal of human life. The possession of perfect freedom and innocent life is a divine prerogative, but the principle of perfection converges towards the principle of happiness, the perfection of freedom in spontaneous love being the ultimate source of joy. The universe, which displays the goodness of its creator, is its own purpose. Spontaneous manifestations of life and human dignity are their own purpose. Man as a moral agent is his own purpose, and his freedom should never be subdued by force or abused as a means to promote ignoble aims.

Creation, A Divine Experiment
The Principle of Universal Equivalence
Evolution, the Free Invention of Laws

Mogens Wegener

Ω. Conclusion: Time=Creation=Grace

By seeing human consciousness - which is a complex of reason, will and emotion - as the final result of a universal urge towards the spontaneous emergence of laws, or habits, of ever higher order and complexity, we do not want to exclude the possibility of maybe infinite mental or spiritual evolution. If the present stage of the development of consciousness on this globe were a summit that could never be surpassed, we would indeed be wretched creatures! But the driving force of evolution is trial-and-error combined with survival of the fittest, and it would be rash to suppose that this is a fact of biology only. However, already when we speak of phylogenetic evolution, the accordance of time is a necessary presupposition for development to take place; and this is even more obvious when we consider the unfolding of ontogenetic potential.[40] That the flowering of mental capabilities is also conditioned by trial-and-error in the sense of training is a psychological fact too common to be emphasized. But what can be said of the "survival of the fittest" in this context?

In order to elucidate that question, we shall consider culture and art. It is commonplace that art represents the expressions of our creative abilities. What is not commonplace is the surmise that these expressions are the more sublime the better they succeed in manifesting the universal in the particular, and that they are the more impressive and fascinating the stronger and more comprehensive the laws embodied in the individual work of art concerned. This kind of strength is spiritual and should not be confused with brute force; my point is that the power of life depends on the scope of the laws it embodies and so its vitality is manifested by its ability to invent and obey its own laws. In order to find evidence in support of this view, we shall turn to history.

It is a well-known fact that the peaks of human culture - the epochal works of art, literature, music, and philosophy - all have survived due to their "fitness", i.e. their suitability to express human feelings, aspirations and goals. This even applies to Christianity if, ignoring its uniqueness, it is compared to other great religions of the world - even the power of Christianity is found in the laws embodied and brought to completion and perfection by its founder. However, the Christian belief is a great paradox, an absolute paradox, indeed; therefore its strength is found in weakness, its pride and honour in humility, and its power to overcome corruption is bound up with the secret of suffering. This may sound like the Baconian motto: *to conquer nature by obeying her*, except that to put up power, vitality and conquest as aims in themselves would be to replace morality with egoism, thus repeating the error of Nietzsche.

Mogens Wegener

Traditionally, Protestantism puts great emphasis on the need of grace. It is therefore strange to compare the protestant origin of the Kantian ethics with its express view of the necessity of God as an instance whose function it is to sanction morality by giving eternal penalty or reward to the will of man. Apparently Kant did not realise that, by assigning to God this purely moral function, he not only alienated man from his creator - he also scorned grace by taking it for granted that it is possible for man to deserve reward from God. Neither did he understand that external sanction, reward or penalty, is foreign to his own ideas of man as his own purpose and duty as categorical.

The point is that to follow a good will up in act is a reward in itself, just as to follow a base will up in act is a penalty in itself - but the truth hereof is first unveiled *sub specie aeternitatis*, as shown by Dante in his *Commedia*. The consequence of this is that *Paradise*, which is a symbol of the fulfilment of our deepest and most secret yearnings, remains closed except to the will that has attained freedom by acting in accordance with the goodness of God. To this purpose - the perfection of goodness in love - grace is indispensable; our evil deeds are all our own, and what good we are able to do is from God. So, without grace, the goodness of will is just an empty posture.

From a protestant view, moral is merely a substitute for spontaneity. But the Lutheran word *simul justus and peccator* [41] is a contradiction in terms - and to sit down, waiting for miracles to happen, is to scorn the exhortation "Wilt thou be made whole? Well then, rise, take up thy bed, and walk!" [42] By contrast, the Thomist saying *gratia naturam non tollit sed perfecit* [43] takes grace to be effective as regards a "piecemeal" improvement of human nature. Of course, grace can never be deserved, for if it could, it wouldn't be grace - but if only theologians were willing to admit that grace, after all, "may work", the immense potential of religious energy latent in modern society might be set free to improve our dreadful world just a little bit.

The present condition of mankind is indeed miserable. But as Leibniz insisted, the actual world - which is the only one to exist - may still be the best of all possible worlds not only in the sense that it is governed by the best laws, producing the richest and most complex outcome from the simplest and most sparing means, but also in the sense that it - better than any other - promotes a steady evolutionary progress towards the realisation of our most lofty hopes. In this situation to advocate pessimism would be but an act of self-mutilation: what we need is a new optimistic metaphysics which can teach us that *TIME* is creation, not annihilation, and a true gift of grace.

Mogens Wegener

Notes

[1] This paper is exceedingly dense, so I found it necessary to provide a summary.

[2] Cf. Descartes on *mathesis universalis*: philosophy is like a tree of which the root is metaphysics, the trunk physics, and the branches all the other sciences.

[3] *Die Wahrheit ist das Ganze!*

[4] For 'iff' read: "if, and only if".

[5] The distinction between the A-series: *past, present,* and *future*, which is absolute, and the B-series: *earlier, simultaneous,* and *later*, which is relative, derives from the Scottish philosopher McTaggart who argued against the reality of temporal becoming and insisted - like Einstein - that the passage of time is a mere illusion.

[6] Cf. the Ockham-system as formalized by McArthur and the Leibniz-system as formalized by Nishimura - see Øhrstrøm & Hasle: *Temporal Logic* .., Kluwer 1995.

[7] Cf. A.N. Prior: *Past, Present & Future*, 1967, *Papers on Time & Tense*, 1968, and the posthumous *Worlds, Times & Selves*, 1977 (ed. Kit Fine).

[8] In the Kripke system, $F_n p$ is compatible with $F_n \neg p$ (different branches).

[9] In the Peirce system, $\neg F_n p$ does not exclude $\neg F_n \neg p$ (indeterminate future).

[10] Cf. *master-argument* of *Diodoros Kronos*, discussed by Lars Gundersen (this volume).

[11] Cf. my joint paper with Øhrstrøm: *A New Tempo-modal Logic for Emerging Truth*, in: J. Faye & al., eds.: *Perspectives on Time*, Kluwer 1996.

[12] *Timaios* 30A, compare also 32C.

[13] Cf. Prof. Mercier's paper (this volume).

[14] Cf. the paper *SFTT* ('Some Free Thinking about Time') by A.N. Prior (this volume).

[15] However, the relativity-specialist P.G. Bergmann already in 1970 spoke of "the breakdown of the principle of relativity" (*Foundations of Physics 1*); and in his classical work: *The Natural Philosophy of Time*, Oxf.1980[2], p.302, G.J. Whitrow, co-founder of the *International Society for the Study of Time*, wrote: *The concept of the relativity of simultaneity on which, in 1905, Einstein based his Special Theory of Relativity, at first appeared to eliminate from physics any idea of an objective world-wide lapse of time according to which physical reality could be regarded as a linear succession of temporal states ... Nevertheless, a quarter of a century later, theoretical cosmologists who made use of the physical ideas and mathemati-cal techniques associated with relativity theory were led to re-introduce the very concept which Einstein began by rejecting.* - Cf. my paper on on: 'God, Time & Creation', *PIRT-Proceedings*, BSPS, Ld. 1994 (Conf. Proc.s "Physical Interpretations of Relativity Theory", sponsored by Brit. Soc. Phil. Sc.)

[16] Cf. P.E. Strawson: *Individuals*, Methuen 1959.

[17] Cf. W.v.O. Quine: *Word & Object*, MIT 1960.

[18] Thus, when Whitrow in his book: *What is Time?* London 1972, claims that in an evolving universe, *there is a single universal scale of cosmic time in terms of which, depending on the choice made of time zero and unit of time, every event has, in principle, its own intrinsic date*, I disagree, insisting that *dates are something we construct* - they are *not* "given out there"!

[19] Cf. my paper: 'Ideas of Cosmology. A Philosopher's Synthesis', *PIRT-Proc.*, BSPS, Ld. 1996, repr. in: Duffy & Wegener, eds.: *Recent Advances in Relativity Theory, selected papers from the PIRT Conf.s 1988-96, Vol.1*, Hadronic Press, Inst.f. Basic Research, Fl.,US, 1999/2000.

[20] Cf. W. Heisenberg: *Physics and Philosophy*, NY 196?.

[21] Cf. J. Bell in: *The Ghost in the Atom*, Davies & Brown eds., Cambr. 1986.

[22] Cf. my papers 'Relativity with Absolute Simultaneity', *PIRT-Proceedings*, BSPS, Ld. 1996[3], as well as those published in *Physics Essays 8*, 1994. For my view today, cf. the ref. of note 19.

[23] Cf. J.D. North: *The Measure of the Universe*, Oxf.1965.

[24] Cf. A. Mercier, 'Gravitation **is** time', quoted from *Gen.Rel.Grav. 6*, 1975.

[25] Cf. e.g. A. Rae: *Quantum Physics: Illusion or Reality*, Cambr. 1994.

Mogens Wegener

[26] Cf. my joint paper with Øhrstrøm: *A New Tempo-modal Logic for Emerging Truth*, in: *Perspectives on Time* (Faye & al., eds.), Kluwer 1996.

[27] Cf. the paper of Tom Phipps (this volume).

[28] Cf. I. Prigogine: *From Being to Becoming*, Freeman 1983.

[29] Cf. my paper on: 'God, Time & Creation', *PIRT-Proceedings*, BSPS, Lond. 1994.

[30] Cf. Nestle & Marshall: *Interlinear Greek-English New Testament*, 1960;
the bracket might be rendered: .. *became nothing of what has become* ..;
in the parenthesis I have retained the indefinite article.

[31] Cf. his *Philosophical Fragments & Concluding Unscientific Postscript*.

[32] Cf. my paper on: 'God, Time & Creation', *PIRT-Proceedings*, BSPS, Lond. 1994.

[33] Cf. my paper on: 'St Anselm's Proof of God' (reprographed), presented at:
ECAP 2 (2nd European Congress of Analytic Philosophy), Leeds 1996.

[34] Cf. e.g. A.O. Lovejoy in: *The Great Chain of Being*, NY 1936 & later.

[35] Cf. the discussion in Øhrstrøm & Hasle: *Temporal Logic* .., Kluwer 1995.

[36] Cf. J.L. Lucas: *A Treatise of Time & Space*, 1973, and: *The Future*, 1989.

[37] Cf. my paper: 'A-priorism in Poincaré, Eddington and Milne', 1996,
in: *Philosophia Scientiae 1*, cahier spécial 1, Entretiens de la session 1994
de l'Academie Internationale de Philosophie des Sciences.

[38] See A.S. Eddington: *The Philosophy of Physical Science*, Cambr. 1939.
Compare Bastin & Kilmister: *Combinatorial Physics*, World Sc. Publ. 1995.

[39] Cf. I. Prigogine: *From Being to Becoming*, Freeman 1983.

[40] A condition of the success of trial-and-error is that the errors are not lethal in the sense that the continuation of trials becomes blocked by lack of time.

[41] At the same time righteous, yet sinful.

[42] The Gospel according to St. John, 5.6-8.

[43] Grace does not suspend nature, but makes it perfect.

APPENDICES

DALE TUGGY

A SHORT TEXT OF LAVENHAM

INTRODUCTION

Richard Lavenham was an Oxford-educated Carmelite friar who probably died some time in the late fourteenth century, perhaps 1383 or 1399. Sources tell us that he wrote approximately sixty-three works, on logical, philosophical, physical, and theological subjects.[1] He has been described as 'on the whole, a rather derivative writer',[2] and this certainly holds of the tract translated here. Lavenham defends the position of a more famous Englishman, William Ockham (c. 1285 - c. 1349), a view which was popular in his own day, and which has been much discussed recently.[3]

The tract has more than a few philosophical shortcomings, perhaps the chief among them being that the perennially popular 'eternity solution' of Boethius and Aquinas is not discussed.[4] Still, it has some pleasing features: it is brief, clear, and it helps the reader to see the intimidating breadth of 'the' problem of future contingents. To stake out a complete position in this long discussion, one must take a stand on many fundamental metaphysical, logical and theological issues.[5] Lavenham helps the reader to recognise some of these issues, and he sketches and defends an Ockhamist answer to some of them.

The following translation is based on a critical text prepared by Peter Øhrstrøm.[6] In the notes I give historical references and attempt to help the reader untangle Lavenham's arguments.[7]

LAVENHAM: TRACT ON FUTURE EVENTS

On the subject of the outcome of future events there are four opinions. *The first* is that all future events will happen necessarily; this was the opinion of the Stoics,[8] and it is still the opinion of laymen. *The second* is that God is in no way foreknowing of future events; this was the opinion of Cicero and of certain Platonists.[9] *The third* is that about future events there is not any determinate truth; this was the opinion of Aristotle in his *De Interpretatione*.[10] *The fourth* is that God determinately knows all future events, but that the events which are future will not happen necessarily but contingently.[11]

The first opinion is false and erroneous because it does away with our free will. This is proved as follows: because whatever sort of activity a man will do, he will necessarily do. Therefore, it is not in the man's power to avoid anything he will do later. And if it is not in his power to avoid something he will do later, it follows that he will not do it freely. Common people and laymen think similarly; when they see that some misfortune has happened to a man, they say that it was his fate, and so it necessarily happened to him.

The second opinion is also false and erroneous according to Augustine in book five of *The City of God*, chapters nine and ten, because this opinion would maintain that God does not now know what is about to happen, which is absurd.

The third opinion, which was that of Aristotle,[12] opposes the Christian faith, in as much as this opinion has to maintain that God no more determinately knows that the Antichrist will be than that the Antichrist will not be, nor does He more determinately know that the day of judgment will be than that the day of judgment will not be; neither does He more determinately know that the resurrection of the dead will be than that the resurrection of the dead will not be. The reason is that with no future contingents that can turn out either way is truth determined. For those propositions, 'The day of judgment will be' and 'The resurrection of the dead will be', are contingent propositions about the future which can turn out either way. Therefore they are not determined to truth,[13] and consequently they are no more determined to being true than to being false, or conversely. The inference is clear, and the major premise is Aristotle's opinion in his book *On Interpretation*. This opinion has to maintain that no contingent proposition about the future is true, and that no such proposition is false. This was Aristotle's intention, as Ockham says about his book *On Interpretation*.[14]

The fourth opinion is the opinion of contemporary people, and of faithful Christians.

Objection: It seems not, because [on this view] necessarily the day of judgment will be and necessarily the resurrection of the dead will be and necessarily the Antichrist will be, and likewise with any future contingent. Therefore, all future contingents will happen necessarily. The inference is clear, and the antecedent is proved as follows: since God has known from eternity that the day of judgment will be, therefore the day of judgment will be. This inference is correct, and the antecedent is necessary, so the consequent [is also necessary].[15] The inference is clear, because from a necessary proposition only a necessary proposition follows in a good inference.[16]

Dale Tuggy

That the antecedent is necessary is proved, because the antecedent is an affirmative, true proposition about the past, whose truth does not depend on the future. Therefore, the antecedent is necessary. The inference is clear in accordance with a common rule.[17]

Likewise, [continues the objector], I argue as follows: Necessarily the Antichrist will be, therefore necessarily the Antichrist will come. The antecedent is proved as follows: God wills that the Antichrist will be, therefore necessarily the Antichrist will be. This inference is correct, and the antecedent is necessary, therefore (so is) the consequent. That the antecedent is necessary is proved, because the antecedent is unchangeably known by God, and every such thing which is unchangeably known by God, is necessarily known by God. Therefore the antecedent is necessarily known by God.[18]

The inference is clear, and the minor premise [is proved] from [the principle that] everything unchangeable is necessary. And the major premise is proved, because if the antecedent is not unchangeably known to God, and the antecedent itself is known by God, then the antecedent itself is changeably known to God, and consequently God knows something changeably. And thus it follows that his mode of knowing would be changeable, that is, that his knowledge would be changeable. The consequent is false and erroneous.[19]

In response to these arguments it is denied that all future events will happen necessarily. I concede this first inference: 'God from eternity has known that the day of judgment will be; therefore, the day of judgment will be.' But I deny that the antecedent is necessary. Then with regard to the proof, where it is argued that because the antecedent is an affirmative proposition about the past, whose truth does not depend on the future, it is therefore necessary - I concede the inference but I deny the antecedent, because its truth depends on the future, as is clear.[20] For if the Antichrist were not going to be, God would not have from eternity known that he was going to be.

To the second argument:[21] I concede, God does not know anything changeably, for neither he himself nor his way of knowing is changeable. And I concede that whatever is known by God is unchangeably known. But it is denied that everything which is unchangeably known by God is necessarily known by God.

Thus ends the tract on future events by Lavenham.[22]

Dale Tuggy

Notes

1. For the sometimes sketchy or contradictory biographical and bibliographical information that we have about Lavenham, see P. Spade, 1973: 'The Treatises On Modal Propositions and On Hypothetical Propositions by Richard Lavenham', *Medieval Studies 35*, pp. 49-59, as well as C. Klingsford, 1937-8: 'Lavenham or Lavynham, Richard' in ed. L. Stephen & S. Lee: *Dictionary of National Biography*, Vol.11 (Oxford) pp. 652-53; and Emden.

2. Spade, P. 1978: 'Richard Lavenham's Obligationes', *Revista critica di storia della filosophia 33*, p. 224.

3. Ockham's several discussions of foreknowledge and future contingents etc., are translated and explained in W. Ockham, 1983: *Predestination, God's Foreknowledge, and Future Contingents* (2nd ed.) trans. M. Adams & N. Kretzmann (Indianapolis: Hackett). For a bibliography of recent discussions of the Ockhamist solution, see W. Craig, 1988: *The Problem of Divine Foreknowledge and Future Contingents from Aristotle to Suarez* (New York: E.J. Brill), p. 289.

4 See Ancius Boethius: *The Consolation of Philosophy* V.3-6, and Thomas Aquinas: *On Truth* Q.2, art.12,14; *Summa Contra Gentiles* I. 67-68; *Summa Theologiae* I Q.14, art.8,13; Q.19, art.8; Q.83, art.1-2; *De Interpretatione* 13-15; *On Evil* Q.16, art.7; *Compendium of Theology* I, 132-33.

5. Calvin Normore has written 2 good introductions to the breadth and history of the discussion, cf. 1982: 'Future Contingents' in N. Kretzmann ed. *The Cambridge History of Later Medieval Philosophy*, Cambr.UP, NY pp. 358-81, and 1985: 'Divine Omniscience, Omnipotence & Future Contingents' in Rudavsky, ed.: *Divine Omniscience and Omnipotence in Medieval Philosophy: Islamic, Jewish, and Christian Perspectives* (Boston: D. Reidel), pp. 3-22.

6. P. Øhrstrøm, 1983: 'Richard Lavenham on Future Contingents', in: *Cahiers de l'Institut du Moyen-Age Grec et Latin 44*, pp.180-86.

7. For interpretation and discussion of this tract together with historical context and references see Peter Øhrstrøm's paper to this volume as well as Øhrstrøm & Hasle, 1995: *Temporal Logic: From Ancient Ideas to Artificial Intelligence* (Boston: Kluwer), pp. 87-102.

8. On Stoic fatalism, see the commentary in A. Long & D. Sedley, 1987: *The Hellenistic Philosophers* Vol.1 Cambr.UP, NY pp. 392-94 and the translated texts referred to there.

9. See Cicero: *On Divination*, Book II, and the interpretation of this in Augustine: *City of God* Book V.9. It is unclear who Lavenham means by 'certain Platonists'; a conjecture is that he is referring to skeptics of the Academy.

10. See *On Interpretation*, Book I, 9. For the different interpretations of this difficult passage see J. Ackrill, *Aristotle's Categories and De Interpretatione* (Oxford) pp. 50-53, pp. 132-43 and R. Sorabji, 1980: *Necessity, Cause, and Blame*, Ithaca: Cornell, ch. 5.

11. One must assume that Lavenham is talking about some future events, and not all of them since, in his (and Ockham's) view, at least some future events are necessary, but not all. My thanks to Paul Vincent Spade for this observation.

Dale Tuggy

12. See note 10.

13. Or, 'they are not determinate with respect to truth'.

14. The relevant part of Ockham's *Commentary on On Interpretation* is translated by Adams and Kretzmann, cf. pp. 96-109.

15. The consequent is 'the day of judgment will be'. The objector is reasoning here according to a principle of all modal logics: If necessarily P, and necessarily if P then Q, then necessarily Q. In logical notation, this is: $(\Box P \wedge \Box(P \Rightarrow Q)) \Rightarrow \Box Q$.

16. Or, 'because a proposition does not really follow from a necessary proposition unless it is a necessary proposition'. His (valid) logical point is that 'P' and 'Necessarily, if P then Q' only imply 'Q', whereas 'Necessarily P ' and 'Necessarily, if P then Q' imply 'Necessarily Q'.

17. The antecedent here is: 'God has known from eternity that the day of judgment will be.' The rule is that all affirmative, true propositions about the past whose truth does not depend on the future are necessary. On this rule see Ockham in Adams & Kretzmann, p. 38, and pp. 46-47.

18. The antecedent now in view is: 'God wills that the Antichrist will be'.

19. The objector is making a *reductio ad absurdum* argument here: the denial of P has an absurd ('false and erroneous') implication, therefore P, where P represents 'God unchangeably knows that he wills that the Antichrist will be'.

20. That is, he concedes that the inference from 'P is a proposition about the past whose truth does not depend on the future' to 'P is necessary' is a proper one, but he denies that 'God has known from eternity that the day of judgment will be' is a true proposition about the past whose truth does not depend on the future.

21. 'Likewise [continues the objector]...' above.

22. I am grateful to John Lawless and Paul V. Spade for their generous help with the translation.

Dale Tuggy

ARTHUR NORMAN PRIOR

SOME FREE THINKING ABOUT TIME

There's a dispute among philosophers - indeed. there has always been this dispute among philosophers - as to whether time is real. Some say yes, and some say no, and some say it isn't a proper question; I happen to be one of the philosophers who say yes. All attempts to deny the reality of time founder, so far as I can see, on the problem of explaining the appearance of time's passage: for appearing is itself something that occurs in time. Eddington once said that events don't happen, we merely come across them; but what is coming across an event but a happening?

So far, then, as I have anything that you could call a philosophical creed, its first article is this: I believe in the reality of the distinction between past, present, and future. I believe that what we see as a progress of events *is* a progress of events, *a coming to pass* of one thing after another, and not just a timeless tapestry with everything stuck there for good and all.

To bring out the difference of viewpoint I have in mind, let me mention a small logical point. Logic deals, at bottom, with statements. It enquires into what statements follow from what - but logicians aren't entirely agreed as to what a statement is. Ancient and medieval logicians thought of a statement as something that can be true at one time and false at another. For example, the statement 'Socrates is sitting down' is true so long as he is sitting down, but becomes false when he gets up. Most modern logicians, however, say that if a statement is true at any time, it's true all the time - once true, always true. Confronted with the example 'Socrates is sitting down', they would say that this isn't really a statement, but only a piece of a statement. It needs to be completed by some unambiguous specification of the time at which he is sitting down, for example, at exactly 3 p.m. (Greenwich mean time) on June 15, 326 BC. And when we say that he is sitting down at this time and date, we don't need to change this 'is' to 'was', because in this sort of statement 'is' hasn't any tense at all - the complete statement tells us a time-less property of a date or moment; that date or moment just is, eternally, a Socrates-sitting-downy date or moment.

Such a notion of what a statement is seems clearly to reflect what I have called the tapestry view of time, and I believe accordingly that this is a point at which logicians ought to retrace their steps. I think the logically primary sense of the word 'statement' is the old sense, the sense in which a statement which is true at one time may be false at another time, and in which the *tense* of statements must be taken seriously. I don't think these are just fragments of 'statements' in some more fundamental sense of the word; on the contrary, the allegedly tenseless statements of modern logic are just a special case of statements in the old sense - they are statements which happen to be either always false or always true, and the 'is' that occurs in them is not really a tenseless 'is' but is just short for 'is, always has been, and always will be'.

This belief, or prejudice, of mine is bound up with a belief in real freedom. One of the big differences between the past and the future is that once something has become past, it is, as it were, out of our reach - once a thing has happened, nothing we can do can make it not to have happened. But the future is to some extent, even though it is only to a very small extent, something we can make for ourselves. And this is a distinction which a tenseless logic is unable to express. In my own logic with tenses I would express it this way: We can lay it down as a law that whatever now is the case will always have been the case; but we can't interchange past and future here and lay it down that whatever now is the case has always been going to be the case - I don't think that's a logical law at all; for if something is the work of a free agent, then it wasn't going to be the case until that agent decided that it was. But if happenings are just properties timelessly attached to dates, I don't see how you can make this distinction.

This general position that I want to uphold has come under fire from different quarters at different times. In the Middle Ages it was menaced by the theologians, many of whom, like Thomas Aquinas, taught that God doesn't experience time as passing, but has it present all at once. In other words, God sees time as a tapestry. Other medieval theologians such as Duns Scotus argued, I think very sensibly, that since time isn't a tapestry, either God doesn't see it that way or he has an illusion about it, and since He hasn't any illusions He doesn't see it that way but sees it as it is, as passing. I would go further than Duns Scotus and say that there are things about the future that God doesn't yet know because they're not yet there to be known, and to talk about knowing them is like saying that we can know falsehoods.

Arthur Norman Prior

God cannot know that 2 and 2 are 5, because 2 and 2 aren't 5, and if He's left some matter to someone's free choice, He cannot know the answer to the question 'How will that person choose?' because there isn't any answer to it until he has chosen.

Nowadays it's not so much the theologians we have to contend with as the scientists, and the philosophical interpreters of the scientists. Many philosophical upholders of what I've called the tapestry view of time claim that they have on their side a very august scientific theory, *the theory of relativity*, and of course it wouldn't do for more philosophers to question august scientific theories. Well, I've tried to find out recently exactly what is the strength of this argument, and I'll discuss it with you now as simply as I can, though I'll have to warn you that it's not very simple. The physical facts seem to be more or less like this: My experience has a quite definite time-order, of which I am immediately aware; and your experience has a definite time-order, of which you are immediately aware; and similarly for any observer, no matter where he is, or how he is moving. Moreover, if you were to calculate the time-order of my experiences, I would agree with your result, and similarly, if I were to calculate yours. The trouble arises when we come to compare one another's experiences - when, for example, I want to know whether I saw a certain flash of light before you did, or you saw it before I did. Even about points like this there is often agreement all round, but we can't depend on it. It could happen that if I assumed myself to be stationary and you moving, I'd get one result - say that I saw the flash first - and if you assumed that you were stationary and I moving, you'd get a different result. I could explain your result by saying that the speed of your movement had made your measuring instruments go haywire; but you could explain my results in the same way. And it appears to be established that in such a case there would be no physical way of deciding which of us is right; that is, there is no way of determining whether the light-signal first crossed my path or yours. And the conclusion drawn in the theory of relativity is that this question, the question as to which of us is right, which of us really saw it first, is a meaningless question; outside our private paths, the time-direction and space-direction just aren't as distinct as that.

Now I don't want to be disrespectful to people whose researches lie in other fields than my own, but I feel compelled to say that this just won't do. I think we have excellent grounds for insisting that the question in question is not a meaningless one, and I'll try and explain what the meaning is.

Arthur Norman Prior

People who are doing relativity physics are concerned with the relations of before and after and simultaneity, but these aren't the first things as far as the real passage of time is concerned - the first thing is the sequence of past, present, and future, and this is not just a private or local matter, different for each one of us; on the contrary, pastness, presentness, and futurity are properties of events that are independent of the observer; and under favourable conditions they are perceived properties of events. We all know what it is to wait for something - an examination, for example; or coming home from the war; or Christmas. What we're waiting for begins by being future; it hasn't yet come to pass. Then a time comes when it does come to pass, when it's present, and we're aware of its presentness, and there's no mistaking it. And then it's past, and we say, perhaps, 'Thank goodness all that's over', and we all know quite well what this 'being over' is, and couldn't mistake it for anything else.

I have a very good friend and colleague in Australia, Professor Smart of Adelaide, with whom I often have arguments about this. He's an advocate of the tapestry view of time, and says that when we say 'X is now past' we just mean 'The latest part of X is earlier than this utterance'. But, when at the end of some ordeal I say 'Thank goodness that's over', do I mean 'Thank goodness the latest part of that is earlier than this utterance'? I certainly do not; I'm not thinking about the utterance at all, it's the *overness*, the *now-endedness*, the *pastness* of the thing that I'm thankful for, and nothing else. Past and future are in fact not to be defined in terms of earlier or later, but the other way round - 'X is earlier than Y means 'At some time X was past and Y was present', and 'X is later than Y' means the opposite of this.

Coming back to this allegedly meaningless question as to whether you or I saw the light-flash first, surely what it means is just this: When I was seeing the flash, had you already seen it, or had you not? In other words, when my seeing it was a present fact, had your seeing it become a past fact, or had it not? And I just cannot be persuaded that such a question is meaningless - its meaning seems to me perfectly obvious. When an event X is happening, another event Y either has happened or has not happened - 'having happened' is not the kind of property that can attach to an event from one point of view but not from another. On the contrary, it's something like existing, in fact to ask what has happened is a way of asking what exists, and you can't have a thing existing from one point of view but not existing from another, although of course its existence may be known to one person or in one region, without being known to or in another.

Arthur Norman Prior

So it seems to me that there's a strong case for just digging our heels in here and saying that, relativity or no relativity, if I say I saw a certain flash before you, and you say you saw it first, one of us is just wrong - or misled it may be, by the effect of speed on his instruments - even if there is just no physical means whatever of deciding which of us it is. To put the same point another way, we may say that the theory of relativity isn't about real space and time, in which the earlier-later relation is defined in terms of pastness, presentness, and futurity; the 'time' which enters into the so-called space-time of relativity theory isn't this, but is just part of an artificial framework which the scientists have constructed to link together observed facts in the simplest way possible, and from which those things which are systematically concealed from us are quite reasonably left out.

This sort of thing has happened before, you know. When that formidable mathematical engine the differential calculus was first invented, its practitioners used to talk a mixture of excellent mathematics and philosophical nonsense, and at the time the nonsense was exposed for what it was by the philosopher Berkeley, in a pamphlet entitled 'A Defence of Free Thinking in Mathematics'. And the mathematicians saw in the end that Berkeley was right, though it took them about a century and a half to come round to it. They came round to it when they became occupied with problems which they could solve only by being accurate on the points where Berkeley had shown them to be loose; then they stopped thinking of the things he had to say as just a reactionary bishop's niggling, and began to say them themselves. Well, it may be that some day the mathematical physicists will want a sound logic of time and tenses; and meanwhile the logician had best go ahead and construct it, and abide his time.

Acknowledgment
This text is reprinted with the kind permission of Dr. Mary Prior, Oxford.

Arthur Norman Prior

INDEX OF PROPER NAMES